Reconceptualizing Teaching Practice

Reconceptualizing Teaching Practice:
Self-study in Teacher Education

Edited by

Mary Lynn Hamilton with Stefinee Pinnegar,
Tom Russell, John Loughran and Vicki LaBoskey

Routledge
Taylor & Francis Group

LONDON AND NEW YORK

First published in 1998
By Routledge
2 Park Square, Milton Park, Abingdon, Oxon, OX14 4RN
270 Madison Ave, New York NY 10016

Transferred to Digital Printing 2006

A catalogue record for this book is available from the British Library

ISBN 0–7507–0869–7 cased
ISBN 0–7507–0868–9 paper

Library of Congress Cataloging-in-Publication Data are available on request

Jacket design by Caroline Archer

Typeset in 9.5/11.5pt Times by
Graphicraft Typesetters Ltd., Hong Kong

Every effort has been made to contact copyright holders for their permission to reprint material in this book. The publishers would be grateful to hear from any copyright holder who is not here acknowledged and will undertake to rectify any errors or omissions in future editions of this book.

Publisher's Note
The publisher has gone to great lengths to ensure the quality of this reprint but points out that some imperfections in the original may be apparent

Printed and bound by CPI Antony Rowe, Eastbourne

Contents

Contents

List of Tables and Figures

Preface

Mary Lynn Hamilton and Stefinee Pinnegar

In August 1996, the first conference sponsored by the Canadian Queen's University and the Self-study of Teacher Education Practices Special Interest Group (S-STEP SIG) of the American Educational Research Association took place in Herstmonceux Castle in East Sussex, England. The idea for this conference grew out of a felt need expressed by members of the S-STEP SIG to meet together as a group in a setting that allowed them to spend extended time examining more carefully what it means to be a scholar of one's own practice. Over a four-day period, eighty participants presented papers, performed ideas, created alternative representations, and lived-and-breathed this notion of self-study. Representatives from four continents (Australia, Europe, North America and South America) attended the conference, bringing with them their curiosity and a range of understandings and interest in the topic. The chapters included in this text illustrate the scope of our work from philosophy to methodology, from examples to processes and practices in self-study. As you read our work, we hope you will gain an understanding of the promise of self-study.

Foreword: Looking Forward:
The Concluding Remarks at the
Castle Conference[1]

Douglas Barnes

I came to the Herstmonceux conference as a complete outsider for, at first, I had even misunderstood the meaning of 'self-study'. Most of my own research has been concerned with talk in classrooms, how students can play an active part in learning and what can so easily prevent it. I had also for many years taught curriculum theory as part of a masters course, so I was aware that it is useful to think about how we develop as teachers, and the conditions under which teachers can also be active learners about the courses they are teaching. This turned out to be of central relevance to the conference.

All the participants were involved in some way in the professional preparation of teachers, and my first impression was that 'caring' seemed to be an underlying concern for them. Almost everywhere I heard about caring for other people and their experiences. I heard about the importance of supporting colleagues, of helping pre-service teachers find their own voices so that they are able to express and organize their experiences in the classroom, and of responsibility for the young students who will be the eventual recipients of all the efforts to help teachers to teach more sensitively and reflectively. Underlying self-study was an essentially *humane* approach to education.

As a newcomer to the self-study group I experienced a typical sense of disorientation because I had not internalized *the ground rules* of self-study. In recent years, I have become convinced of the importance of the concept of 'ground rules' in understanding not only education but many other aspects of our experience. It was my former student and co-author Janina Sheeran (1991) who both brought the idea to my attention and who provides from her research materials the example that will help to make my point. Janina, who was studying the setting of written work, observed a biology lesson. Its topic was the difference between things living and not living, and on the blackboard was a list of seven characteristics that separated the two. The teacher, finding that the time was drawing to a close, hastily set some written homework. He began, 'I want you to devise seven tests that would enable you to decide whether . . .', here he hesitated; and then, pulling a bunch of keys from his pocket, continued: '. . . whether these keys are living or not living'. The class went away and when they returned to the next

---

[1] The conclusion of Douglas Barnes' foreword on the Conference forms the afterword of this text, see page 247.

biology lesson most had made an attempt to outline seven tests. Since some had hardly tried to do so, Janina decided to ask them what had gone wrong. Their answer was, in essence, 'What's the point? We know that keys are inanimate'. They had failed to grasp one of the essential ground rules of education, that most schooling is concerned with a *what if?* world that has no more than a symbolic relationship to the world of action. Students who do not grasp that ground rule do not do well at school. I asked myself, 'So what are the ground rules of self-study?'

As I read the conference papers and attended the earlier discussions it became clear that the concept of 'self-study' was a broad one. The concept seemed to include being a responsible and reflective teacher, collaborating with colleagues in planning and reviewing courses; and collecting evidence from students about their perceptions of the courses they were experiencing. So far the papers seemed to cohere well; self-study was about gathering colleagues and students together to understand better the progress of a course. Other papers seemed different. Reflecting upon one's own history as a teacher would, perhaps, fit, but did an account of the collecting of information about a device for evaluating students belong with the other topics? Perhaps self-study was a kind of action research. This, however, did not match those papers where teacher educators, who had returned to the classroom, reflected on their experiences or those which explored ways of improving communication between colleagues. The range seemed extraordinarily wide. Perhaps this was appropriate at an early stage of the life of this group while its members were finding out where the boundaries of the topic lay. In the future there might come a time to tighten relevance and work towards agreed-upon boundaries.

As I attended the presentation and discussion of papers, a distinction appeared that divided them into two groups. On the one hand, there was reflective investigation of one's own teaching, often highly informal. On the other, was a version of self-study that approached formal research with all the priorities and concerns that implies. The difference appeared to be related to the different audiences to whom the self-study was to be addressed. When the reflective investigation of a course was solely intended to enlighten those who were teaching it, there could be an emphasis upon openness: these studies were at best characterized by sensitive and open communication between colleagues and between faculty and students. Such studies could be systematic and based upon collected material. Since everyone concerned had been involved in its collection and interpretation, its validity could be assumed. There was no need for persuasive accounts of methodology.

Other examples of self-study were, in contrast, intended for a wider audience. Some were intended to be published, others to meet the requirements of a research degree, or to put pressure upon administrators to liberalize the conditions under which the course was taught. These papers made it clear that once self-study becomes public, once it is involved with the micro-politics of status and power in academia, then the validity of its methods, its evidence, and its interpretive arguments become extremely important, because the political implications of any findings open the methodology to question. Those members of the group whose papers fell into this category were profoundly concerned with validity and persuasiveness and the standing of their studies in the institutions where they worked. For them, how to achieve validity in the evidence used in self-study ought to provide the central question for the conference to address. (It occurred to me that there are other powerful audiences besides the academic ones. Since many teachers buy books they provide a means to avoid the powers of the academic community, but this does mean writing books that address teachers' concerns.)

The differences between these two kinds of self-study seem to lie in the audience for whom they are intended, whether any documents written were solely for those involved or for a wider and more influential readership. However, it is also possible to represent the difference in terms of differences of purpose, and in one of the last sessions of the conference five purposes for self-study were suggested. These were:

1 To uncover the real story of what was going on in a course;
2 To exert political power upon those who control the conditions under which teaching takes place;
3 To construct new knowledge (traditional research);
4 To enhance the self-knowledge of the participants;
5 To celebrate the achievements of a course.

This seems a line of thought that could usefully be taken further.

The second group thus showed a profound concern for the public validity of their studies, especially the collection and display of evidence, so that the main question they posed could be phrased as 'What counts for rigour in self-study?' They felt an urgent need to be able to demonstrate that self-study methods led to identifiable improvements in pre-service education. Some participants called for a change in academic norms for evidence, and others felt that their work had been undervalued by colleagues, whose positivistic preconceptions about the nature of knowledge led them to undervalue more impressionistic data. This seemed to be a particular problem for younger academics who had still to establish their status in the eyes of senior colleagues and, for that reason, I felt that this concern, though real enough, should not be allowed to dominate the discussions of self-study. It became clear that faculties of education differed radically from one institution to another in the extent to which they value and support qualitative forms of research. Some members of the conference were fortunate enough to have strong support from senior colleagues who value this kind of study. Beyond the problems that derived from academic expectations about evidence, however, was the sense that the overall cultural values of dominant groups in some countries were inimical to qualitative approaches such as self-study. For example, certain kinds of education practice had been made threatening to teachers in the UK by the fact that ministers of state had publicly attacked the use of group methods in schools: in these ways politicians can manipulate the cultural context of education. Those who urged economic individualism nevertheless feared the possibility that young people might develop a critical habit of mind.

For me, the most persuasive papers were those that modelled the whole process of self-study. Some participants had reported the work done by them and their colleagues by rapidly summarizing the kind of evidence they had collected and then moving quickly to discussing their conclusions. Such papers were often interesting and worthwhile, but I was wanting the *process* of self-study to be made plain. The papers that did this began by explaining the institutional context, quoted next (rather than summarized) some of the evidence used, illustrated the processes of interpretation, including alternative views, outlined any changes made in the course being studied, and discussed general conclusions. Papers that had done this drew their audience into the process by which the conclusions had been reached.

Throughout the conference I asked myself what the conditions were for the success of any example of self-study, but I became convinced that any adequate answer would be very complex. Three major topics would have to enter any discussion: *reframing*, *collaboration* and *openness*.

It was Donald Schön who used the term *framing* to refer to teachers' taken-for-granted views about classrooms, students and the curriculum. He distinguished *theory-in-action* from conscious beliefs about schooling, arguing that although teachers are often only partly aware of their theory-in-action, it has far more influence on how they teach. Merely to change teachers' conscious beliefs was not enough to change their classroom practices. Genuine innovation depends on changes in the unconscious frames of reference that shape their perceptions of what is possible in their lessons. If Schön's assertions are right, the central task for both teacher education and the improvement of our work as teacher educators, must be seen as a matter of *reframing*, making changes in how the various aspects of the task of teaching are perceived by teachers. That, of course, includes university teachers. Changed patterns of work need to become changed ways of understanding what is going on in classes. (One member of the conference who had returned to classroom teaching for a time had found that the more profound changes in his thinking didn't take place until weeks after the classroom events that provoked them. Reflection and critical reconsideration were crucial.) Radical changes in well-practised methods are very threatening to teachers: some teachers in both schools and universities found it hard to take the risks. For too many teachers: 'My teaching is me'. I remembered Lawrence Stenhouse's contention that teaching should be a matter of evaluating hypotheses about the likely effects of teaching; the outcomes of each lesson should provide an opportunity to improve the hypotheses. If success and failure in a lesson are seen as an evaluation of a teacher's deeper self, as for some teachers it is, the effect is to inhibit change and therefore learning. There is no doubt that successful self-study can change teachers profoundly, as witness the teachers who took part in the PEEL project in Australia.

The *collaboration* of a supportive group of colleagues, or even, as in one example, a single partner, had been essential to the success of self-study. It has become a cliché that good teaching is a form of learning, but this does not necessarily happen in isolation. Trusted colleagues help by validating one's experiences, ensuring that they make sense by asking for clarification, by offering alternatives and by reminding one of one's own values. Paper after paper showed the part that had been played by the collaboration of a group of colleagues, but the possibility of such collaboration depends upon other characteristics of the institution, including what I am calling *openness*.

Openness proved to be a central theme of the conference, for, in several ways, it is essential to the success of self-study. Many of the papers reported profound changes in the form of authority taken by senior staff: the exercise of *positional* authority had to give way to an openness to colleagues' views and experiences, so that administrative and other decisions were debated and negotiated. Indeed, the nature of relations between colleagues became critical, since self-study, by making public the details of courses and teaching, made everyone feel more vulnerable. This needed to be matched by an equal sensitivity to the perspective of students who, in learning to become teachers, found themselves in an equally vulnerable position. One participant in the conference insisted on the importance of 'telling my story' to the pre-service teachers, so that they knew in some depth the person who was helping them to acquire the necessary attitudes and skills. Several other participants spoke of the importance of helping pre-service teachers to 'find a voice': the students needed to play an active part in their own learning, to forward reflection upon their experiences and the changes taking place in their thinking and feeling in the face of their new places in schooling. Moreover, for the purposes of self-study, their accounts of what happened provided an essential source of evidence. The phrase 'empowering the learner' was also used, of pre-service teachers, of teachers in general and of school students. Pre-service teachers should be involved in identifying goals, choosing and managing their own learning activities, and reflecting and interpreting what happens. At best, they would be full participants in the process of self-study, and that would include taking part in the decisions about future action. The parallel between schools and institutions for teacher education becomes plain; both should be critical learning communities not just for students but for everyone taking part. This brought us back to the inappropriateness of positional forms of authority, which would prevent a school (or for that matter a faculty) from becoming a genuinely self-critical and collaborative community. The papers contained many hints about the effects of interpersonal relationships upon learning but I thought there was a need for more accounts of self-study that spelt out in detail all such matters that had affected its progress.

Since the purpose of teacher education is to shape how student teachers will act when they eventually find themselves in schools, it is of central importance to see to it that their learning becomes deeply embedded in their perceptions of schooling and of their own future role in schools. The learner's existing way of thinking is as important as the new patterns that are to be learnt. This is a point at which much well-intentioned teaching fails. I remember observing a geography lesson in a country school. The teacher gave out to each student a copy of an excellent aerial photograph of the area; one could see the road, rail and canal that ran through the valley, its cultivated fields, and the pastoral enclosures on the hillsides above. The photograph seemed an ideal starting point for the fourteen-year-old students to reflect on the nature of the country-side and its activities. All one needed to do to begin discussion was to ask, 'What can you see?' But the teacher asked, 'What geographical information can be obtained from the shapes in the picture?' and was met with silence. By setting up a frame of reference that was alien to the students' existing way of thinking, he had managed to detach them from what they knew best, their everyday lives. That moment has remained in my memory as a reminder of a mistake that it is all too easy to make at any level of teaching: that of trying to impose one's own way of thinking upon the students, without helping them to relate what they know already to the new forms of thought that they need to take over.

For beginning teachers, book learning is almost useless. It is no use to offer them the thoughts of an experienced teacher, for these will merely be reinterpreted in the light of their preconceptions. *Reframing* by the student teachers themselves *is* crucial. New ideas are more likely to shape their behavior when they are working in schools if these have become integrated into the frames of reference that guide their understanding and choices. This implies that the roles of the students in their own learning is critical for, without self-examination and a willingness to reflect, they will not benefit from the course, however appropriate it seems. That is why it is so valuable to involve students in the processes of self-study since it will demand of them precisely the critical reflec-tion that they require as learners.

Introduction: Reconceptualizing Teaching Practice

Mary Lynn Hamilton and Stefinee Pinnegar

You may have picked up this book because with a title like *Reconceptualizing Teaching Practice: Self-study in Teacher Education*, you were hoping for answers. You may have expected to find another treatise on how teacher education ought to be reformed or could be reformed. Others of you, focusing on the second segment of the title — *Self-study in Teacher Education* — may have picked up this book expecting to find an explanation of self-study research methodology. Ironically, we think all of you will be happy with the chapters found in this book. The structure of this book and the breadth of the chapters' contents serve both sets of readers. The individual chapters are good examples of self-study research because the context for the studies is teacher education practice. Collectively, the sections provide insight into teacher education as an enterprise and capture the promise of improvement in teacher education. More fundamentally, these studies exist at the juncture between research and practice. As a result, reading this book provides answers for reconceptualizing teaching practice and for studying the teaching practices of teacher educators.

As a teacher educator committed to the education of excellent teachers, you can read these chapters as guideposts for reforming teacher education practices. Each chapter provides an account of how teacher educators recognize discrepancies between their beliefs and their educational practices, altered their practice to harmonize with their beliefs and simultaneously gained new insights into the education of teachers. A central tenet for the contributors to this book manifests itself as a commitment to examining one's own practice to bring into action the values that underlie their practice. In his analysis, Barnes suggests openness, collaboration, and reframing as the defining features of the kinds of work revealed in these chapters. This is not to say that being open, collaborative, and reframing your own practice will necessarily lead to either improvement or understanding in teacher education generally or in your specific location. However, a teacher educator must indeed be open to ideas from other teacher educators, from other disciplines, and from students themselves in order to help students develop their teaching potential. Further, such a teacher educator must be willing to risk collaborating with the student, who will become a teacher, and other colleagues interested in the education of teachers.

We maintain that this kind of openness and collaboration will potentially lead one to think and act differently in teacher education practice — reframing. Self-study of teacher education practices is a formalization of reframing. Those involved in self-study

systematically collect evidence from their practice, allowing them to rethink and potentially open themselves to new interpretations and to create different strategies for educating students that bring their practice into concert with the moral values they espouse.
In their individual chapters, the contributors to this book have revealed how studying
one's practice leads to the reframing of practice and, ultimately, the continual reconceptualization of teacher education. As you read these chapters, we suggest using the
categories openness, collaboration, and reframing as touchstones to help you consider
both self-study and the reconceptualization of teaching practice.

Openness

Howard Smith, in providing a careful investigation of what the term self-study of
teacher education practices might mean, demonstrates the importance of openness in
program-wide collaborations through analysis of a self-study group's meetings. Further,
he gives insight into communication structures necessary for the development of community through collaboration. Russell and Upitis provide an important echo of Smith's
work. Their email records reveal the strength of open communication and the ways in
which conversations, that may initially appear confrontive, can lead productively to
reconceptualization and reform — not just of practice, but of programs as well. Gipe's
use of her teaching portfolio as a self-study for professional development demonstrates
how teacher educators can take a careful, systematic look at their practices in relationship to their beliefs. When teacher educators are open about their beliefs concerning
teaching and commitment, they must make sure that the two are in harmony. She
further articulates the way in which making such private arguments public can be a
strategy for improving the status of teaching. If other teachers in an institution also
committed themselves to providing coherence between belief and practice, it could lead
to the improvement of teaching as well. In their chapter, Cole and Knowles, provide a
public look at their private dilemmas about research in teacher education and the general dismissal by academic communities of both qualitative research and a commitment
to good teaching. Indeed, this is an open and public statement about those concerns
nearest to their hearts. This is a courageous manifesto of their concerns about the role
and status of self-study research in teacher education practice.

Collaboration

Loughran and Northfield argue that collaboration is a fundamental requirement in self-
study research. Collaboration enhances the integrity of the researcher and is more likely
to ensure the reforming of practice. In terms of reconceptualizing teacher education,
their strategies for engaging collaborators result in different relationships with teacher
education practice. For example, straightforwardly asking students for insights, not so
much about a practice but about what they learned about a practice, is intriguing.
Further, their own relationship with each other and their explication of it is an excellent
example of the ways in which working with collaborators not only improves practice
but gives one the courage to utilize the best teaching strategies available. The possibility
of the multilayered impact of collaboration is evident in the Tidwell and Heston chap-

ter, where they explore the elicitation of practical arguments among students, between student and professor, and among professors. When you look at the Johnston, Anderson and DeMuelle chapter, it provides insight into the use of collaboration in research and development of teaching practice. Methodologically, it presents a technological innovation for data collection. As reform, it points out the impact and results of collaboration.

More straightforwardly, the chapters found in the examples of the collaborative self-study section reveal exemplary practices of collaboration in teacher educator research as well as offer strategies for collaboration in and across teacher education practices and programs. Lomax, Evans and Parker's use of memory work is a brilliant research strategy based on collaboration. The chapter displays the way in which interpretation emerges in collaborative structures and the interrelation between the inquiries of teachers and students. In terms of reconceptualizing teaching practice, it forces teacher educators to confront, reexamine, and possibly reinterpret their past practices in light of current situations. The LaBoskey, Davies-Samway and Garcia chapter reveals the way in which cross-institutional collaboration can be especially helpful, not just in developing a community to support the study of teacher education, but also as a community for disseminating, developing, and examining teacher education programs and practices.

Reframing

The integrated narrative provided by Conle, Louden and Mildon offers an intriguing insight into the process of reframing. Using a collaborative process of reframing, they integrate into one narrative their separate lived experiences and personal interpretations of abstract ideas. This integrated narrative represents how collaboration results in the reframing of meaning.

Richards utilizes self-portraits as a research methodology to reframe her own practice, and also introduces her students to a strategy for reframing their practice. In addition, the topics of the self-portraits that her students choose to draw provide insights into students' conceptualizations of the difficulties they face as they become teachers.

On an individual level, Oda's chapter begins with the question about whether her cultural heritage has any impact on what her students learn about issues of race and diversity, and how she, as an Asian-American, supports them in developing their awareness. She seeks evidence about whether her status as an Asian-American causes her students to reframe their ideas about issues of diversity and, in the process, begins to think of herself and her purposes in teaching multicultural issues differently.

Wilcox provides an even more complex view of the process whereby studying one's teaching practices results in a constant reframing of an understanding of the self and the practice. She exemplifies this by looking at herself and her research, and examining their impact on her professional development.

Hutchinson provides intriguing insights about reframing. Throughout her work she appears to constantly ask — 'How might I think differently about what I am doing and how might my students help me do that?' In the process, she provides evidence of the ways in which she helps them think differently. Thus, her research study gives insight into the importance of seeking to reframe practice. Finally, Wilkes' dilemmas present a heuristic for instigating, guiding and enhancing the rethinking of teaching and learning both for systematic study of practice and for the reform of practice.

Part I

Philosophical Perspectives

Introduction

Tom Russell

What is self-study? Where did it come from, and where is it going? To whom does it appeal, and why does teacher education in particular require an unusual and specialized term such as 'self-study?' In the chapters in this opening section, John Loughran, Jeff Northfield and Howard Smith write thoughtfully and perceptively about their experience of self-study. They draw conclusions from their experiences with a view to helping others engage in self-study, and their numbered lists of issues related to self-study and developing collective knowledge can be read as 'guidelines' for those embarking on self-study. One goal of this section overview, however, is to discourage reading these chapters solely for guidelines.

Teacher education is a uniquely perilous enterprise. In virtually all other domains of teaching, what one teaches and how one teaches are independent, although both 'what' and 'how' are relevant to the learning that results. But in teacher education, what and how we teach are interactive, and we ignore this interaction at our peril. Just as actions are said to speak louder than words, so how we teach may speak more loudly than what we teach. Teacher education is the easiest domain of teaching in which to experience one's self as a 'living contradiction' (Whitehead, 1993).

For many reasons, rooted in culture and tradition, teacher education has seemed inattentive to the peril of the living contradiction, but those who partake of self-study seem captivated by it. This seems to tell us something about where self-study of teacher education practices came from and is going. There may still be some truth in the 'Mickey Mouse' characterizations of pre-service programs, and some teacher educators see self-study as one route out of that dilemma. While self-study may seem like a lonely and isolated activity, the Loughran–Northfield and Smith chapters indicate that it is quite the reverse. The goal is to turn the focus of inquiry on to the self, as expressed in the teaching activities of teacher education. This involves new forms of data-gathering and communication with the individuals one teaches, as one is teaching, and it also involves sharing with one's teaching colleagues.

Refreshingly, the self-study field is new enough that there are no experts, and the field is likely to prosper and go further if it resists the tendency to see some people as experts simply because they began self-study earlier or appear to have written more about it. Who are the experts for the academic? What is to be gained by creating an uneven playing field? There is only one way to understand self-study, and that is to experience it personally.

In 1993, Hugh Munby and I began to talk about the 'authority of experience' to open up for each other a discussion about the ways in which personal experience can convey authority that might be contrasted with the authority of others' experiences ('Been there, done that — Do it my way') or the authority of scholarly argument ('Research shows that . . .'). At that time, our attention was on how new teachers learn from experience:

> We use the term *authority of experience* because of our concern that students never master learning from experience during pre-service programs in a way that gives them direct access to nature of the authority of experience. If Schön is correct that there is a knowledge-in-action that cannot be fully expressed in propositions and that learning from experience has its own epistemology, then our concern is that learning from experience is never clearly contrasted with learning that can be expressed and conveyed in propositions. (Munby and Russell, 1994, p. 92)

Self-study is about the learning from experience that is embedded within teachers' creating new experiences for themselves and those whom they teach. Like new teachers, teacher educators must learn to learn from experience and self-study is a way for teacher educators to do that. I invite readers to delve into these first two chapters by reading between the lines, listening for the original experiences of Loughran and Northfield and Smith. These chapters can and should be read for guidelines about self-study, but any such reading will be incomplete without also examining the experiences that support the conclusions. Then readers should create their own self-study exercises and activities, not alone but with students and colleagues. After focusing on one's personal learning from self-study experiences, one is finally in a position to define self-study and to contribute to self-study by sharing the results with others. Our goal may well be the reinvention of learning to teach, enabling others to understand learning from experience by showing them how we do it ourselves.

References

MUNBY, H. and RUSSELL, T. (1994) 'The authority of experience in learning to teach: Messages from a physics method class,' *Journal of Teacher Education*, **45**, 2, pp. 86–95.

WHITEHEAD, J. (1993) *The Growth of Educational Knowledge: Creating Your Own Living Educational Theories*, Bournemouth: Hyde Publications.

1 A Framework for the Development of Self-study Practice

John Loughran and Jeff Northfield

Introduction

Interest in self-study is increasing as many teacher educators review the manner in which teaching about teaching is carried out in schools and faculties of education. This questioning arises, in part, from an increased desire and corresponding need by teacher educators to ensure that their teaching practice is congruent with the expectations they have of their student-teachers' developing practice. Hence, the growing need for teacher educators to 'practise what they preach'.

Reflection on practice and self-study are becoming important components of the push for closer scrutiny of an individual's pedagogy in teaching about teaching, and they are linked to ideas about the development of knowledge through better understanding of personal experience. Studying one's own practice sometimes leads to what Whitehead (1993) describes as 'experiencing yourself as a living contradiction' (p. 8).

Such an interpretation hinges on the understanding and recognition that ideas and aspirations may not be matched by teaching practices. In self-study, recognizing the dissonance between beliefs and practice is fundamental to action. While it is important to attend to experiencing self as a living contradiction, it may be equally important to include others in the interpretation of and response to the contradiction. While the term 'self-study' suggests an individual approach, attempting to better align beliefs and practice solely from an individual perspective may be a significant paradox within the term 'self-study'.

In this chapter, we contend that it is working with an important 'other' that matters. Otherwise, self-study may simply be seen as rationalizing or justifying one's actions or frames of reference. We argue that if self-study is to lead to genuine reframing (Schön, 1983) of a situation so that learning and understanding through reflection might be enhanced, then the self in self-study cannot be solely individual. The experience of an individual is the focus of the study but the individual need not be, and should not be, the sole participant in the process. The way self-study has come to be characterized, and some of the associated concerns surrounding its practice, are important in understanding how self-study might be better recognized and defined in practice.

The idea of self-study has evolved from several significant educational perspectives. In some ways, self-study appears to be related to the development of Schön's

7

(1983) ideas about reflection on practice. For example, Munby and Russell (1994) have developed Schön's ideas to highlight the 'authority of experience' as a key to the way teachers may better understand teaching and learning. Furthermore, there is no educational change without 'people' change. By focusing on personal practice and experience, teachers may undertake genuine inquiry that leads to a better understanding of the complexities of teaching and learning.

Self-study may be defined as a participant study of experience and it has therefore inevitably been queried as a form of research. Thus, questions are rightly raised such as, 'Is the outcome of a self-study merely personal reflections, or does self-study aspire to generalizable forms of knowledge?' are rightly raised. There appear to be at least three responses to this question. The first explores the relationship between two ways of gaining knowledge about educational practice. Richardson (1994) distinguishes between two forms of research on practice: formal research and practical inquiry. We would suggest that self-study is an important form of practical inquiry. Richardson argues that, 'Both forms . . . may be conducted by the practitioner, and at times, practical inquiry may be turned into formal research . . . One could suggest, then, that practical inquiry may be foundational to formal research that will be truly useful in improving practice' (pp. 7–8).

A second response, from which some debate has developed, has been to argue that participant research has unique features that deserve acknowledgment and recognition as a distinct genre of research (Wong, 1995; Baumann, 1996; Northfield, 1996). A third response is to learn from observing the professional development that occurs when practitioners gain the confidence and skills to reframe and reflect on their experiences. Self-study is thus seen as an indication that a professional is willing to accept that experience is a major source of improvement in personal practice. This type of professional development has been well documented in the PEEL project (Baird and Mitchell, 1986; Baird and Northfield, 1992) and demonstrates how important such experiences are in the lives of schoolteachers. We believe that a similar situation also exists for teacher educators.

Encouragement of self-study thus becomes an option for all those committed to the improvement of professional practice. In fact, self-study may be one way of helping teacher educators grasp the sense of excitement in their teaching in teacher education programs that Tom (1996) describes as generally lacking due to the 'external forces which sustain mundane and unimaginative teacher education . . . [and] underlying beliefs which deter teacher educators from questioning the traditional content and structure of our field' (p. 19). The recent growth of interest and practice in self-study certainly addresses Tom's (1996) assertions.

Questioning the theoretical underpinnings of a practical venture in self-study is both important and necessary as teacher educators attempt to address their pedagogical concerns in order to maintain the spark that is so important for teaching and learning about teaching. Such questioning is vital to teacher education if the importance of the knowledge base for learning about teaching is to be recognized and valued in the educational community, particularly so in terms of better articulating the pedagogy of teacher educators. The need for such recognition and articulation prompted recent collections by Russell and Korthagen (1995) and Loughran and Russell (1997), in which the need to highlight teacher education practices is portrayed as a crucial issue for schools and faculties of education.

Opening the Classroom Door: A Case Study of Self-study

This chapter builds on what we have learnt in a self-study of Jeff Northfield's experiences during a one-year teaching allotment in a secondary school where he taught mathematics and science and was the Home Group teacher for one class of students in their first year of secondary school (Year 7). At the same time, he was the Director of Pre-service Education in the Faculty of Education at Monash University, an academic role with administrating, teaching and research responsibilities in teacher education, teaching and learning.

In some ways, Jeff's return to teaching can be seen as a teacher educator trying to regain some of the important contact with schools, and with the teaching role within that context, that are so easily lost (or at least diminished) through the demands of an academic appointment. (See Russell, 1995, for a similar return to teaching by a teacher educator.) The desire to reacquaint himself with schools was important for many reasons, both professional and personal. At the forefront of his thinking was the value of 'recent and relevant' experience. Such recent and relevant experience was an important pragmatic response to his professional concerns for his own teaching in the preparation of the young teachers for whom he was responsible in the Teacher Education program at Monash University. There was also a desire to share the excitement of teachers (such as those in the PEEL project, as described in Baird and Mitchell, 1986, and Baird and Northfield, 1992) who appeared to be making a difference in classrooms as they worked to teach in ways that helped their students learn for understanding. This approach to teaching and learning was at the heart of the teaching approaches espoused in the teacher education program. Thus, Jeff's desire to teach in a school was one way of attempting to better understand the strategies he was urging his students to use in their school teaching experiences. Finally, there was perhaps also a yearning for the pleasant memories of teaching associated with those times from much earlier in his teaching career. Therefore, an opportunity for a self-study was a real possibility. The complexities of teaching, learning, personal and professional beliefs and practice would be more available in a real context rather than in a contrived situation.

During his year teaching 7D, Jeff kept a daily journal of his teaching activities, including descriptions, reactions and interpretations associated with his teaching and his students' learning. The journal was an important part of Jeff's self-study of his teaching experience and he used it both to document and to reflect on his experiences as he attempted to teach his students in a manner that would encourage them to learn for understanding. In this return to secondary school teaching, 'Jeff the researcher' became 'Jeff the practitioner' and worked from a self-study/practical research perspective through to a more formal, more widely available and accessible research knowledge as documented in Loughran and Northfield (1996).

Opening the Classroom Door draws on three main data sources: Jeff's daily journal, interviews conducted by Carol Jones with twenty-two of the students in the class, and student writing (from both regular classroom tasks and specific responses to classroom experiences). It is noteworthy that Jeff's journal was also read by some of the teachers in the school and provided a stimulus for extended discussions about students, teaching and learning. Subsequent discussions with interested staff provided opportunities for reframing situations and experiences that could well have been missed or overlooked if the journal had remained a personal 'closed' book. At the end of the year, when Jeff reviewed the journal, he developed twenty-four theme statements about teaching and learning, which were in essence the culmination of a year's self-study. The theme statements were grouped under five headings:

- Nature of learning
- Creating conditions for learning
- Student perspectives on learning
- Process of teaching and learning
- Overall reactions to the experience

Each statement summarized significant experiences and suggested possible interpretations of important issues related to teaching and learning. Yet this alone is not the extent of the self-study, nor is it alone what we would argue defines self-study.

Throughout Jeff's year in the classroom, an important 'other' was involved. Carol Jones, a research assistant and an experienced teacher, spent time in Jeff's classes observing his teaching. She also worked with and interviewed the students. Her presence in the class helped her to get to know the students and to be accepted as an observer who had no teaching or assessment status. Thus, her interview data were most interesting, revealing a student voice and perspective on the classroom experiences that would normally be easily missed in the daily rush and bustle of classroom practice. Similarly, the students' writing was equally useful as they completed specific learning tasks and other regular classroom activities and offered insights into practice that could inadvertently be overlooked in more 'normal' circumstances. Thus, an important element of self-study was highlighted: self-study is set within the complexity of the teaching and learning environment (in this case, schools and classrooms) and it should aspire to retain and use this complexity in the search for understanding.

As teacher educators, we are always trying to understand more fully the schooling situations for which we are to prepare and support teachers. We are also searching for more effective ways to prepare teachers for their professional lives. It is, therefore, not surprising that we see the opportunity to spend an extensive period of time in school classrooms as a valuable learning experience. First hand experience must surely allow for a better understanding of current learning issues and could therefore better inform approaches to teacher education. In one sense, then, the value of recent and relevant experience for teacher educators could almost be regarded as self-evident. However, we now argue that the connection between school experience and improvement in teacher education is not quite that clear. On the one hand, we would argue that greater opportunities should exist for teacher educators to work in schools and classrooms, but on the other hand, we contend that the experience alone is not sufficient. Certain conditions for learning about teaching and teacher education need to be established to make the effort worthwhile. These conditions are the precursors to our learning about self-study.

Two conditions made this particular experience worthwhile, and both involved other individuals. The first condition was the involvement of Carol Jones. Jeff needed an opportunity to reflect on students' responses to his teaching and Carol helped him to do this. Carol was also able to interview students, to provide a student perspective on the classroom activities, and to act as a colleague as the teaching and learning situations were interpreted from the perspectives of all participants, their backgrounds and aspirations. From the daily journal record and the variety of data gathered from the class, a more holistic sense of the whole situation began to emerge. Carol, therefore, provided important conditions to begin learning from experience.

The second condition for learning was the analysis of the journal and other data that led to the writing of our book, which could not have been written without the involvement of a colleague who was able to remain at a distance from the experience and see the trends developing over the year. *Opening the Classroom Door: Teacher Researcher Learner* (Loughran and Northfield, 1996) describes the progress made in understanding teaching and learning and the associated implications for teacher education. Thus, the data analysis by an 'other' was similarly important in the reframing for learning.

Through this study of Jeff's teaching practice, we came to better understand what we believe to be important aspects of the nature of self-study and the way in which knowledge and understanding can be gained through such practice. This chapter presents the assertions that we are now prepared to make about the nature of self-study and the knowledge and understanding gained through it. For us, these assertions offer a way of considering how self-study might be viewed, understood and practised so that the outcomes may be communicated to others and thereby lead to learning that is useful and applicable for more than just the individuals directly involved.

While Jeff's return to high school teaching was an important event, it was the collaborative nature of the analysis of the event that stimulated development of our emerging views on self-study. As we were both in constant contact throughout Jeff's teaching year (by virtue of our close professional relationship through our teaching and research in pre-service education), the discussions, insights and episodes that emerged became a continuous source of reflection on practice for both of us. However, in the formal analysis of the data, the classroom events served as a touchstone (Lakatos, 1970; Walker and Evers, 1984) for the development of a better understanding of teaching and learning for both of us. This, then, was the key to our collaboration in self-study. It would have been impossible to construct the following assertions had we not had an honest relationship built on common principles of pedagogy that allowed us to examine the issues in a critical and professional manner.

The Nature of Self-study and the Knowledge and Understanding Gained

We offer the following statements to encourage discussion of various features of self-study. In the emerging tradition of self-study, these ten statements are intended to provide prompts for the reader's personal experience in such a way that their meaning and implications might resonate with the reader.

1   Self-study defines the focus of study (i.e. context and nature of a person's activity), not the way the study is carried out

In the documentation and dissemination of any study, understanding the context is important so that the issues raised and conclusions drawn might be viewed in ways that help readers to relate the learning to their own situations. However, even though understanding the context and the nature of one's work is important and is a shaping factor in self-study, self-study itself should not be construed as simply coping with the pressures or constraints of these factors. We see self-study as the development of an understanding, of reframing and reconsidering action within those constraints. That is why defining the context becomes crucial, for the portrayal of the context shapes the focus of the study, but not the study itself. A wide range of strategies, both quantitative and qualitative, can be used for gathering data, and these are determined by the study rather than being predefined.

2   Even though the term 'self-study' suggests an individual approach, we believe that effective self-study requires a commitment to checking data and interpretations with others

Checking data and interpretations with others is crucial to self-study. It is through the involvement of others that data and interpretations can be viewed from perspectives other than one's own and therefore be scrutinized and professionally challenged. The value of the involvement of others becomes evident in practice and is well demonstrated when interpretations, conclusions or situations resonate with others who have had the opportunity to analyse the data independently. Clearly, an extension of this is that working with others tests the validity and reliability of the data sources. In this case of self-study, further understanding was gained by considering the data and experiences with the critical friend, Carol Jones, with the first author (John) in preparing the book, with teachers who read the journal during the year, with readers who discussed the book and their ideas and experiences, and with the students who (four years later) have begun to review their experiences with Loughran. This situation, if effectively described, can be the subject of continual self-study from a number of perspectives.

3   It is very difficult for individuals to change their interpretations (frames of reference) when their own experience is being examined

This is an aspect of self-study that is common to many other forms of study but is perhaps most quickly recognized in self-study. However, the willingness to review existing frames of reference must be seen as a criterion of quality in self-study and an indication that the study is not being used to rationalize existing frames of reference. As an individual is so deeply involved in a personal working environment, it is often very difficult to step back and reconsider the experiences from another viewpoint. It may well be that one's own experience is too personal to seriously question one's own frames of reference, despite the best intentions to do so. Being so personally involved in the experience may limit the ability to see beyond the experience. It could therefore, be reasonable to suggest that, in some instances, such personal involvement negates the ability to recognize oneself as a living contradiction, even though this recognition may well be the 'stated' basis for self-study.

---

[1] As an extension to this self-study, John returned to speak with Jeff's former students when they were in Year 11 to discuss with them their understanding of their Year 7 experiences with Jeff. Each student was given a copy of the book (*Opening the Classroom Door*) and these discussions now extend us as we reconsider our interpretations of Jeff's teaching year by further exploring the students' understandings of these events in light of the book and their own memories of the events. In essence, this reconsideration challenges us both to continue to learn from the teaching and research associated with Jeff's return to high school teaching.

4   Colleagues are likely to frame an experience in ways not thought of by the person carrying out the self-study

This point is a natural progression from points 2 and 3 in that the need to work with others broadens the possibilities for validation and clarification as well as reframing. The essential characteristics of self-study provide both the strengths and weaknesses of this approach to research. The strengths lie within the detailed experiences in very complex settings over long periods of time by a participant who is committed to better understanding the situation. The uniqueness of each context, the personal involvement, the bias and the emotional investment all have the potential to limit the value of any study when attempts are made to communicate ideas more widely. Satisfying the fundamental requirements of reliability, generalizability and validity remains an essential element if self-study aspires to communicate new understandings. These same requirements need to be interpreted and applied in particular ways when considering self-study approaches.

People engaging in self-study are very conscious of the specific and complex contexts from which their findings emerge. It is important that findings are seen to be tentative and those who do self-studies may be reluctant to engage in wider communication. Generalizability is not a claim that can be made by the self-study researcher without wider interaction with colleagues. Such interactions allow validation of experiences and ideas and, thus, self-study reports can be considered as an invitation to readers to link accounts with their own experiences. In this sense, generalizations are best described as 'naturalistic' (Stake and Trumbull, 1983) and readers will require adequate descriptions of context if they are to be able to make links to their own situations and experiences. In self-study, the generalization criterion is addressed in the way that the study is conducted. Ideally, perspectives and final drafts are developed with significant others and continued (or discontinued) and further shaped and refined to form a report that remains tentative but, more importantly, acts as an invitation to abstract from the self-study described to the reader's own situation.

The concepts of reliability and validity are directly queried when terms such as subjectivity and bias are used to question a self-study. In the end, it is the reader who assesses reliability and validity. If an account is considered 'authentic' and 'a useful contribution to better understanding my situation', then a reader is accepting the account as reliable and valid for personal purposes. From this perspective, reliability and validity are enhanced if the report:

- includes sufficient detail of the complexity and context of the situation for it to 'ring true' for the reader,
- provides and demonstrates some triangulation of data and a range of different perspectives around an issue,
- makes explicit links to relevant educational literature and other self-study accounts and literature.

Again, the requirements for reliability and validity are addressed in the way the self-study is developed. They include the involvement of others, and the interplay of ideas, questions and challenges introduced through interaction with others. Involving the ideas and perspectives of others is an important way of addressing reliability and validity.

5   Valuable learning occurs when self-study is a shared task

The learning in self-study is intensely personal, but self-study itself requires collaboration. In many ways learning through self-study is a 'shared adventure' (Loughran and Gunstone, 1996). The value of the 'shared adventure' is that the learning outcomes broaden the understanding of the individual whose situation is the focus of the self-study and the significant 'other' with whom the sharing of the adventure occurs. It is not an 'expert–novice' relationship, nor that of a 'critical friend', but a shared adventure in which the participants are jointly involved in developing the study and learning through collaborative experiences. In this approach, the intensely personal aspects of the study that might otherwise be simply accepted without challenge or scrutiny are able to be professionally and constructively challenged from within the study itself. In so doing, new understandings may emerge as situations become better clarified and questioned. Alternate interpretations may lead to shared generalizations.

6   Self-confidence is important

In spite of the previous point about shared adventure, the intensely personal nature of self-study experiences requires an important trait that shapes the individual's approach to self-study. A high level of self-confidence is necessary, as 'successful' experiences have unintended outcomes and closely held assumptions and ideas are queried. Self-confidence is a most intriguing aspect of self-study. One needs to be comfortable with the sense of vulnerability necessary to genuinely study personal practice, and the overarching need to learn through self-study inevitably creates personal conflicts and a sense of dissonance. Self-confidence is thus an important personal characteristic if self-study is to be a professionally rewarding learning experience.

7   Self-study outcomes demand immediate action, and thus the focus of study is constantly changing

Learning through self-study unavoidably means that the results of self-study create new opportunities for self-study. Therefore, as learning opportunities arise, they need to be grasped and acted upon. Thus, the situation of self-study is ever changing and developing because the researcher must continue to give first priority to managing the context that is simultaneously being studied. Researchers are therefore obliged to continually adjust their activities to improve their interactions with others.

8   There are differences between self-study and reflection on practice

'Reflection' has various interpretations and often means many things to many people, and 'self-study' is in danger of being viewed similarly. However, if reflection on practice is defined from the Deweyan perspective (Dewey, 1933) as has been most common in the literature (for example, see Bode, 1940; Hullfish and Smith, 1961; Zeichner, 1981; Schön, 1983; Baird, 1991; Loughran, 1996), then the recognition of a problem or a perplexing situation becomes the impetus for reflection. Flowing from this, reflection involves not simply a sequence of ideas, but a con-sequence — a consecutive ordering in such a way that each determines the next as its proper outcome, while each outcome in turn leans back on, or refers to, its predecessors. The successive portions of reflective thought flow out of one another and support one another . . . there is a goal to be reached, and this end sets a task that controls the sequence of ideas. (Dewey, 1933, pp. 4–6)

Reflection then is a thoughtful process within an individual, yet clearly, considering the previous point about a shifting focus, we suggest that self-study may best be regarded as a sequence of reflective instances as the problematic situation is not only reframed and redefined, but is also changed as a result of the intended action designed to resolve the problem.

Self-study builds on reflection as the study begins to reshape not just the nature of the reflective processes but also the situation in which these processes are occurring and — as has been an important theme in this chapter — the persons involved. Reflection is a personal process of thinking, refining, reframing and developing actions. Self-study takes these processes and makes them public, thus leading to another series of processes that need to reside outside the individual.

Reflection on practice may be regarded as a description of the way professionals should go about their work and career. It is essentially a professional development model and a powerful guideline based on a respect for personal experience as a basis for new knowledge and understanding being generated. Self-study can be considered as an extension of reflection on practice, with aspirations that go beyond professional development and move to wider communication and consideration of ideas, i.e. the generation and communication of new knowledge and understanding. Reflection is important in self-study but it alone is not self-study. Self-study involves reflection on practice.

9   Dilemmas, tensions and disappointments tend to dominate data gathering in self-study

Just as reflection is sparked by dilemmas, tensions and disappointments, so too are these important in self-study, as they tend to dominate the data gathering and to occupy the study's centre of attention. As self-study tends to be directed by problems, dilemmas and tensions, it is inevitable that these elements control the data-gathering. This means that, in many ways, successes tend to be glossed over in an almost 'to be expected' fashion as the mind focuses on the unexpected and the unexplained. Thus, surprise and curiosity spring from self-study and shape it, but are drawn from unresolved situations. This is why confidence is again an important issue in self-study. Constant attention to apparent 'failures' is demanding and somewhat unrepresentative of the total situation being experienced.

10   The audience is critical in shaping self-study reports

Just as self-study is not an individual task but is best seen as a collaborative enterprise, so too the reporting of self-study is influenced by the intended audience of the report. If self-study is to move beyond the individual, it needs to resonate with others in similar situations. Therefore, the way self-study is reported is important in helping to make the findings clear and meaningful to others. Obviously, then, the form of reporting is shaped by the audience and an understanding of the relevant needs and concerns of this audience.

Overview

The importance of collaboration may seem to contradict the personal nature of self-study (see points 2, 3, 4, and 5 above), but it is essential for checking that focus, data collection and interpretations do not become self-justifications and rationalizations of experience. Collaboration provides some confidence that experiences and interpretations can be offered more widely for consideration by others, an important aspect of any study.

For Jeff, the return to teaching was often a confusing and unsettling experience. The conditions rarely seemed to be suitable to initiate different teaching and learning activities with the class. His journal entries frequently outlined disappointments as he searched for understanding of his context. The daily nature of teaching and its unpredictability appeared to dominate his reflections. As he began to understand the students' perspective, their responses to the demands of schooling often made more sense than the learning attitudes and outcomes he was seeking. At the same time, the overall experience with the class was enjoyable and satisfying. What tended to be documented in the journal and discussed with others were the surprises, dilemmas and tensions, perhaps giving a more negative picture of the experience. Yet it is through the shared adventure of this self-study that we have come to understand the features (listed above) that we find important in describing and defining self-study. Our experiences have enabled us to define our knowledge and practice in self-study, and we hope that the manner in which we portrayed this knowledge resonates with others and is valuable and helpful for their practice.

The Future of Self-study

Teacher knowledge generation (teacher research) depends on teachers finding ways to share critical experiences. This tacit knowledge must be made explicit if we are to consider alternate frames of reference that may lead to deeper understanding of teaching and learning. There is always a danger that individuals will interpret situations in ways that reinforce existing perceptions. Genuine study of classrooms is associated with a willingness to consider alternate frames of reference, and colleagues are an important source of ideas and support as the teaching and learning are reviewed.

In addition to encouraging self-study, we believe its proponents have a responsibility to critically analyse the nature of the process and the features of the new knowledge it yields. In the end, the value of self-study depends on providing convincing evidence that it can be undertaken with rigour. This requires addressing the issues of quality, reliability, and validity if self-study is to continue to make a contribution to knowledge and understanding.

Self-study will inevitably be judged on the credibility of the individual (the self). It is impossible to separate the substance of self-study from the credentials and reputation of the person who undertakes it. In the end, appreciating self-study depends on how much personal experience is valued as a source of new knowledge and understanding. Portraying this well to others is an important measure of self-study itself.

References

BAIRD, J.R. (1991) 'Individual and group reflection as a basis for teacher development', in HUGHES, P. (ed.) *Teachers' Professional Development*, Melbourne: ACER, pp. 95–113.

BAIRD, J.R. and MITCHELL, I.J. (eds) (1986) *Improving the Quality of Teaching and Learning: An Australian Case Study — The PEEL Project*, Melbourne: Monash University.

BAIRD, J.R. and NORTHFIELD, J.R. (eds) (1992) *Learning from the PEEL Experience*, Melbourne: Monash University.

BAUMANN, J.F. (1996) 'Conflict or compatibility in classroom inquiry? One teacher's struggle to balance teaching and research', *Educational Researcher*, **25**, 7, pp. 29–36.

BODE, B. (1940) *How We Learn*, New York: Heath.

DEWEY, J. (1934) *Art as Experience*, New York: Capricorn Books.

HULLFISH, H.G. and SMITH, P.G. (1961) *Reflective Thinking: The Method of Education*, New York: Dodd, Mead and Company.

LAKATOS, I. (1970) 'Falsification and the methodology of scientific research programmes', in LAKATOS, I. and MUSGRAVE, A. (eds) *Criticism and the Growth of Knowledge*, Cambridge: Cambridge University Press, pp. 91–196.

LOUGHRAN, J.J. (1996) *Developing Reflective Practice: Learning about Teaching and Learning through Modelling*, London: Falmer Press.

LOUGHRAN, J.J. and GUNSTONE, R.F. (1996) 'Self-study in Teaching and Research'. Paper presented at the Annual Meeting of the American Educational Research Association, New York.

LOUGHRAN, J.J. and NORTHFIELD, J.R. (1996) *Opening the Classroom Door: Teacher Researcher Learner*, London: Falmer Press.

LOUGHRAN, J. and RUSSELL, T. (eds) (1997) *Teaching About Teaching: Purpose, Passion and Pedagogy in Teacher Education*, London: Falmer Press.

MUNBY, H. and RUSSELL, T. (1994) 'The authority of experience in learning to teach: Messages from a physics method class', *Journal of Teacher Education*, **45**, 2, pp. 86–95.

NORTHFIELD, J.R. (1996) 'Quality and the self-study perspective on research'. Paper presented at the Annual Meeting of the American Educational Research Association, New York. (ERIC Document Reproduction Service No. ED 397 034.)

RICHARDSON, V. (1994) 'Conducting research on practice', *Educational Researcher*, **23**, 5, pp. 5–10.

RUSSELL, T. (1995) 'Returning to the physics classroom to re-think how one learns to teach physics', in RUSSELL, T. and KORTHAGEN, F. (eds) *Teachers Who Teach Teachers: Reflections on Teacher Education*, London: Falmer Press, pp. 95–109.

RUSSELL, T. and KORTHAGEN, F. (eds) (1995) *Teachers Who Teach Teachers: Reflections on Teacher Education*, London: Falmer Press.

SCHÖN, D.A. (1983) *The Reflective Practitioner: How Professionals Think in Action*, New York: Basic Books.

STAKE, R.E. and TRUMBULL, D. (1983) 'Naturalistic generalisations', in BELOK, M. and HAGGERSON, N. (eds) *Naturalistic Research: Theory and Practice*, Meerut, India: Anu Books, pp. 1–14.

TOM, A. (1996) 'Principles for redesigning teacher education', *Journal of Primary Education*, **6**, 1 and 2, pp. 19–28.

WALKER, J. and EVERS, C. (1984) 'Towards a materialist pragmatist philosophy of education', *Education Research and Perspectives*, **11**, 1, pp. 23–33.

WHITEHEAD, J. (1993) *The Growth of Educational Knowledge: Creating Your Own Living Educational Theories*, Bournemouth: Hyde Publications.

WONG, E.D. (1995) 'Challenges confronting the researcher/teacher', *Educational Researcher*, **24**, 3, pp. 22–8.

ZEICHNER, K. (1981) 'Reflective teaching and field-based experience in teacher education', *Interchange*, **12**, 4, pp. 1–22.

2 Self-study and the Development of Collective Knowledge

Howard A. Smith

Introduction

This chapter reports a study of the relationships among ten individuals (five females, five males) who met seven times in six months while they were engaged in personal self-study projects. As they evolved, the purposes of this study were to explore: (a) the relationships among individuals engaged in their own self-study projects, and (b) the development of collective knowledge when these same individuals met as a group. Self-study researchers speak of the importance of sharing their information with others, but how might this sharing best be achieved? What group conditions support both individual and collective enterprises when the group focus involves self-study in a teacher education setting? This 'study of self-study' sought to capture in part the influences that exist between the individual mind and the collective socio-cultural surround that continuously shapes, and is shaped by, the thoughts and activities of its individual members (see Bohm, 1994).

The following statements give a sense of the conclusions drawn from the study:

- The group had differential effects on individual members and an important role in promoting self-study research.
- In the absence of explicit feedback, members were unable to determine their impact on others.
- The cognitive constructivist model is useful in describing group functions.
- Affect played a powerful role in knowledge development and group proceedings.
- Junior members were very aware of the authority of position or knowledge.
- Electronic mail had limited influence on group processes.
- Members believed that the group had not achieved a full cycle of development in its short history and hoped that the group would resume meeting.

Background Perspectives

I came to self-study from educational psychology possessing a cultural psychological and semiotic bent. Thus, I hoped to explore some key issues that were raised for me by the concept of self-study in teacher education. For example, to what extent does self-study involve western views of the self as an independent entity versus other views, such as the Japanese, which perceive the self as interdependent? As an example, these contrasting views may be illustrated by two firms trying to enhance productivity in the United States. A Texas corporation told its employees to look in the mirror and say 'I am beautiful' 100 times before coming to work each day, while a Japanese firm in New Jersey had its employees hold hands and tell the other person that they were beautiful (Markus and Kitayama, 1991).

Secondly, how should we understand the word 'study' and its apparently distinctive role in western thinking? The term connotes deliberate and sustained effort and is epitomized by the heavy, muscular statue of Rodin's thinker. This view may be contrasted with a delicate wooden Japanese figure from the sixth century that underlines the fragile, hesitant, and effortless view of thinking in an oriental culture. Study also tends to be associated with linear verbal streams of representation, a view that represents only one theory of thought (Bruner, 1996).

Thirdly, and similarly, who and what do we include with the terms 'teacher' and 'teacher education'? Do not these expressions also have strong cultural roots and restricted meanings? Because most of us tend to think only in terms of educational systems, we hold rather narrow views of who is a teacher and what activities count as teacherly. In turn, these views have implications for what constitutes teacher education and for what types of activity qualify as self-study in teacher education.

Finally, what kinds of self-phenomena are open to study and under what conditions? For example, on occasion, people exhibit a fully masterful control of events, are perfectly attuned to the task at hand, lose all consciousness of self, and distort time as a clock-based concept. This state is called 'flow' (Csikszentmihalyi, 1990) and is entered into by those skilled in tasks that are neither too easy nor too hard for them. Whether or not teachers who experience flow can also engage in self-study is a matter for investigation.

These were some of the questions that I hoped to raise and have discussed upon joining my local self-study group. In addition, I came to the first meeting of that group with plans for my own self-study project: to examine how my assessment practices in educational psychology supported or contradicted our new institutional objectives in teacher education. However, upon noting the diversity of the group's members at its first meeting, I decided to examine a pervasive matter in cultural psychology: the relationship between individual and group cognitions.

Conceptual Bases of the Research

For most of the history of western academic thought, researchers have focused on individual cognitions without acknowledging the central influences on thought of the surrounding collective. However, at least two distinct streams of research have rectified this imbalance, sometimes inadvertently. First, some recent studies have characterized personal development among family members as an increasing diversification among the family members involved. Much of this diversification is created by active decisions of the individuals themselves as they choose and then negotiate their places within their own preferred communities or collectives (e.g. Plomin, Chipuer and Neiderhiser, 1994; Scarr, 1992). That is, individuals choose, shape, and are shaped by the groups to which they belong.

Second, researchers have emphasized that personal meanings are derived from and in activity with other members of the culture. The activities themselves tend to be culturally valued and linked to cultural survival (e.g. Lave and Wenger, 1991). These assertions are supported by the cultural psychological perspective that declares all knowledge to be constructed, distributed, mediated, and situated (Bruner, 1990; Vygotsky, 1978). Lotman (1990), who introduced the notion of the semiosphere, offered additional comment. He argued that semiotic systems, not just the individual human intellect, conduct intellectual operations and rework and enhance information. According to Lotman, 'thought is within us, but we are within thought' (1990, p. 273).

These claims were advanced by Nichol (1994), who argued that individuals are in large measure controlled by collective thought and knowledge and that feeling and thought interpenetrate one another in profound ways. For example, a recent and well-publicized American trial (the O.J. Simpson case) served to underline intriguing questions about the mutual influences that exist between individual and collective judgments over what constitutes reasonable doubt. This case demonstrated clearly that different collectives offer differing perspectives on the 'same' phenomenon and that individuals within collectives are influenced likewise. The obvious involvement in thought of feeling, emotion, or attitude (Bartlett, 1932) underlines the fact that thought and knowledge are not objective dispassionate phenomena. Recent work in human biology (reviewed in Goleman, 1995) supports the latter finding.

To summarize, this study uses group processes and dialogue to detect the flow of meaning (Nichol, 1994) among ten members of a self-study group created in 1995 at the Queen's University Faculty of Education. As one member of this group, I set out to: (a) document evolving relationships within the group as each member undertook his or her own project, and (b) explore the influences of individual and collective contributions on the development of collective knowledge.

The Faculty's Self-study Group: Its Formation and Operation

In late June of 1995, Tom (see p. 22 for information about the group's membership) sent an electronic message to the entire Faculty of Education community inviting expressions of interest in self-study. Specifically, Tom mentioned the objective of working toward a conference on Self-study of Teacher Education Practices to be held in August, 1996 at the University's International Study Centre, a fifteenth-century castle at Herstmonceux, England. In addition, Tom mentioned the possibility of meeting as a group in the fall and the likely contributions of two visitors to the Faculty of Education who would be supporting the Herstmonceux conference. The email message concluded with a list of deadlines leading to the August 1996 event.

The first meeting of the Self-study Group (SSG) took place at noon on 7 September 1995 (see Table 1 for a chronology of main events). Of the nine persons who attended this meeting, eight remained to become contributing group members. Two others joined the group later: Sylvia at the second meeting and Angela at the fifth. In the end, the group consisted of 10 academics, 5 females and 5 males, with extraordinary diversity in disciplinary background, institutional experience, academic rank, research experience, and familiarity with the self-study literature.

1   **Angela**, female, working on her PhD., one year at the Faculty, cross-appointed to the University's Instructional Development Centre, and familiar with self-study.
2   **Callum**, male, an overseas visitor to the Faculty for a full term and experienced in self-study.
3   **Cari**, female, associated with the Faculty for 12 years (the last 4 on a tenure-track appointment), and new to self-study.
4   **Chris**, female, tenured, with 9 years at the Faculty, and new to self-study.
5   **Howard**, male, tenured, with 25 years at the Faculty, and new to self-study.
6   **Hugh**, male, tenured, with 25 years at the Faculty, and familiar with self-study.
7   **Peter**, male, untenured, with 2.5 years at the Faculty, and experienced in self-study.
8   **Rena**, female, tenured, associated with the Faculty for 13 years, Dean for one week at the group's first meeting, and new to self-study.
9   **Sylvia**, female, the Education Librarian for 15 years, and new to self-study.
10 **Tom**, male, tenured, with 19 years at the Faculty, and experienced in self-study.

As the participants chose, both actual and self-assigned names were used for this chapter. (As a sidenote, the process of assigning names raised an interesting question: To what extent did choice of name reflect one's perceived comfort, status, and power in the Faculty?) Disciplines included Adult Education, Educational Psychology, Curriculum Theory, Measurement and Evaluation, Music Education, and Science Education. At the time of the group's first meeting, several members were already working on projects while the remainder soon decided to pursue self-study endeavours. Table 1 provides a concise overview of the chronology of the group's seven meetings and related events culminating in the conference at Herstmonceux Castle.

Table 2.1: Chronology of main events involving the self-study group.

	Date	Event
1995	Jun 29	Tom sends open invitation to Faculty of Education
	Sep 7	First meeting of the SSG (9 attended)
	Sep 21	Second meeting of the SSG (9 attended)
	Oct 5	Third meeting of the SSG (9 attended)
	Oct 19	Fourth meeting of the SSG (8 attended)
	Oct 31	Abstract of conference paper due
	Dec 4	Fifth meeting of the SSG (9 attended)
1996	Feb 7	Sixth meeting of the SSG (8 attended)
	Feb 27	Seventh meeting of the SSG (9 attended)
	May 31	2500-word summary of conference paper due
	Jun 4–7	Six members present papers at CSSE
	Jun 30	Full conference paper due for electronic dissemination
	Aug. 4–8	Self-Study Conference at Herstmonceux Castle, England

Seven noon-hour meetings were held between early September, 1995, and the end of February, 1996. Nine persons attended five of the meetings, and eight attended the other two. An eighth partial meeting at the end of March was attended by only four persons and lasted thirty minutes. The meetings were supported by a steady flow of email, usually from Tom and usually about details of the August 1996 conference. SSG members also received the electronic communications sent to members of AERA's Special Interest Group on Self-study of Teacher Education Practices, the official sponsor of the Herstmonceux conference.

I attended every meeting of the SSG and took notes concerning speaker and topic. During the meetings, my dual role as observer and participant likely reduced my effectiveness on both counts. My notes of the meetings were supplemented by audiotapes and transcripts organized by Tom. In May 1996, I interviewed every member of the group individually, including an email interview with Callum, who by this time had returned to his home country. Interviews varied in length from 40–90 minutes. Most of the information reported here was obtained from these interviews. The date following a quotation from an interview indicates when the event or interview took place and is displayed in the numeric form recommended by the International Organization for Standardization (e.g. 1995–05–15 represents 15 May of the year 1995).

Results and Discussion

The major findings of the study are presented and discussed in the context of the eight major themes raised in the May 1996 interviews.

1   How did the Self-study Group (SSG) influence you and your own project?

The group had different effects on the individual members. Angela changed her view of her ongoing work from seeing it as isolated to perceiving it as supported collectively. Callum was particularly aware of how important the formation and bonding of the group was to its success. Cari saw the group as a mentor group with important human resources. Chris found that, for reasons beyond explanation, the SSG made it easier for her to write her reflective notes. Neither Howard nor Rena would have conducted their studies without the group, while Hugh felt that his work was legitimated by it. Peter found the SSG a validating and reassuring experience after he had shared a situation with it (see question 3 below). Sylvia, for the first time, felt accepted as an academic group member. Tom was impressed by the fact that the SSG was able to meet as it did.

The overall influence of the group was substantial. Of the ten members, only three — Tom, Callum and Peter — were highly likely to attend the Herstmonceux conference when the SSG began. Hugh was highly doubtful about attending, and no one else planned to go. In fact, ten members completed either ongoing or new studies, nine attended the conference at Herstmonceux, and six presented their work at the Canadian Society for the Study of Education conference at Brock University in June 1996. In addition, the SSG received financial support from several sources within the university, no mean feat during a time of fiscal constraint. Finally, most members reported feeling much better about going to Herstmonceux as part of a group rather than attending alone. The cumulative evidence suggests that the group as a whole reached a level of performance that most of its members would not have achieved by themselves.

2   *How do you think you influenced the group as a whole?*

Most members stated that this question was difficult to answer and reported being uncertain about influencing the group at all. Upon reflection, most were able to provide instances when they had asked questions or made comments that resulted in group discussion or action. Callum stated that he tried to avoid pushing any particular agenda but on occasion would throw in an idea when he sensed a lack of direction or when he thought someone needed support. The general sense of the group members was that of working as a collective.

Several members stated that they approached the group meetings with particular attitudes and hoped that their attitudes would be noted. For example, Cari reported that, by joining the group, she was making a commitment to it and wanted the group to know that she was pursuing significant questions. In fact, her contributions in this regard were noted specifically by Chris, Sylvia and Hugh. Tom stated that he was there 'to take' more than 'to influence', but hoped that he was being supportive. In my view, he succeeded. For example, when Cari distributed the first abstract to 'oohs' and 'aahs' at the third meeting, Tom said immediately 'we're a support group' (1995–10–05). In addition, he carried out such actions as offering a comfortable setting in which to meet and distributing same-day positive email statements about the group's meeting that had just concluded.

On a number of occasions, a member's question or comment was important for some of those present, even if the initiator was unaware of this influence. For example, when asked how she thought she had influenced the group, Angela said 'I'm not sure that I did' (1996–05–24). Yet she introduced the word 'hypomnemata' at her first meeting and provoked a brief, vigorous discussion that resulted in her bringing to the next meeting a written definition and description of the concept. Also at the first meeting, Angela asked if people kept teaching portfolios. Cari and Chris responded to the question immediately while, later on and back in his office, Tom was prompted to take an empty binder from his bookshelf and place it near some course materials so as to begin a teaching portfolio.

In general, members able to provide examples of their own influence at the meetings based them on communications that they had received at the time or later. For example, Rena believed that her presence as Dean had an impact on group proceedings, because of her judgment on the private communications that she had received from different members following the meetings. These and other data underline the value of responding directly to fellow members about the value of their contributions, which they are otherwise unlikely to understand. This finding has particular implications for those engaged in self-study for the improvement of their own teaching: the more frequent and complete the students' (or observers') feedback about teaching strategies and methods, the better able teachers will be to study aspects of their own teaching.

3   *Who had the greatest influence on the group's direction?*

Tom's name came up most frequently in the context of organizing the meetings and other matters. Cari said: 'he was a champion for the process' (1996–05–16). However, for ideas and related contributions, members believed that everyone offered something to the group. Otherwise, the interview data reveal that different individuals had different impacts, often for quite different reasons, on members sitting around the table.

For example, for some members the most compelling incident took place on 4 December at the SSG's fifth meeting. On that occasion Peter recounted, to use his words, the 'almost . . . totally crippling paralysis about being deconstructed and not being put back together' (1996–05–24), a reference to his ongoing work with Callum. This openness was helpful to and welcomed by, in particular, Angela, Callum, Cari and Tom, although for different reasons in each case. However, Peter himself was unaware of his impact at this time. Mentally, he had already dealt with the matter and saw the incident more as an opportunity to take a risk and share a meaningful experience with the group. He believed also that previous exchanges with Callum had provided the necessary support for him to share his experiences in this way, and he considered Callum to be the strongest influence on the group. Further, Peter found the group's response to his sharing to be validating and reassuring as different members jumped in and shared similar experiences. This event served as a useful exemplar to underline the distinctive, complex, nonlinear and reciprocal influences that group members can have on one another against the backdrop of whole-group endeavour.

4 To what extent was the group's knowledge constructed, distributed, situated and mediated? Did some form of collective thought evolve over the course of the meetings?

Members believed that assumptions of the constructivist model were appropriate to describe how the SSG functioned. Some members believed that by the third or fourth meeting the group's collective sense had been established, although more development remained to be done. On this later point, several members believed that the SSG did not achieve a complete cycle of development. For example, Tom did not have the sense of a shared knowledge within the group and Hugh observed that none of the papers represented a construction of the group. Instead, each member focused on his or her own project. Angela noted that the group did not reach the stage of closely examining the premises of each project or really using the drafts and abstracts to respond to the writings instead of merely critiquing them.

5 What roles did thought and feeling (or emotion) play in the group, and how were thought and feeling connected?

Members acknowledged occasions when the entire group had been very (an emotionally-tied word) focused intellectually on a topic raised by a member, although most of the 'thinking' was done individually outside the meetings. However, for many members, the SSG was remembered for its emotional support, warmth and sensitivity. These qualities existed despite a variety of personal and professional tensions that existed, or had existed, among different pairs of members in the group. Within the group, it was possible to support someone even if that support might not have occurred in dyads outside the meeting.

    The key to establishing this supportive tone seemed to lie in the first ten or fifteen minutes of the meeting as members arrived, ate lunch, and opened a wide range of brief conversations that were punctuated by jokes, wry comments and laughter. The discussion at these times was often 'very funny, even surreal' (Sylvia, 1996–05–16). Hugh noted the large proportion of time at the beginning of meetings spent laughing. He stated, 'I must happily admit that initially I was a bit bemused by it and a little concerned that we might be losing sight of what we were there for; then it was quite apparent that that was not happening' (1996–05–22). In fact, it seemed that these initial moments permitted the sharing of a great deal of information and promoted the building of a group identity. The outcomes of these openings are consistent with research that shows the high value of jokes and laughter in helping people to think more broadly, associate more freely, and solve problems demanding creativity (Goleman, 1995). The beginnings of meetings were bolstered by Tom's tea and coffee and, on occasion, by others' shared food or drinks.

In general, the few details that members could recall about the SSG's functions were forceful reminders of the constructive and selective nature of human memory (e.g. Bartlett, 1932). For example, Tom remembered the affect of the meetings, but could not recall sending his initial open invitation to the Faculty (1995–05–27). And I, who carefully collected all such correspondence for this study, could not recall this pivotal memo either until I saw it in my file. These results show how little memory is tied to the specifics of a situation in the absence of affect at the time, and how important affect is to the recall of an event (cf. Goleman, 1995; Nichol, 1994).

The thought-feeling relationship deserves comment from another important perspective as well. According to at least one female member, the main contribution of Peter's emotionally-linked account at the 4 December meeting (see question 3) was to link thought and feeling explicitly by saying how he felt about his situation. This statement gave permission for the females to do likewise in the kind of forum that has so often slighted their 'irrational' contributions in the past. This study supports others in underlining the enduring ties between the rational and the emotional and shows the value of fostering group discussions that link both thoughts and feelings. The latter linkage seems especially important for self-study research that can be suffused with emotional elements. Members reported that other emotional benefits of the meetings include the promotion of knowledge and, especially, the increased liking of other group members, who typically were widely dispersed around the Faculty serving in a variety of institutional roles.

6 Did the many and varied 'authorities' present at the meetings affect the proceedings?

Group members acknowledged that every person in the group was an authority on something. Beyond that, more senior members did not see authority as a particular issue while more junior members did. More junior female members made the most extensive and perceptive comments about group functioning. These findings showed clearly that authority was a factor at the meetings, even when more senior members did their best to assume an equality of membership. For example, even though Rena asked the SSG's very first question ('How do we define self?') and made a number of other academic inputs, members remembered her in her role as Dean. They appreciated her support of the research through her presence, remembered her administrative acts, and recalled her arrivals and departures better than anyone else's.

Given that authority, usually of position or knowledge, is likely to be an ongoing issue in group functioning, what can members do to minimize its effects? Callum suggested that 'the lead as to what is acceptable and how to risk and raise issues must come from the perceived leaders' (1995–05–28). More generally this view suggests that, to enhance comfort and to encourage full participation within the group, senior members should be the first to take risks by raising substantive events and (building on the preceding question) issues that affect them emotionally.

7   How did email support group development?

Meetings were supplemented by a steady flow of email, usually from Tom. Group members saw the email as organizational and not intended to advance group dialogue. Sylvia believed that the email added to group cohesiveness, while Chris believed that email enhanced the sense of belonging to something even if individual messages could be deleted with the press of a button. However, all members agreed that the critical events happened at the meetings where they could see people and use collective energy to advance the group's agenda.

Members addressed other characteristics and shortcomings of email. For example, Angela mentioned that there are questions and answers at live meetings where individuals can try out their interests and determine who will share their perspectives. Peter and Tom noted that email is used in different ways by different people: some individuals try to hold significant conversations on email while others use email more for basic contact, that is, an electronic means of asking, 'How are you doing?' without really wanting to know the answer. Hugh observed that 'email has declared its limits. It is not a vehicle for discussion. There's more to discussion than sharing words. . . . The medium has no way of checking up on whether or not the recipient of a message has understood it' (1995–05–22).

These results have implications for scholars who are moving increasingly toward email exchanges as substantive undertakings. It is clear that email has some important limitations even if verbal information (sometimes enhanced with 'smileys') can be disseminated in large volumes to widely-dispersed recipients. Research is needed on how to set the stage for maximally productive email communications among members of working groups that are concerned with interpersonal relationships.

8   What else should be noted?

The formation and workings of the SSG were generally very positive. A number of papers were critiqued and completed, there was some sharing of book titles and contents, and a wide range of academic and institutional concerns were discussed. These accomplishments were remarkable given the fact that the group had only seven full meetings over two full academic terms (eight months). In retrospect, however, even more could have been achieved. Several members missed not having meetings later in the spring and wished that the group had continued meeting beyond 27 February for motivational, emotional, and intellectual reasons. Although anyone could have called for another meeting at any time, no one did.

As noted above, there is a general sense that the SSG did not achieve a full cycle of development. Because the group's main purpose to prepare for the Herstmonceux conference has been achieved, a reformulated objective will be necessary should the SSG continue to meet. At that time, the group can move toward addressing some of the matters that still need attention, such as examining the basic assumptions of the projects and responding to the writings in a meaningful way.

Two other points are worth mentioning in this context. The first point involves the role of recognized experts in self-study research (the topic of current focus) who are external to the Faculty and who may participate in some or all of the group's proceedings. On the one hand, experts can offer invaluable information and advice that help to advance group and individual knowledge. On the other hand, to promote group cohesiveness and willingness to risk, experts should be seen as sharing their uncertainties and feelings along with everyone else. The present data suggest that the group's more junior members see the expert along with more senior members as models for determining what is acceptable in the group and for what passes as knowledge in the given research domain.

The second point concerns the records kept by members of the SSG. Although they collected extensive documentation on their own individual and independent projects, Angela was the only person who maintained a journal following the group's meetings. Several members noted references or themes of interest during the meetings but did not supplement these notes with post-meeting reflections. Given the composition of the group and its focus on self-study in teacher education practices, the lack of journaling may be surprising at first blush. However, this fact may be another sign that the group did not achieve the in-depth and engaging analysis of issues and projects that it could have.

Finally, the relationship between individual and group cognition deserves attention. Although the group of interest here was the SSG, every member belonged to a number of other groups, including the group of all faculty engaged in the development of a new teacher preparation program during the period of the SSG's existence in 1995–96. Clearly, some of the SSG's proceedings and individual projects were devoted to this other major interest. It is important to note, then, that every group exists in some broader context and that group members have many other allegiances. However, within the SSG's confines and despite the group's short history, a collective personality developed that elicited particular forms of behavior from the individuals present. In addition, and perhaps obviously, members of the group possessed some kinds of information that were unique to them. Less obviously, the names of individuals who had key roles in establishing this information were often forgotten. Knowledge was often coupled with affect in a manner that supports earlier claims by Nichol (1994) and others that lived thought is founded in emotion. Although the present study of the individual–group interface is incomplete in many ways, it provides information about the workings of a particular group and raises issues for further investigation.

References

BARTLETT, F.C. (1932) *Remembering: A Study in Experimental and Social Psychology*, Cambridge: Cambridge University Press.

BOHM, D. (1994) *Thought as a System*, London: Routledge.

BRUNER, J. (1990) *Acts of Meaning*, Cambridge, MA: Harvard University Press.

BRUNER, J. (1996) *The Culture of Education*, Cambridge, MA: Harvard University Press.

CSIKSZENTMIHALYI, M. (1990) *Flow: The Psychology of Optimal Experience*, New York: Harper & Row.

GOLEMAN, D. (1995) *Emotional Intelligence*, New York: Bantam.

LAVE, J. and WENGER, E. (1991) *Situated Learning: Legitimate Peripheral Participation*, Cambridge: Cambridge University Press.

LOTMAN, Y.M. (1990) *Universe of the Mind: A Semiotic Theory of Culture*, London: Tauris.

MARKUS, H.R. and KITAYAMA, S. (1991) 'Culture and the self: Implications for cognition, motivation, and motivation', *Psychological Review*, **98**, pp. 224–53.

NICHOL, L. (1994) Foreword, in BOHM, D. *Thought as a System*, London: Routledge, pp. ix–xv.

PLOMIN, R., CHIPUER, H.M. and NEIDERHISER, J.M. (1994) 'Behavioral genetic evidence for the importance of nonshared environment', in HETHERINGTON, E.M., REISS, D. and PLOMIN, R. (eds) *Separate Social Worlds of Siblings: The Impact of Nonshared Environment on Development*, Hillsdale, NJ: Erlbaum, pp. 1–31.

SCARR, S. (1992) 'Developmental theories for the 1990s: Development and individual differences', *Child Development*, **63**, pp. 1–19.

VYGOTSKY, L. (1978) *Mind in Society: The Development of Higher Psychological Processes*, Cambridge, MA: Harvard University Press.

Part II

Methodological Perspectives

Introduction

Stefinee Pinnegar

The chapters in this section have been selected because we feel they provide evidence that while the methods and methodologies of self-study are not much different from other research methods, self-study is methodologically unique. Our purpose here is not another challenge in some kind of paradigm war, but instead, an attempt on our part to explain why although participant observation, ethnographic, grounded theory, or statistical methods might be used in any single study, self-study involves a different philosophical and political stance. It is not a need to claim truth but a need to assert certainty that underlies most traditional research methods. Debates about validity, reliability or other appeals for foundational criteria for knowing rest more on a desire to be able to assert with certainty a particular claim of meaning or of relationships among phenomenon than on a desire to understand the meaning of situations or phenomenon.

Faulconer and Williams (1990) argue that using the methods developed according to theories based in modernist traditions allowed the researcher to be objective and to treat the researched as objective. This made it possible to treat findings from research as determinant, atemporal, and generalizable; and, therefore, statements from research projects that followed appropriate methods could be asserted with certainty. During the postmodern movement, this idea came under attack. As a result there have been a plethora of critiques of modernist (usually numerically based) methods. In this process, researchers, usually those proposing more interpretive research methods have argued that the subjects of research are temporal, indeterminate, and particular. However, these researchers have continued to stumble over issues of the subjectivity of claims made using such interpretive methods. To counter this claim, these researchers have continued to argue for the position of the researcher as a position of objectivity. Fenstermacher (1994) for example, argues the need to make 'warranted claims' about practical knowledge. Guba and Lincoln (1985) propose alternative terms for validity, reliability, and generalizability but have continued to assert the ability of the researcher to make such claims.

In contrast to even this position, researchers, who embrace self-study through the simple act of choosing to study their own practice, present an alternative representation of the relationship of the researcher and the researched. In their chapter, Russell and Upitis provide a clear representation of how the nature of self-study research is temporal rather than atemporal. This occurs as they explore the development of understanding in a practice context. Their presentation of email communications between a new dean and a faculty member is framed first in their understanding at the time of a communication and then reframed by an analysis from their current professional practice. As relationships of trust change, the interpretation of what is communicated changes both in the present and retrospectively in the past. Their chapter reveals the nuances that underlie this process.

All of the chapters included in this section strongly demonstrate the reciprocal relationship between the researcher and the researched. Richards' chapter provides evidence that student journal entries led to her own construction of a self-portrait in order to examine how she talked in her courses. Tidwell and Heston articulate the use of a process of elicitation of practical arguments with students and with other faculty members providing a clear record of several layers of the interaction of researcher and researched. First, Tidwell demonstrates the way in which it impacts on her students' development then how her use of their articulated understandings influences her practices with them. Next she and Heston show how attending to the voice of teacher education students tutoring reading leads to programmatic changes in a teacher education program. Finally, they demonstrate how faculty members, reflecting together on their individual practice, change their collective practice as well as their teacher education program.

As each of these studies reveal, self-study researchers must attend to process, product, content and context. Wilcox clearly outlines the context, content and process of both her work as an educational developer and in her collection of the data upon which this analysis was framed. Richards' self-portraits focus on the individual, but the individual is engaged in practice that includes others and often elements of the setting. The Tidwell and Heston chapter articulates the multiple layers of professional practice and the various elements to which teacher educators must attend.

Self-study research always presents evidence of meaning and relationship among phenomenon from the authority of their own experience (Munby and Russell, 1994). Wilcox's articulation of her four claims for her work as an educational developer captures the strength of the authority of experience as a warrant for knowing in self-study research.

As a community of self-study researchers, we ask that the researcher provide evidence not just that they studied the phenomenon named in their research project, but that such study resulted in a reframing of their beliefs (learning) and changes in their professional practice. The various chapters in this section clearly do this, as do other chapters in this volume as a whole. In addition, the researcher must present, in voices in addition to their own, believable evidence of changes in practice or claims of understanding in meaning (Loughran and Northfield, 1996). The self-portraits of Richards' students, the work of Tidwell and Heston's students, the Russell and Upitis reframings are examples of attempts to provide such evidence.

The chapters in this section, as well as the chapters in this entire book, demonstrate that self-study research seeks as its hallmark not claims of certainty, but evidence that researchers, however stumblingly, demonstrate in their practice the understandings they have gained through their study. Self-study researchers seek to understand their practice settings. They observe their settings carefully, systematically collect data to represent and capture the observations they are making, study research from other methodologies for insights into their current practice, thoughtfully consider their own background and contribution to this setting, and reflect on any combination of these avenues in their attempts to understand. They utilize their study to represent for others what they have come to understand in their own practice and ultimately to perfect and improve the quality of their own practice setting. For these reasons, this section provides evidence that self-study is not a collection of particular methods but instead a methodology for studying professional practice settings.

References

FENSTERMACHER, G. (1994) *The Knower and the Known: The Nature of Knowledge in Research on Teaching: Review of Research in Education, 20*, Washington, DC: American Educational Research Association, pp. 13–56.

FAULCONER, J.E. and WILLIAMS, R.N. (1990) *Reconsidering Psychology: Perspectives from Continental Philosophy*, Pittsburgh: Duquesne University Press.

GUBA, E. and LINCOLN, Y. (1985) *Naturalistic Inquiry*, Beverly Hills, CA: Sage.

LOUGHRAN, J. and NORTHFIELD, J. (1996) *Opening the Classroom Door — Teacher, Researcher, Learner*, London: Falmer Press.

MUNBY, H. and RUSSELL, T. (1994) 'The authority of experience in learning to teach: Messages from a physics method class', *Journal of Teacher Education*, **45**, 2, pp. 86–95.

3 Turning to the Artistic: Developing an Enlightened Eye by Creating Teaching Self-portraits[1]

Janet C. Richards

My beliefs about the practical and practitioner nature of self-study serve as catalysts for the self-study methodology I describe in this chapter. Central to my beliefs are the following definitions: Self-study 'is conducted by practitioners to help them understand their contexts, practices, and in the case of teachers, their students. The outcome of the inquiry may be a change in practice, or it may be an enhanced understanding' (Richardson, 1994, p. 7). Self-study is mainly qualitative research that is focused inward (Cole and Knowles, 1996). It is 'a deliberate attempt to collect data systematically that can offer insight into professional practice' (Clift, Veale, Johnson and Holland, 1990, p. 54).

One picture is worth a thousand words! When I create self-portraits of my actions and 'teacher talk' in the classroom this old adage holds true. Self-portraits (i.e. drawings or sketches that depict the ways we view our inner and outer selves) have the capacity to reveal our self-perceptions and constructions of reality (Dobbert and Kurth-Schai, 1992; Harmon and Gregory, 1974; Pitman and Maxwell, 1992). Drawing self-portraits allows us to uncover and become sensitive to what we consider significant about ourselves. Creating self-portraits forces us to look carefully at who we are and helps us confront our strengths and shortcomings (e.g. consider the notable self-portraits created by da Vinci, Rembrandt and Van Gogh).

Creating Self-portraits: A Four-step Recursive Cycle

In order to create a self-portrait, I find that it is helpful to implement a four-step recursive cycle of thought and action. The first step involves a conscious effort on my part to monitor a particular aspect of my teaching that I wish to explore. Decisions to initiate this self-monitoring phase can be triggered by my own concerns about pre-service teachers' learning or by my pre-service teachers' uncertainties and confusions.

---

[1] **Author's Notes:** The pre-service teachers whose self-portraits appear in this chapter have graciously given permission for their drawings to be shared. Special acknowledgments go to USM pre-service teachers Jan Hansen, Stephanie Scheppens, and Soni Damien for their artistic expertise, and to Stefinee Pinnegar, colleague at Brigham Young University, Provo, Utah, for her suggestions concerning this chapter. Please note that Bayview School is a pseudonym.

For example, a pre-service teacher recently wrote in her journal, 'Dear Dr. R., I can't figure out all of my notes — you talk fast!' When I read this message, I immediately made a conscious decision to monitor my speaking rate during lectures and seminar discussions in order to determine if I needed to speak slower. This self-monitoring stage also may be stimulated because I want to pause, consider and document specific dimensions of my teaching that I think are particularly noteworthy.

In step two, I carefully consider the teaching problem or event, posing questions to myself such as, 'How have I contributed to this dilemma?' and 'How did I come to be this way?' (Kapuscinski, Browne, Krentz, Cooper and Goulet, 1995, p. 103). I reflect both in a systematic and in a non-sequential, intuitive way until I develop some insights into my behavior. Reflection demands that we stop and take stock of our actions, 'looking inward at our thoughts and thought processes, and outward [at the teaching context. Through reflection] we become aware of ourselves' (Kemmis, 1985, p. 141).

In the third step, I document my discoveries by creating a teaching self-portrait. Drawing forces me to publicly disclose parts of myself that I may prefer remain hidden. Drawing also forces me to see myself with an 'enlightened eye' (Eisner, 1991). As Eisner (1985) notes, 'it is to the artistic we must turn, not as a rejection of the scientific, but because with both we can achieve binocular vision' (p. 199).

Finally, I reflect further about the portrait's content, searching for insights into my professional decisions and attempting to develop some deeper understanding about my actions. I ask myself, 'Am I ready to alter this situation?' and 'How might I do things differently?' (Kapuscinski et al., 1995, p. 103) until I come up with some alternative behaviors.

Recently, following the described four step process, I created the following self-portrait depicting my instructional delivery during an initial meeting of a field-based reading methods course. The audience is a group of pre-service teachers enrolled in their first reading class (see Figure 3.1).

After creating this portrait and reflecting upon its content, I recognized that, just as I had suspected, I talk too much on the first day of class. My justification is that the pre-service teachers need to know such large amounts of information. Yet, studies show that teachers who reduce the complexity of their 'teacher talk' maintain student attention and provide a classroom atmosphere that motivate students to make self-discoveries (Chilicoat, 1992). Additionally, decreases in the amount of 'teacher talk' and increases in student interactions aid students' future recall of information, encourage students to accept some responsibility for their own learning, and promote student independence, autonomy and mutual learning (Anderson, 1991). Moreover, good teaching is NOT telling and delivering information. Rather, good teachers maximize opportunities for learners to construct their own knowledge by engaging them in challenging learning activities mediated by a competent facilitator 'or in collaboration with capable peers' (Vygotsky, 1978, p. 86). As a reading teacher educator, more effective ways for me to help pre-service teachers come to individual and shared understandings about teaching reading at Bayview School include:

1   leading an interactive discussion in which I draw out, extend and build upon the pre-service teachers' beliefs and background knowledge about elementary schools and the teaching and learning of literacy;

Figure 3.1: A self-portrait depicting the author's 'teacher talk' in the classroom: 'I talk too much'.

2 displaying slides, photographs, and videos showing former pre-service teachers and their students working at Bayview School;

3 inviting a group of former pre-service teacher program participants to share their perceptions, experiences and knowledge;

4 forming collaborative groups and encouraging the pre-service teachers to work together, framing questions and concerns about their future activities at Bayview School;

5 sharing authentic teaching cases written by former pre-service teacher program participants (see Richards, Moore and Gipe, 1996; Shulman, 1992; and Silverman, Welty and Lyon, 1994 for information on teaching cases).

Self-portraits and Pre-service Teachers

I have found that creating self-portraits also provides opportunities for pre-service teachers to develop a conscious awareness of their own performances with students and to address discrepancies and 'incongruities between what they intend . . . [and] espouse, and their actual teaching behaviors' (Osterman and Kottkamp, 1993, p. 86). After drawing my teaching self-portraits, I share them and my reflections about their content with my pre-service teachers. I also model the four-step cycle that I use to complete my drawings. Then I help the pre-service teachers explore and document their own teaching practices by leading them through a similar process of self-awareness and reflection. Understandably, many pre-service teachers initially experience difficulties when I ask them to document and objectively evaluate their own actions and behaviors in the classroom. Because they are in the beginning stages of teacher development, they lack the self-awareness and stock-taking abilities acquired by most seasoned teachers. (See Diamond, 1988; Fuller and Bown, 1975; Huberman, 1989; Pigge and Marson, 1997; and Ducharme, 1993 for discussions of stages of teachers' professional development.) Consequently, they tend to overlook and discount their own contributions to classroom dilemmas. As a result, rather than looking at their own performances, my pre-service teachers often create drawings that depict problems with individual students (e.g. 'John never listens. He also disturbs others').

The contents of these initial drawings provide wonderful teachable moments. The pre-service teachers and I interact collegially, discussing the meaning of each illustration, offering suggestions, and posing thought provoking questions until the pre-service teachers are ready to construct a valid self-portrait that appraises and evaluates their own practices. Once these second or third drawings are completed the pre-service teachers share them with their peers. Because teachers and teaching contexts differ, we note the uniqueness of each portrait. We also talk about the effectiveness of some of the teaching behaviors displayed in the portraits (e.g. see Figure 3.7, 'I always remember to display a visual'). Since there is no one correct method of teaching (see Loughran, 1996) we help one another brainstorm and formulate possible solutions to practices that may need improvement. In addition, I remind the pre-service teachers to keep their completed self-portraits in a portfolio so that they can review their drawings often. Comparing and reflecting upon one's past and present practices in an ongoing careful and deliberate way are crucial to teachers' ongoing professional growth.

The following self-portraits were created by pre-service teachers in an advanced reading methods course. The drawings illustrate problem areas that are typical to many novice teachers — too much 'teacher-talk', not following through on group management plans, not staying focused on lessons, and not giving students sufficient time to complete work (see Figures 3.2–3.7).

When I reviewed the preceding portraits, I was confronted with an intriguing phenomenon. Many of the drawings revealed that my pre-service teachers talk too much in the classroom, just as I do. Recognizing the similarities in our teaching behaviors helped me to reevaluate my actions as a teacher educator and to consider how my behaviors have the capacity to impact my pre-service teachers' conceptions of teaching. Thus, in a synergistic gestalt, my pre-service teachers' self-portraits coupled with our mutual, shared reflective dialogues, influenced my thinking and provided an important

Figure 3.2: A pre-service teacher's self-portrait: 'I need to stay focused on a lesson'.

dimension to my growth as a teacher educator (Garcia and Litton, 1996; Kremer-Hayon and Zuzovsky, 1995; Loughran, 1996).

Summary

In this chapter I present a practical method for documenting and studying teaching practices. Creating self-portraits provides opportunities for teachers to identify classroom behaviors such as too much 'teacher talk' that are not congruent with their students' growth. Self-portraits also call attention to teachers' decisions and actions that are particularly exemplary and beneficial. Additionally, drawing and sharing self-

Figure 3.3: A pre-service teacher's self-portrait: 'I don't give students enough time to enjoy completing their work'.

portraits of teaching behaviors allow teacher educators and pre-service teachers to collaborate as partners and to engage in a synergistic process of mutual learning that promote an enhanced understanding 'of the nature and impact of their performance' (Osterman and Kottkamp, 1993, p. 19). For example, sharing my self-portrait illustrating too much 'teacher talk' stimulated my pre-service teachers to create their own self-portraits. In turn, reviewing my pre-service teachers' self-portraits helped to reveal the similarities in our classroom discourse as well as the possibility that my actions as a teacher educator have the capacity to impact my pre-service teachers' conceptions of teaching. It is my hope that readers of this chapter will consider creating their own self-portraits. Equally important, I hope that the ideas offered in this chapter will stimulate teachers to devise other practical methods for researching and documenting their professional decisions and actions based upon their particular teaching contexts and individual styles of self-discovery.

Figure 3.4:   A pre-service teacher's self-portrait: 'I talk too much'.

References

ANDERSON, V. (1991) 'A teacher development project in transactional strategy instruction for teachers of severely reading disabled students'. Paper presented at the annual meeting of the National Reading Conference, Palm Springs, CA.

CHILICOAT, G. (1992) 'Promoting student achievement through clear teacher presentations', *Illinois School Journal*, **72**, 1, pp. 3–14.

CLIFT, R., VEALE, M., JOHNSON, M. and HOLLAND, P. (1990) 'The restructuring of teacher education through collaborative action research', *Journal of Teacher Education*, **41**, 2, pp. 104–18.

COLE, A. and KNOWLES, J.G. (1996) 'The politics of epistemology and the self-study of teacher education practices', in RICHARDS, J. (ed.) *Empowering Our Future in Teacher Education: Proceedings of the First International Conference on Self-study of Teacher Education Practices*, Sussex, England: Herstmonceux Castle, pp. 67–73.

Figure 3.5: A pre-service teacher's self-portrait: 'I talk too much'.

DIAMOND, C. (1988) 'Constructing a career: A developmental view of teacher education and teacher educator', *Journal of Curriculum Studies*, **20**, 2, pp. 133–40.

DOBBERT, M. and KURTH-SCHAI, R. (1992) 'Systematic ethnography: Toward an evolutionary science of education and culture', in LECOMPTE, M., MILLROY, W. and PREISSLE, J. (eds) *The Handbook of Qualitative Research in Education*, New York: Academic Press Inc, pp. 93–159.

DUCHARME, E. (1993) *The Lives of Teacher Educators*, New York: Teachers College Press.

EISNER, E. (1985) *The Art of Educational Evaluation: A Personal View*, London: Falmer Press.

Figure 3.6: A pre-service teacher's self-portrait: 'I have problems with group management'.

EISNER, E. (1991) *The Enlightened Eye: Qualitative Inquiry and the Enhancement of Educational Practice*, New York: Macmillan.

FULLER, F. and BOWN, O. (1975) 'Becoming a teacher', in RYAN, K. (ed.) *Teacher Education: 74th Yearbook of the National Society for the Study of Education, Part 2*, Chicago, IL, pp. 25–52.

GARCIA, S. and LITTON, E. (1996) 'A self-study of the bicultural factors that influenced our development as teacher educators and agents for social justice', in RICHARDS, J. (ed.) *Empowering Our Future in Teacher Education: Proceedings of the First International Conference on Self-study of Teacher Education Practices*, Sussex, England: Herstmonceux Castle, pp. 8–12.

HARMON, M. and GREGORY, T. (1974) *Teaching is . . . Experiences and Readings to Help you Become the Kind of Teacher you Want to Become*, Chicago: Science Research Associates.

Figure 3.7: A pre-service teacher's self-portrait: 'I always remember to display a visual'.

HUBERMANN, M. (1989) 'On teachers' careers: Once over lightly with a broad brush, *International Journal of Educational Research*, **13**, 4, pp. 347–61.

KAPUSCINSKI, P., BROWNE, N., KRENTZ, C., COOPER, E. and GOULET, L. (1995) 'The invisible work of program change in teacher education: A reflective case study', *Teaching Education*, **7**, 2, pp. 103–10.

KEMMIS, S. (1985) 'Action research and the politics of reflection', in BOUD, D., KEOGH, R. and WALKER, D. (eds) *Reflection: Turning Experience into Learning*, New York: Nichols, pp. 139–63.

KREMER-HAYDON, L. and ZUZOVSKY, R. (1995) 'Themes, processes and trends in the professional development of teachers', in RUSSELL, T. and KORTHAGEN, F. (eds) *Teachers who Teach Teachers: Reflections on Teacher Education*, London: Falmer Press, pp. 155–71.

LOUGHRAN, J. (1996) *Developing Reflective Practice: Learning About Teaching and Learning Through Modelling*, London: Falmer Press.

OSTERMAN, F. and KOTTKAMP, B. (1993) *Reflective Practice for Educators: Improving Schooling Through Professional Development*, Newbury Park, CA: Sage.

PIGGE, F. and MARSO, R. (1997) 'A seven year longitudinal multi-factor assessment of teaching concerns development through preparation and early years of teaching', *Teaching and Teacher Education*, **13**, 2, pp. 225–35.

PITMAN, M. and MAXWELL, J. (1992) 'Qualitative approaches to evaluation: Models and methods', in LECOMPTE, M., MILLROY, W. and PREISSLE, J. (eds) *The Handbook of Qualitative Research in Education*, New York: Academic Press, pp. 729–70.

RICHARDS, J., MOORE, R. and GIPE, J. (1996) 'Pre-service teachers' cases in an early field placement', *The Reading Professor*, **18**, 2, pp. 60–75.

RICHARDSON, V. (1994) 'Conducting research on practice', *Educational Researcher*, **23**, 5, pp. 5–10.

SHULMAN, J. (1992) *Case Methods in Teacher Education*, New York: Teachers College Press.

SILVERMAN, R., WELTY, W. and LYON, S. (1994) *Teaching Methods Cases for Teacher Problem Solving*, New York: McGraw-Hill.

VYGOTSKY, L. (1978) *Mind in Society*, Cambridge, MA: Harvard University Press.

4   Self-study Through the Use of Practical Argument

Deborah L. Tidwell and Melissa I. Heston

Research in beliefs and practices suggests a strong relationship between what a teacher believes and how teaching occurs in the classroom (Richardson, Anders, Tidwell and Lloyd, 1991). This relationship between beliefs and practice is an important one because it underscores the need for recognizing one's own beliefs as an initial step in the active process of changing one's practice (Fenstermacher, 1986; Richardson, 1990). This active process of change is driven by a desire to improve the practice of one's own teaching, wherein the desire to 'improve' requires changing current practice. In order to understand how to change, one must look at what is being done and why (examining the beliefs underlying the practice being examined).

In fact, it can be argued that the foundation of good teaching is based in making connections between practice (actions) and beliefs (knowledge). Through self-reflection of one's own teaching, the teacher is able to make connections between what she believes and how she externalizes those beliefs through her actions. This grounding of practice within beliefs is the cornerstone of action research, wherein the teacher reflects on the efficacy of the learning–teaching environment in an effort to make sense of the dynamics within that environment. Self-study of one's own beliefs through examination of teaching practice bridges explicit actions (teaching) to new knowledge about one's own practice. Such knowledge informs future action and illuminates instructional decisions, creating praxis, '. . . informed, committed action that gives rise to knowledge . . .' (McNiff, Lomax and Whitehead, 1997). As labeled by McNiff et al. (1997), praxis evolves from the study of one's own educational practice, where the values that underlie the practice are uncovered and discussed in light of other people's views. Through this process arguments for or against such practice lead to new knowledge. Practical argument works well in self-study because it is a successful discussion-based approach that elicits teachers' beliefs through examining teacher talk related to practice (Richardson et al., 1991; Tidwell and Montecinos, 1993). This heuristic device is post hoc in nature, where a teacher reviews a particular teaching moment after the fact and reflects through talk about practice and correlate beliefs. In this talk, according to Fenstermacher (1994), a teacher's 'premises (about a particular action) are grouped together, they are reasonably well developed, and they relate to the action in a recognizable way' (p. 26). He explains the dynamic of the practical argument as involving two voices, that of the teacher and that of the Other. The Other plays an important role by providing necessary prompts for eliciting the teacher's rationales and reasonings for practice. Fenstermacher describes this Other as a critical friend of the teacher, first engaging in descriptive discussions of practice and then moving to more evaluative talk.

Fenstermacher's (1994) conception of practical argument is based in an Aristotelian notion of practical reasoning. Practical reasoning relates to an individual's actions and requires individuals not only to think about logical connections that conclude with a description about their world, but also to put that conclusion into an action. This is the process by which an individual makes a decision to do something because it is something that is good, has value, and is the best action to take. Practical argument is a more formal approach to practical reasoning, and use of structure provides a gateway to the discussion of praxis.

While the voice of the teacher is the focal point of the practical argument process, the role of the Other is crucial. The Other elicits format. In the elicitation process, the Other is familiar with the professional and theoretical grounding of educational practice as well as the teacher's instructional work. The voice of the Other provides important prompts at crucial moments to allow the teacher opportunities to think about actions by forcing the teacher to examine the reasons behind specific actions.

This chapter describes two specific uses of practical argument in teacher preparation: (a) self-study of effective clinical instruction through the examination of practical argument discussions of university students; and (b) self-study of effective instruction in professional education courses through practical argument discussions of practice among university faculty.

Part I: Practical Argument in a Clinic Setting

This section describes how I have used practical argument in a reading clinic setting to help me study my own teaching practice. Each semester university students enrolled in the remedial reading clinic courses tutor a child in a one-to-one setting for a total of 30 hours throughout the semester. These tutors are videotaped each week and, following each taping, they preview their tapes using specific practical argument question prompts to help guide their thinking about their teaching. In this initial viewing, each tutor views the tape from two perspectives: the perspective of the tutor, talking about her own practice and actions; and the perspective of the Other (stepping outside herself as the tutor) and asking herself questions, using specific prompts to help discover her own premises/reasons for specific instructional actions.

After previewing a video, the tutor then shares the tape with a clinic supervisor acting in the role of the Other (a faculty member or a graduate assistant). During this process the tutor guides the Other (supervisor) through the practical arguments developed from previewing the lesson. During this presentation, the Other also provides additional elicitation, if needed, but more importantly, engages in a critical discussion of the tutor's premises for instruction. This part of the practical argument provides the tutor with an opportunity to question her own reasoning about her practice, and to begin to reconstruct the rationales behind her instruction.

The greatest impact of practical argument for the pre-service and in-service teachers is in developing their own reflections in and understandings of the relationship between teaching and a child's learning (Tidwell, 1995). Initially, tutors tend to discuss more concrete components within the teaching situation, such as the step by step actions of the child. There is usually minimal discussion about the reasoning behind the instruction. Even with elicitations provided by the Other, tutors typically find it difficult to elaborate beyond the concrete elements of their practice. Over time the quality of the practical arguments change from a concrete 'what happened' focus to a more abstract belief-based discussion. These more sophisticated practical arguments include rationales for practice, connections between a child's actions and subsequent instructional changes, critiques of both positive and negative aspects of instructional moments, less dependency on the supervisor's Other voice for argument elicitation, and the development of new knowledge about the nature of instructional practice.

Practice and Program Reflection

As a faculty member involved with courses in a reading clinic setting, I have found students' practical arguments to be very helpful in informing me about my own teaching practice as well as informing me about the overall reading education program. I use the students' practical arguments to examine how their talk relates to my intentions for teaching. In this manner I am attempting to determine the effectiveness with which my instruction helps students make connections between reading theory and practice. Effectiveness in this setting is evaluated through the students' language use, problem solving, application of knowledge to practice, and implementation of change over time. In a similar manner, I can make connections between the students' talk and the overall purpose of our reading education program, to prepare informed and thoughtful teachers.

How a tutor uses the assessment procedures and instructional practices presented in Remedial Reading and Tutoring provides information about the effectiveness of the course itself. Typically these two courses are taken by seniors in their final semester prior to student teaching, by post-baccalaureates completing state specified Reading Endorsements, and by graduate students as their initial course work in a Reading Education master's program. Inherent in the curriculum of these two courses is the necessary background knowledge provided by prerequisite courses in reading education: language development, emergent literacy, reading and writing processes, children's literature, effective practices for classroom reading instruction, and informal reading inventories.

I use the following components of the reading clinic tutorial experience to help inform me about my teaching: the tutor's instructional plan (concepts related to instruction, lesson plan, and post-lesson debriefing notes), the tutor's teaching of the lesson (video tape), and the practical argument (self-evaluation in writing and the oral presentation). To illustrate these components, I have chosen tutorial work from Jean, a graduated nontraditional baccalaureate returning to school for a reading endorsement. Although every student's work in the clinic is unique in its own way, Jean represents the typical clinic tutor. Following these examples I provide a discussion of how such data informs me about my own teaching, closing with an explanation of how the practical argument process is also used to inform me about the reading education program as a whole.

Concepts related to instruction

The concepts are derived from baseline data about the client gathered during the early part of tutoring. This baseline data provides the information to create goals for a client's instructional program. Within each goal, specific concepts about literacy are developed and used as the objectives for the clinic instruction. For example, Jean's client was experiencing difficulty recognizing words when reading. One goal developed was to improve understanding and use of word recognition strategies. Within that goal, concept objectives directly addressed the specific needs of that client. In this case, the young reader had no strategies for approaching unknown words other than stopping and sounding out each letter one at a time. This created a stilted, incomprehensible reading experience and greatly affected his understanding of the text. Concept objectives were designed to directly address his lack of effective strategy choices when approaching an unknown word (such as, Reading past an unfamiliar word and thinking about what I have read can help me figure out a word). These concepts can be seen as the connective tissue between the initial plan of action for the lesson (the lesson plan) and the tutor's practical argument rationales about the completed lesson. During the self-evaluation of a lesson, the tutor uses practical argument prompts to help make connections across the plan of action, the actual teaching actions, and the lesson's underlying purpose (objective).

Lesson plan

Plan of action refers to the actual step-by-step lesson plan itself. Each step in the lesson plan is labeled with a concept focus. The rationales for a lesson are indirectly stated in the plan by the labeling of concepts. (The direct rationales for the lesson are elicited through the practical argument process.) The actions within the lesson are placed within an overlying format of reading–writing–reading. This preset lesson design is time flexible, but encourages the tutor to develop literacy lessons that flow from a specific reading experience into a related writing experience and back into a connected reading experience. This lesson frame is based on a belief that literacy instruction is more meaningful when authentic reading and writing tasks are connected (authentic in this context meaning reading texts that have not been altered by readability formulas, and writing created by the client).

Post-lesson debriefing notes

At the close of each tutoring session, the tutor spends 10–15 minutes writing a reflective response to the lesson as a whole. This debriefing time provides the tutor an opportunity to respond affectively to the lesson, describing what 'went well' or 'poorly' as well as personal responses to the client or the lesson. The tutor also reflects on how she felt the client responded to the lesson. Any suggestions for changes to the next lesson are included in the debriefing notes.

The following are excerpts from Jean's debriefing notes for lessons in February and April. They are broken into three sections: Tutor responses, client responses, and subsequent tutorial decisions.

7 February

T   Although I did 3 assessments in one day Nathan was game. I did the CAP (Concepts About Print) last because I thought he would do well. I think I'd only do 2 assessments if I were to do it over, and I would add something to make Nathan experience success.

C   Nathan kept working until the very end even though he was pretty tired. (His mom later told me he was in Fort Dodge last evening.) He was very frustrated by the PP ON (pre primer oral narrative) 'Just Like Mom' and missed words after awhile that I think he would usually know. Ex. go, at, with, of

TD   Make a PB&J sandwich and write about it so it has real-life meaning after reading the whimsical version of making a PB&J sand in the book we read and will reread.

10 April

T   I liked this lesson because I really liked the books I was using.

C   Nathan seemed to like the stories and paid attention.

TD   None

Video tape

Tutors are videotaped during the teaching of a lesson. Taping is once per week for each tutor, lasting approximately 30 minutes. Since the lessons run one hour in length, videotaping varies so that every tutor is taped in the beginning, middle and end of the lesson during the semester. The tutor views the tape and chooses a minimum of two teaching events for use in the self-evaluation of her teaching.

Self-evaluation in writing

The tutor views the videotaped lesson privately, chooses instructional moments to highlight, and through the practical argument process writes a self-evaluation of those instructional moments using three prompts. The examples provided are for Jean's same two lessons in February and April.

Prompt 1: What is happening here? This prompt asks the tutor to provide the gist of the instructional moment. This requires the tutor to think about the actions of the client and the tutor, understand what is happening in that instructional moment, and synthesize the actions into a main point or focus.

7 February

Nathan is reading the PP ON (pre primer oral narrative) passage Just Like Mom from the QRI II. He is becoming very frustrated.

10 April

Nathan and the tutor are successfully doing a DLTA (Directed Listening Thinking Activity) using The King, the Mice, and the Cheese.

Prompt 2: How did I know what was happening? This prompt asks the tutor to provide the specific events that led to the gist revelation. This description of the child's and tutor's actions is the most concrete aspect of the practical argument, tying the gist or major point of the moment to concrete actions.

7 February

As Nathan reads he became so frustrated that he would stare at 'Just Like Mom' and not pronounce it until a long pause happened. At the end he mispronounced a few words I think he usually knows.

10 April

Nathan seems very engaged by the story. He makes predictions sometimes, but doesn't sometimes. As the story progresses he makes more predictions that are logical.

Prompt 3: Why was I doing that? This prompt asks the tutor to explain her reasoning for her actions. This is the most difficult aspect of the practical argument self-evaluation because it asks the tutor to connect her beliefs about teaching and learning to the actions within the lesson, and to provide the rationale for the gist of the lesson.

7 February

I wanted to try one oral passage even though Nathan frustrated at the PP word list (score of 110) because I hoped words in context might be more helpful.

10 April

Nathan needs more understanding of story structure in order to aid his predictions during reading and retells afterwards. I did a Directed Listening Thinking Activity (DLTA) because he would be able to listen (he wouldn't lose comprehension because of decoding problems) and figure out the pattern of the story. After reading *Eek! There's a Mouse in the House*, we did the DLTA with *The King, the Mice, and the Cheese*. The two stories had many similarities in structure and some differences so we did a Venn diagram to compare and contrast them. I wanted Nathan to see that the same story patterns are sometimes used over and over. If he senses that pattern developing he will be better able to predict the future events in the story.

Oral presentation

After completing the self-evaluation through practical argument, the tutor presents the selected videotape moments to a small group of peers and her supervisor, and elaborates on the written self-evaluation. It is during this practical argument oral presentation that the supervisor, as the Other, can encourage the tutor to represent more clearly the what or gist of her lesson in light of the how or concrete description. Peers can also contribute as the Other, providing thoughtful questions related to the context of the lesson and all can help the tutor construct the why or the rationale behind the teaching actions.

Self-study of Practice Informed Through Practical Argument

The intent of the clinic courses is to provide university students with appropriate assessment measures for literacy and to help them learn how to use assessment information in developing appropriate and effective instruction. Using Jean's work in the clinic, I demonstrate how practical argument helps inform me about my own teaching practice.

From the onset of the semester, students' language began changing in the terminology that was used when writing about their students and in the focus of their discussions during oral presentations of their practical arguments. As was typical of most students, Jean wrote lengthy initial debriefing notes about her lessons. However, the more she experienced practical arguments, the less she 'debriefed' (provided affective responses) about the lesson. This was a typical pattern across most students.

During her written self-evaluations, Jean initially described gist or what statements that were step-by-step explanations of her child's actions. Often her what and how descriptions were indistinguishable. By the end of the semester, she was able to synthesize her client's actions and her own teaching actions into gist statements, and provide specific step-by-step descriptions (how) to support her gist statements. This change of her discussion of practice over time relates well to her study of practice in the classroom. Jean's practical argument discussions provide insight into the connections she was making with her class work and her tutoring experiences.

Being able to understand what you are doing and to explain the reasoning behind your actions incorporates both language use and problem solving. Initially, Jean talked at a concrete level when discussing her rationales for teaching. When asked why she did what she did in her February lesson, Jean initially discussed why in terms of her own tasks to complete ('I wanted to try one oral passage even though Nathan frustrated . . .'). In contrast, by the end of the course Jean related her practice not only to instructional needs of the client ('needs more understanding of story structure'), but to the underlying metacognitive point to the practice ('. . . wanted Nathan to see that the same story patterns are sometimes used over and over . . . better able to predict the future events in the story'). Often practical argument provided me with a greater depth of understanding about my students' progress and about the impact (or lack there of) of course instruction on my students. As the semester progressed, Jean increased her discussion of rationales for her teaching during her practical arguments. Clearly, she was able to make connections from class lecture and activities and from practice with her client to better understand the reasons why she was doing what she was doing.

This insight into students' knowledge can also uncover what is missing from instruction. In my teaching, I was attempting to provide ongoing assessment techniques for use during instruction. At no point in any of the students' practical argument discussions did they highlight these ongoing assessment techniques. Through the use of their Other voice during practical arguments, supervisors attempted to elicit possible ongoing assessment procedures being used during tutoring (How do you know your client is improving? What can you do to better understand what your client is thinking?) to no avail. Through the rationale discussions it was discovered that students did not find the need for ongoing assessment as they had already assessed at the beginning of the semester. This misunderstanding about the need for and use of ongoing assessment was prevalent across the students in all sections of the course. Clearly, this was a misunderstanding not addressed well by my instruction. I began to rethink the ways in which I have tried to make ongoing assessment connect with my students' own tutorial work. I realized that the push I had made earlier for assessment baseline data had encouraged students to view assessment as a pre-instruction or post-instruction phenomenon. While

I believed in the importance and value of ongoing assessment through instruction, my actions were suggesting a very different belief.

The February and April lessons of Jean are just a few examples of how the rather involved practical argument process used in the clinic setting provides an opportunity for me to examine the effectiveness of my teaching. The practical arguments presented by my students about their own videotaped teaching provide a window into the ways students are making sense of course content and connecting that content to previous study. More importantly, this process is ongoing throughout the semester. It provides me with immediate feedback about my students' interpretations, applications, and adaptations of both course content and intent. This immediate feedback allows me the opportunity to regroup as an instructor and approach the content and intent from a different and perhaps more effective perspective.

In the example of my students' lack of ongoing assessment through their tutoring instruction, I was able to readdress this issue in class using a practical argument approach toward my own instruction to them: describing the gist of what I believed was happening (students were not using their instruction as ongoing assessment of their client's progress), how I knew this was happening (a step-by-step description of what students were doing), and why I wanted to have students think about instruction as a vehicle for ongoing assessment (the rationale). From this experience, I was able to use my own instruction as a model for using instruction to assess progress.

Reading Program Informed Through Practical Argument

In a similar sense, educational programs can be informed through practical arguments. In the case of Jean, her responses to her practical arguments provided insights into her previous experiences in reading. Jean came to the course with a great deal of knowledge about the learner in the classroom, with a great deal of experience in the public schools and, specifically, in small group instruction. In her practical argument oral presentations she often related her classroom experiences with small groups of children to her one-to-one tutoring in the clinic. Many of the strategies she used with her client she had originally learned through a prerequisite course and had tried in a small group setting in an elementary classroom field experience. She often commented on the advantages or disadvantages of using a particular strategy in a small group setting compared to a one-to-one setting. The undergraduate reading program (which she completed recently) appeared to have provided her with many effective real class experiences.

What is powerful about practical arguments is that (a) practical arguments allow students the opportunity to connect what they know with what they are doing through a specific context and within a narrow focus; and (b) students' practical arguments serve to inform my own self-study of my instruction. Through practical arguments, patterns begin to emerge from students' language and rationales. Examining program effectiveness through practical arguments becomes especially interesting in light of students' difficulties with misunderstandings or lack of knowledge. Is it the course (specifically my instruction) that is creating the difficulties? Or are the difficulties stemming from the students' previous course work and learning experiences? To determine the answers to these questions it is best to examine several groups of students over a period of time. After evaluating students' practical arguments from the first three semesters of their implementation in the reading clinic, a programmatic problem was discovered. The practical arguments seemed devoid of any 'meaty' discussions about emergent literacy issues. In probing further, it was discovered that students had many misunderstandings about phonemic awareness, invented spelling, and the overall assessment of beginning readers and writers. This became a programmatic issue, as two prerequisite courses were supposedly providing the emergent literacy experiences needed. Through faculty discussions of patterns of student knowledge (or lack of knowledge) in other classes and continued examination of the practical argument data from clinic tutoring, a programmatic change occurred in the focus of two courses in the reading program.

While practical arguments are admittedly a time consuming and energy draining process, the benefits outweigh the distractors. For me (and for my students), practical arguments provide a framework for talking about practice. It forces me to think about my teaching in a very honest way, to tie what I think I am doing to what is understood by my students, and to relate my practice to a purpose. A bit humbling at times, but always informative and often enlightening.

Part II: Practical Argument Among Colleagues

As a beginning teacher educator, I never questioned (much) the pedagogical appropriateness of my instructional techniques. Although my classes were generally small (25–35 students) I relied heavily on lectures using highly sequenced overheads, occasionally supplemented by a small group application activity or class discussion. I was confident that I was teaching well as long as I covered the required content, my students were generally satisfied with the course, and their test performances reflected my norm-referenced assumptions about the nature of learning within the university context. As I look back, much of what I knew as a developmental and educational psychologist about children's and adolescents' learning was not well reflected in my instructional practices. However, I was teaching 'adults', and good teaching evaluations from my students assured me that I was doing what I was supposed to be doing. Fortunately, I became increasingly aware that the content I 'taught' (or rather presented!) was not being reflected accurately in my students' class discussions, written work, and exam performances. For example, I considered the role of disequilibrium in learning essential for future teachers to understand. My students, however, consistently indicated that teachers should work to reduce or avoid disequilibrium rather than strive to create and use it to stimulate their students' learning. As I came to recognize these kinds of discrepancies between my teaching and my students' understanding, I resolved to teach 'better'. I would spend more time on concepts that were difficult, give more examples, make my explanations more detailed, and so on.

I did not become aware of a need to teach 'differently' rather than 'better' until I was asked to teach a sophomore level course in classroom evaluation for pre-service teachers. I can best be described as a skilled and knowledgeable amateur rather than an expert in this content area. I was very excited about this particular teaching challenge. I had experienced considerable emotional trepidation during my graduate course work in this area. I also had been much more consciously aware of my own efforts at active meaning making (resolving disequilibrium!) in this content area than in other areas that had been easier for me. I had not considered myself particularly good at mathematics, but I came to understand that the mathematics *per se* were quite simple, and I found the concepts intriguing. Ultimately, I developed considerable confidence about my own ability to understand and apply classroom evaluation concepts, and I wanted my students to develop similar degrees of confidence and understanding. Because of my personal learning experiences, I believed that I could structure this course and my students' learning experiences more effectively by taking an 'insider's view' of the learning process (Duckworth, 1996, p. 112). I 'knew' what the problems would be; I had experienced them myself. I 'knew' what my students would really need to know about classroom evaluation; I used much of this content as a teacher and thought I could discriminate between what would be truly meaningful and useful to the students, as opposed to what would merely display my own expertise while greatly confusing them.

Although I did not realize this at the time, I had begun a new journey in my development as a teacher. The focus of my teaching shifted from making sure that I covered the content to trying to understand the sense my students were making of the content. Of course, I 'knew' that teachers had to think about how their students were thinking, but I did not really understand what this meant until I had to think about my own understanding of classroom evaluation, and how to convey that understanding to my students. I learned more about both teaching and learning while working in this new and less familiar domain than I ever had while working in my area of expertise. Other than course syllabi examples, I received virtually no guidance from senior faculty teaching this particular course. I also chose to teach my section of the course in a once a week, two hour block at night. These two factors allowed me to feel quite free to take risks in my teaching that I would never have tried in the courses I usually taught.

I began by deciding that what these pre-service teachers really need to understand about classroom evaluation could be organized into three major areas: (a) the philosophical and practical aspects of norm-referenced and criterion-referenced assessment; (b) basic test construction techniques and guidelines; and (c) the statistical procedures most commonly used in classroom assessment. I chose to make the philosophical and practical aspects of norm-referenced and criterion-referenced assessment the central theme of the course. Classroom test construction and statistical procedures were subsumed within this theme. While other instructors of this course tend to present statistical procedures in an intensive unit, I presented the mathematics of assessment in small progressive chunks that built upon each other week by week. Much of class time was spent in small group classroom assessment construction activities, and these activities were designed to keep the students focused on the conceptual and practical components of norm- and criterion-referenced assessment. Although I did not give up lecturing entirely, I spent considerably more time trying to engage students in thinking about problems of classroom evaluation and how we might solve those problems rather than in presenting highly organized lectures on reliability, validity, item analysis, standardized test scores, and so on. On the whole, it was the most exciting class I had ever taught. I had a noisy, active classroom, and everyone seemed to be learning and learning well! I thought I had never 'taught' better. I was, of course, in for a stunning surprise.

I chose to give the students an open book, open note final that required students to select a conceptual approach to assessment (either norm- or criterion-referenced) and defend their choice as appropriate for their classroom needs. Students had to complete and interpret a variety of statistical procedures. Although the students generally did the computations and interpretations well, it quickly became clear that students were woe-fully confused about norm-referenced and criterion-referenced assessment. During the course, many of my students, particularly those majoring in elementary or early child-hood education, claimed to be firmly committed to criterion-referenced assessment. However, most of the students, who indicated that they believed a criterion-referenced assessment approach was most appropriate for their classrooms, then described and defended their choice based largely on norm-referenced assessment assumptions. 'What! How could they do this? Didn't they learn anything!?' Never before had the critical importance of the meanings which students construct for themselves been more evident to me.

Thus began my own journey toward understanding the teaching–learning process as it really happens in my own classroom. Although this journey began largely as a solitary one, it has since become much more communal. For the past two years, a small group of faculty have met weekly to discuss their beliefs about the multiple and inter-related natures of education, learning, and teaching. In this chapter, I will describe the process by which we as a group began to use practical argument to guide our work; I will also provide illustrations of the way in which practical argument has enhanced my understanding of my beliefs and practices, the degree to which these beliefs and prac-tices are congruent, and how incongruencies can serve as a basis for action.

The Group

Our discussion group consists of four women and one man who regularly teach under-graduate coursework in developmental psychology, classroom evaluation, classroom management, educational psychology, early childhood education, and special education. Two participants are tenured, and one participant is an adjunct instructor. Group mem-bers range in age from their late 30s to their late 40s.

As individuals, we possess a wide variety of background experiences. For exam-ple, Kathie (names used with permission) has extensive teaching experience in special education; Annette is a former school psychologist; Linda has extensive experience evaluating early childhood programs and leading school reform efforts; Rob has a background in philosophy and instructional technology; and I have a background in developmental psychology and early childhood education. It is, in many ways, a rather heterogeneous group bound together by our shared interest in enhancing our teaching and improving the quality of teacher education in general.

Our Basic Process

The focus of each meeting is identified in advance and we have established a pattern in which we take turns preparing, circulating, and informally presenting course syllabi, descriptions of assessment techniques, examples of learning activities, and brief thought pieces on a variety of topics. Because we have talked with each other so much both during regular meetings and in other contexts, we have developed fairly clear under-standings of what we each do in our classes. Thus, during discussions, group members can act as informed Others, asking questions which challenge the presenter to clarify his or her terminology and conceptual positions, and the ways those positions match with actual practice. We audiotape each meeting and these audiotapes are later transcribed, edited for accuracy (e.g. 'It's Vygotsky, not Gotsky'), and the transcripts are duplicated and distributed to participants.

We have a relatively implicit set of group governance rules. First, the presenter and his or her material are the focus of the meeting. When we act in the role of informed Other, we ask questions, listen, and identify and describe ideas in the presenter's discussion which seem particularly important to the presenter. Second, our goal is to help the presenter reflect further on his or her practice in ways that he or she finds useful. We generally try to follow the lead of the presenter, pursuing his or her line of thought rather than our own. And third, we avoid giving advice to the presenter since such behavior devalues the importance of the presenter's reflection on his or her own work. Indeed, advice-giving impoverishes both the quality and the quantity of our shared thinking.

In March 1996, group members agreed to prepare position papers on how we think about our students' learning. In May, the group chose to work with my learning paper which has been provided below in a slightly abbreviated and edited form. The remainder of this paper will provide two illustrations of our group process and describe the insights I gained into my beliefs about learning and teaching and how those beliefs are translated into classroom practice.

Learning

How do I think about learning? More specifically, how do I think about my students' learning? What does it mean for them to learn? How do I think that happens? My thinking in this area has undergone a tremendous transformation in the past few years due to a number of experiences. When I began teaching, I definitely had a 'telling' model; I expected my students to listen to what I said, take accurate notes, to believe what I told them, and to connect what I was telling them with what they were reading or doing. Fundamentally, I was pursuing Ausubel's model of meaningful receptive learning. I developed considerable skill at taking large chunks of information, and breaking them into small sequential pieces which I then presented in a lecture format. Throw in some humorous examples, and the occasional small group application activity, and viola! Any reasonably competent student could learn if he or she made an adequate effort. After all, I had been able to learn this way (I think).

The information-processing model also influenced my thinking in regard to teaching and learning. This occurred as I taught information-processing to my students in undergraduate courses in educational psychology. Although I largely stuck with a lecture approach, my overheads became quite colorful with different chunks of information written in different colors to help students partition these into little coherent units of knowledge. I also began using colored chalk, which my students loved. These changes, however, were largely superficial. The more profound change occurred as I began to apply the 7 +/− 2 notion for how much I should put into a single class. I also began to use more extreme examples, actually rather bizarre examples, on the principle that novelty and shock helps learners to retain.

My students, however, still made 'mistakes'. They would make odd, rather idiosyncratic interpretations of developmental and learning theories, be limited to the examples I gave rather than being able to generalize from the examples, and talk about one theory while using inaccurately described examples from another and often conflicting theory. Indeed, perhaps most frustrating was my sense that even though the students 'knew' the information, it was only in a rather meaningless, disconnected way. No matter how long we spent on the principles of operant learning, for example, the students still tended to define a reinforcer as a reward, and a punisher as some unpleasant experience that we knew *a priori* that learners would dislike. What is particularly interesting about this process is the fact that I really thought Piaget's constructivist model was right, but it did not seem to translate at all into how I taught Piaget or anything else!

In the past few years, two major experiences have led me to think about learning from a more constructivist framework than I ever had when I 'taught' Piaget's theory of cognitive development. The first experience arose as I taught an undergraduate measurement and evaluation course. During this process, it became clearer and clearer to me that philosophical orientations about the nature of human beings and their learning determine how we assess and evaluate student performance. As I began to grapple with these relationships, I increasingly tried to get my students to grapple with these same notions. After all, how could they evaluate meaningfully if they really did not understand the philosophical underpinnings of the evaluation model they were using. Without the philosophy, evaluation simply became an algorithmic task: put the numbers in here, crunch the numbers there, look at the numbers, and assign grades based on those numbers as if the numbers inherently had real and generally understood meaning.

As I tried to 'make' my students grapple with the philosophical aspects of evaluation as well as with the mechanical ones, I again found students' misconceptions cropping up. For example, as part of their final exam, students were asked to select and then defend their selection of either a norm-referenced or a criterion-referenced system. Although I thought that the students had 'gotten' this, the students often selected one system and then defended their select with rationales used to justify the other system. The students had grappled, and in their grappling, created a tangle web of inconsistencies and contradictions that clearly showed that they had indeed learned a lot, but they had not learned it with any particular accuracy. Why had this happened? What did I need to do better or differently? Had I failed to present the information in an organized enough fashion for the students to keep it straight? Had the students simply not had enough time and practice to develop an accurate and coordinated understanding of the basic ideas of norm-referenced and criterion-referenced testing? And then I read Duckworth (1996).

This little text helped me to transform my understanding about my students' learning. I began to reflect back on all my frustrations with students' superficial fluency with the concepts I was teaching and their underlying misconceptions which seemed to remain largely unchanged despite my best lectures, small group activities, and our small and large group discussions. I did not really understand that what I was facing when I taught were long-established knowledge structures regarding the nature of human beings, learning, schooling, and grading that my students had created over the past 12 or more years. Yikes! No wonder using a relatively traditional approach (lecture) did not actually cause much change in the students' thinking. It did not help them to reflect on their own beliefs about these concepts and principles; it did not provide them with real opportunities to confront the inconsistencies or inaccuracies in their own understanding;

it did not really have anything to do with learning (even in the most behavioristic sense of change). My teaching had to do with telling, no matter how many active learning experiences I tried to provide. Then again, why should I expect my students to grapple with the inaccuracies and inconsistencies in their understanding when I was not grappling with the clear evidence that what I was doing was causing little if any change in their thinking.

So how do I think about learning now? I start from the premise that my students by and large view learning as a passive mental activity that involves mostly just taking in what the teacher says. That is, I assume their understanding of the real nature of learning as active meaningful cognitive or intellectual change is at best limited to well-intentioned, but largely unreflective lip service about the need for hands-on activities, the use of manipulatives, making learning 'fun', and teaching to all learning styles. My goal is to help them identify and confront their highly inadequate notions (very much like my old ones) of learning by having them grapple actively with their own learning and the learning they see in children.

For me, learning has become defined as a very personal and active striving to understand something meaningful which has the potential to transform one's intellectual life. It is a joyful, ongoing struggle to make more and more sense of the world in all its complexity. Thus learning involves developing an alert awareness of all the opportunities which exist from moment to moment for further learning. And, in order to teach something, one must take the time to discover how the learner is thinking about that something.

In reviewing the transcript of our discussion, it was evident that much of what I now try to do in class is informed by three fundamental beliefs: (1) the value of frustration; (2) the importance of transforming students' understanding; and (3) the need to restructure students' emotional frameworks for learning. These beliefs, however, conflict to some extent with other elements of my framework for teaching and learning. It was only in our practical argument discussions that these conflicts became clear enough for me to use them in reflecting further on my own beliefs about practice. I also realized that if I truly valued frustration, transforming student understanding, and restructuring emotional frameworks for learning, then I would have to do more to create an environment in which these are explicitly and genuinely encouraged.

The Value of Frustration

The notion of frustration provides one critical element in my framework for thinking about my teaching and my students' learning. Frustration in this context refers to my own frustration and the frustration that my students experience. Although the term frustration has a relatively negative connotation, I actually use it in a broader sense which includes concepts such as disequilibrium, confusion, and cognitive dissonance. Since I take (or at least try to!) a constructivist orientation to learning, I believe entering a state of frustration is essential to true learning. However, for my students, frustration on their part is often interpreted to mean that either I am not doing my job as a teacher, or that they are somehow intellectually incompetent. Although I explicitly talk to my students about the value I see in frustration, it is difficult for them to let go of the traditional notion that confusion is bad.

Many of the activities I use in class are designed specifically to create frustration and confusion on the part of my students in the hope that this will lead them to reflect on how they learn and how they feel about their learning. Ultimately, I want students to feel comfortable with not knowing, with being frustrated and confused; I want students to find this a wonderful place to be, even though it does not always feel particularly wonderful, especially at first. I want my students to come to understand and fundamentally believe that the essence of learning is to wrestle intellectually with problems and solutions, and become comfortable knowing that solutions will always remain more or less uncertain. However, in our group's discussion of my own frustrations, it became clear that to some degree I still hold a relatively 'traditional' notion of teaching and learning. This traditionalism is clearly reflected in the transcript excerpt below. (Transcripts have been edited slightly to promote readability.)

Excerpt 1

M: . . . I just read a paper by one of my graduate students and we read all these different sources and as I read her final synthesis paper, I'm thinking, 'We haven't made any progress. She knows tons more information, but she hasn't really transformed her thinking because she's still condemning families, she's still talking about children of poor families not getting love, she's still . . .'

. . . I'm thinking, 'Now how is it that we got through this whole semester talking about this, and yet when she was asked to go back on her own, and she's a bright student and try to grapple with it, she winds up back in the almost exactly same place that she was when we started.'. . .

. . . it was very frustrating to me to read that and then read another paper from another student and say, 'Ah, this student really got it'. And I don't know if that student had it beforehand. Maybe it doesn't make any difference what we do. . . .

L: It's interesting that you use that word 'frustrating' again.

M: It's frustrating to me because I want to have control — that's a good point. I want to mold them. I keep forgetting that they're not little tabula rasa and I can't just write my own wisdom on their own slates for them to keep with them forever and ever and expect it to have any meaning. I like to transform my students to be more like me or at least more thoughtful. I want them to become more thoughtful about what they think, rather than automatically processing information . . .

. . . I want my students to think like me. I want them to think real critically and real complexly. Maybe that's egotistical on my part to say that's what I do, but to think at least more complexly and more critically about their own thinking and to be more hesitant about jumping to conclusions, about assuming that they know.

L: But you are an 'expert'.

M: That's true, I have a little piece of paper that says I know a lot. But always in the back of my mind when I jump to those conclusions, there's always this little voice that says, 'now, now, now'. And I don't know that they have that little voice that says 'now, now, now, let's know that you jumped to a conclusion, and that's okay, but just remember — you jumped to a conclusion, so don't treat it like it's reality'.

K: But did you have that voice when you were their age?

M: That's a good question . . .

    . . . No, I don't know whether I did or not.

L: It took you awhile to get to this point.

M: That's true, it did take me awhile to get to this point. It took me six to eight years of teaching to get to this point.

K: You want to save them the work that you went through to get to this point and kind of jump them up there.

M: Yeh.

R: But you can't.

M: Don't tell me that.

R: Here's what I meant to say. I think one thing is she (M) has the assumption she can jump them up some, but if her model of learning is right, there's a limit to how much you can jump them up at any given time. Isn't that right? Because they have to sort of go through the process. Is that kind of in there?

M: Right.

Thus, one source of my frustration arises from my sense that students are not getting where I want them to be. If I truly believe that students construct their own knowledge in their own time, then it is a contradiction in my thinking to say, 'I want all my students to reach this particular level of understanding by this particular time'. Despite the fact that I believe that students construct their knowledge, I still want to mold them as if they were pieces of clay. Moreover, I had failed to realize that by valuing frustration and choosing the activities I use, I was creating a situation in which my own frustration was guaranteed to be higher than was the case when I pursued a more traditional framework for teaching and learning. My current framework forces me to reflect much more on the nature of the understandings each student is developing. In my previous framework, I could more or less ignore this by attributing it to individual differences in students' intellectual capabilities. Now, I have to take much more responsibility for the development of student understanding, while at the same time I must acknowledge that my ability to control this process is limited.

Acquiring Knowledge vs Transforming Understanding

One of my goals is to shift my students' framework for learning from one of acquiring knowledge to a framework which emphasizes the transformation of understanding. In a traditional approach to learning, errors are viewed as a failure to acquire knowledge accurately. While working within that approach, I always emphasized the importance of paying attention to children's errors as keys to understanding children's thinking, but I rarely paid any attention to my students' errors on multiple choice questions as keys to understanding their thinking. In the learning framework I am now trying to pursue, errors are opportunities for transforming understanding. Thus I have to pay close attention to the errors that my students make as individuals; that is, I need to attend closely to how my students are thinking about what I want them to understand. To do this, I have found that I must take the time to engage in some kind of one-to-one dialogue with each student, even when there are ninety of them.

These dialogues and the other activities used to explore my students' thinking are often major contributors to my sense of frustration. I 'know' that transforming cognitive structures takes considerable time and that learners are generally resistant to data that conflict with their understanding of something. However, I still feel exasperated when students seem to be thinking about something at the semester's end in much the same way as they did at the semester's beginning, despite having been given and asked to work with contradictory data. I find myself saying, 'Why don't they understand this yet? Why are they still thinking about this concept in such a limited and primitive way?' To have this response contradicts my own position that transforming students' understanding takes time, and that each of my students will make progress in large part according to their own timetable and not according to my timetable (a semester). If I truly have a constructivist orientation toward learning, then I must be able to tolerate wide individual differences in the degree and nature of progress that my students make while I work with them.

Reconstructing Feelings and Attitudes Associated with Learning

In the course of our group discussion, it became evident that I had an implicit goal for my students regarding their learning. Many of my students report having strong negative feelings about particular content areas. Mathematics and science are most frequently identified as sources of fear and anxiety, but art, literature, and social sciences are also mentioned in this context. Thus, I do a wide variety of activities which can be classified as being math or science or literature, but I do not talk about them as such. Rather, I try to get students engaged in aspects of math, science, and other content areas by focusing their attention on some aspect of the real world to which they had not previously paid much attention (Duckworth, 1996). For example, students are asked to spend some time watching ants, we talk about what they noticed, identify questions that they wondered about as they watched the ants, and then watch the ants again to see if we can answer these questions. We also spend time watching the moon and keeping a journal of those observations, experimenting with floating and sinking using fruits and vegetables, and trying to make sense of poems written in English some six hundred years ago. I encourage students to talk explicitly about their feelings and attitudes toward these activities.

Typically, students initially consider all of these activities as quite odd for a course called, 'The Development of Young Children'. Almost inevitably, in the course of one of these activities, each student will develop a strong curiosity about what is being observed, and do some modest pursuit of the area on his/her own without any expectations of credit. When I see this happen, I experience an incredible sense of elation and satisfaction. However, I also regret that my students do not find their curiosity equally aroused by all of the activities we do.

During our discussion in regard to changing students' attitudes toward learning, Annette noted that there is a strong psychoanalytic theme to this process. I have since learned that Richardson (1990) suggested that 'a psychoanalytic approach to teacher education' (p. 13) might be useful. I was unaware of this psychoanalytic theme in what I was attempting to do, but as the transcript excerpt below makes clear, this theme does seem to underlie much of my practice.

Excerpt 2

M: Annette, did you have questions?

A: Yes, I did. If you think about how you turned out given the way you were taught and the way you learn and then that you were able to come to this new position . . . Does it make you uneasy that you might be throwing out some of the ways that you were taught and learned as you teach from a new position?

M: That's a really good question. No, it doesn't because, when I think about . . . I also have to point out that actually part of my entire educational career was fairly different from what many of these kids experience . . .

. . . My mom always enrolled me in these things that I hated at the time. Classes at the museum about Native Americans and about animals and about Africa. I learned Swahili one year for a few weeks. I mean, just all this kind of stuff. I took ballet and I took music lessons and I took dance — other kinds of dance. So, there was always this kind of underlying background that you just . . . that school is important, but that there's a lot more. There's always learning going on. You read everything and I had models for kind of continuous education. I think that in some ways it's hard for me to look at that and say that . . . I don't know. I've lost the whole thing.

A: Actually, I think that's important to know because you said earlier that you'd like students to be like you. To have a joy for learning and have an attitude about learning similar to yours. It seems like you're saying that you'd like to see that occur through the new teaching–learning model that you're using in your classrooms.

M: I would.

A: But yet, you just described a whole background and upbringing that in your case is probably very different from the majority of the students that you have.

M: That's true, but I also think about this. These people are going to be, most of them, early childhood educators. It worries me tremendously when they say things like 'I hate science', 'I hate math'. They're afraid of particular subject areas and then we're going to turn little kids over to them and say 'We want you to teach in a way that teaches children to love . . . that doesn't teach them to love learning, but builds upon kind of an instinctual built-in kind of obsession for finding out new things'. I think they (teachers) go in and they take it out of them (children). In fact, the students know they take it out of them. That's one perception that my students all share; somewhere along the line, they all say, 'Kids are so great when they're 3 and they're 4 and they love to learn and they're so curious. How is it we destroy that curiosity?' I know that without really transforming how they think about teaching, they're gonna go right back in there and destroy that curiosity. It takes a really lucky set of opportunities and sequences perhaps to rebuild that level of learning. Some of these students scare me.

A: You know what? I'm seeing a parallel here between psychoanalytic therapy and what you're trying to do in your class. I'm wondering if . . .

M: Say more about this, Annette, because I have no idea what you're talking about.

A: In psychoanalytic therapy, you take the adult back to early childhood and restructure their personality. What you're trying to do almost is take your students back to early learning as a child. You're trying to strip away all their defenses that they've learned about learning or something and put them in situations where they can approach learning as a child so they can, as an adult teacher, they can model that and construct in that way in their own classrooms. If that's true, if there's a parallel here, then you wouldn't expect them to get this in one semester or even two semesters because psychoanalytic therapy goes on for years. Do you see the parallel?

M: Yes, I do. That's a fascinating parallel, I think. I guess I would rather think of it as short term cognitive therapy. Cognitive behavioral therapy. I understand — that's a very interesting sort of thing.

A: It sounds like you're trying to reconstruct.

M: That's a very helpful way to think about it because I really am trying to reconstruct their emotional framework for approaching learning. I'm seeing this happen. I guess now that we're back to it, I do think for at least some of the students, it really is working. I think it works better for the experienced teachers than it does for the undergraduates. When we do this moon journal thing, where they have to go and watch the moon, they all start off saying, 'This is a really stupid activity'. But once they start looking at the moon and make it kind of become a part of it, it is really interesting to watch them go from, 'Why are we doing this? This is silly, but I'll do it because she said we have to do it', to 'Where is that darn moon? I drove out into the country to find the moon'. I'm reading in their moon journals and they're saying, 'I drove out to the country'. Someone else said, 'My wife called me at 5:30 in the morning to tell me to get up and look at the moon'. It's not only having an impact on them, but they're sharing it with their families, and their kids, and whole families are getting into going out and looking at the moon and thinking about the moon and talking about the moon. That's the essence of what little kids are about with learning. It's not about understanding everything all at once and getting the answers right on the test. It's about being totally fascinated with what you're looking at and just wondering about it. The wonderful thing with an adult is we have resources so we can go find answers to our questions. As a 3-year-old, our resource is to ask our parents, who don't know the answers. As 20- or 30- or 50-year-olds, we can go and we can get on the World Wide Web. I had a student turn in a moon journal that was full of stuff about the moon. She just went and downloaded all this junk off the web. The other thing is that not everybody really understands it, or they get to the point where they feel a touch of the excitement and then it's like they shut down . . .

. . . I want these people to get in touch with the real world around them and have respect for it and that means looking at ants and looking at floating and sinking . . .

. . . The world is right there to be explored. We miss the opportunity; we don't see it.

Essentially, I want to return my students to early childhood, and a time when learning was inherent in living, rather than learning being something that we do in order to live later. I hope to restructure my students' early emotional framework for learning much as a psychoanalyst tries to restructure a client's early emotional framework for living. As Annette noted, psychoanalysis takes time, and it may be quite unreasonable of me to expect that what I do in a single semester will allow such a restructuring to occur. And, to the extent that I create learning experiences which are unpleasantly rather than pleasantly frustrating, I may actually be a contributor to the very frameworks I wish to transform.

The Need to Build a Safe Learning Community

Practical argument discussions have led me to think more deeply about the importance of building a classroom community in which students feel comfortable taking intellectual risks and pursuing their intellectual interests. It puzzles me greatly that my students will privately grapple with their confusion in their journals and talk about how they think about their learning and the learning of others, but they will not substantially engage in this same behavior publicly. This conundrum is not easily resolved. Creating a learning community in which students feel safe taking intellectual risks takes time. The time spent doing this limits how much I can spend on doing things that more directly relate to the content of the course. However, it has also become clear that community building must come first. I cannot expect my students to arrive ready to engage in intellectual risk-taking; for them, such risk-taking has often carried a high price in terms of either the humiliation of being wrong, or socially stigmatized as 'too smart'.

What Changes Will I Pursue?

As a function of our practical argument discussion, I have identified several things I plan to change or to do better. First, I will need to monitor my own sense of frustration more closely, keeping in mind that the pedagogical techniques I am using are quite likely to cause me more frustration, in both a positive and negative sense, than the more traditional techniques I previously used. I also need to review my expectations more critically, remembering that the transformations I am trying to elicit in my students take considerable time and effort, particularly on their part. Being impatient for results seems a sure way to undermine both what I am doing and my own motivation to keep trying to improve what I am doing. Perhaps most importantly, I need to focus more heavily conceptually and pedagogically on building a classroom climate which supports intellectual risk-taking in an authentic manner. I must be willing to trade some breadth of content for the opportunity to enhance my students' processes of learning and their processes of thinking about that learning.

Looking Ahead

For both of us, we have found practical argument to be a useful framework for studying our own teaching practices, either individually (Deb) or collaboratively (Melissa and company). It is through this process that we have come to know our selves better as teachers, and our work as professionals. We are currently making plans to expand our uses of practical argument and to inaugurate this process amongst colleagues across the university as well as in teacher education. For us, this is a plausible task as our institution is noted for its teaching focus, and has a university-wide center for teaching excellence. As we, our colleagues, and our students develop our processes of self-reflection, we hope we will all become more authentic as we participate in the teaching/learning process.

References

DUCKWORTH, E. (1996) *The Having of Wonderful Ideas and Other Essays on Teaching and Learning* (2nd ed.), New York: Teachers College Press.

FENSTERMACHER, G.D. (1986) 'Philosophy of research on teaching: Three aspects', in WITTROCK, M.C. (ed.), *Handbook of Research on Teaching, 3rd Edition*, New York: Macmillan, pp. 37–49.

FENSTERMACHER, G.D. (1994) 'The place of practical argument in the education of teachers', in RICHARDSON, V. (ed.) *Teacher Change and the Staff Development Process: A Case in Reading Instruction*, New York: Teachers College Press, pp. 23–42.

McNIFF, J., LOMAX, P. and WHITEHEAD, J. (1997) *You and Your Action Research Project*, London: Hyde Publications.

RICHARDSON, V. (1990) 'Significant and worthwhile change in teaching practice', *Educational Researcher*, **19**, pp. 10–18.

RICHARDSON, V. and ANDERS, P. (1990) 'The role of theory in descriptions of classroom practices'. Paper presented at the annual meeting of the American Educational Research Association, Boston.

RICHARDSON, V., ANDERS, P., TIDWELL, D. and LLOYD, C. (1991) 'The relationship between teachers' beliefs and practices in reading comprehension instruction', *American Educational Research Journal*, **28**, pp. 559–86.

TIDWELL, D.L. (1995) 'Practical argument as instruction: Developing an inner voice', in HINCHMAN, K.A., LEU, D.J. and KINZER, C.K. (eds) *Perspectives on Literacy Research and Practice: Forty-fourth Yearbook of the National Reading Conference*, Chicago: National Reading Conference, pp. 368–73.

TIDWELL, D. and MONTECINOS, C. (1993) 'Negotiating a mandate: Secondary teachers' understandings and implementations of multicultural education in the language arts'. Paper presented at the annual meeting of the National Reading Conference, Charleston, South Carolina.

5   Claiming to Understand Educational Development

Susan Wilcox

In this chapter I make explicit knowledge claims about the process of educational development and the nature of educational development (ED) work. These claims, which represent my personal understanding of ED, arise from critical reflection on my own experiences as a developing educator and educational developer.

Background

The site for my research is the educational practice associated with efforts to improve university teaching and learning. Within higher education, there is an area of work — and a related body of literature and field of scholarship — that focuses on improving the quality of education provided by institutions. In Canadian universities, instructional development and faculty development are the most commonly used terms for improvement activities and the improvement process. The usual role of the institution in instructional/faculty development is to establish and support a unit, or at least a committee, which is responsible for facilitating educational improvement. Instructional/faculty developers are usually academics who take on the role of planning and providing programs, services and activities for their colleagues and institutions. Since the overall intention of this work is to improve the quality of education — teaching and learning — through a developmental process, I refer to it as educational development.

I am an educator, a member of the faculty at a Canadian university, where I do educational development work. My research began with interests arising from my development work; I wanted to:

1   improve my practice — more accurately, to practise well;
2   communicate effectively with others regarding educational development, and to engage in meaningful dialogue with my colleagues;
3   have a sense of ownership about my work and authenticity in it, and to effectively manage and evaluate my work and direct my own development.

The purpose of my research is to help me establish and sustain a legitimate educational development practice; to come to a deeper understanding of the development process and myself as an educator/developer, and to make a contribution to educational knowledge.

In this chapter, starting from the particulars of my own situation, I theorize about the educational development process. More specifically, I make four claims about educational development and give a justification for each.

Framework

My ED practice is based on the premise that educational development is an educational approach to the improvement of teaching (teachers improve instruction by learning to teach in ways that support student learning). Educational development refers to the process of educating teachers, and to the process of learning to teach. As an educator/ educational developer, I am engaged in ED in both senses — I am an educator (of teachers) and a learner (of educational practice).

Similarly, my inquiry into ED is based on the premise that it, too, is educational. By this I mean that the process and outcomes should be educative in the Deweyan sense; I contend that the research experience should lead to meaningful learning, helping me and others meet educational goals.

As an educator, the ethical ideal that governs and acts as a standard for my practice is fidelity to persons through caring. As a scholar, my pursuit of knowledge is guided by commitment to the ideal of truth (to try to be honest, not to intentionally delude myself or others). These two interests — in persons and in knowledge — form a framework for my educational research and practice: I fuse fidelity to the development of persons (myself and others), and fidelity to the development of knowledge (my own and others'), through a commitment to persons as knowledge-builders.

In my ED work, I try to express my commitment to persons as knowledge-builders by constructing, engaging in, and reflecting on educative ED experiences — on my own and with other educators. The concept of self-directed learning (Candy, 1991) supports my commitment to developing teachers as knowledge-builders, because it is based on the idea that all persons are ultimately responsible for conducting their own search for personally meaningful knowledge. Therefore, in my ED work, I try to facilitate self-directed learning — my own learning and the learning of faculty I work with. My intention is to model a self-directed approach to ED, to present an approach to ED that invites self-directed learning, and to respond with care to the challenge of faculty who engage in the process of ED in a self-directed fashion.

Nature of the Inquiry

Throughout this study, I focus on what I know of ED and how I came to know ED through the experience of constructing an educational practice in the field of educational development, and through critical reflection on that practice. My research follows what often is called by Moustakas (1990) the 'heuristic tradition'. I have used my experiences as a developing educator/educational developer as a case study, theorizing about the educational development process on the basis of the particulars of my own situation. I want to ensure that my personal conceptions of educational development are explicitly and critically grounded in my personal experiences as a beginning educational developer, and to broaden current conceptions of ED that are portrayed in the literature.

Method

Procedure

My claims are based on an analysis of (a) daily journal entries concerning my educational development work made from August 1994 until February 1995; (b) journal entries kept sporadically from 1987 until 1996; and (c) documents produced in my work over a period of approximately one year in 1994–95.

The six month educational development journal was kept to help me better understand my approach to ED work. In 1995, I reviewed the entries twice, writing comments on the text as I reviewed it. In effect, through this analysis, I engaged in a process of dialogue with myself — I commented on earlier entries, questioned my motives and underlying assumptions, made suggestions, connected various entries one with the other, and noted underlying themes. I did not have a formal procedure — instead, I responded to the text as I would have done if the journal had been submitted to me by one of my adult education graduate students, with the additional step of sometimes using the entries as jumping-off points for new entries.

In April 1996, I reviewed all journals kept from 1987 until that time. Although these journals were not kept regularly, most of them included detailed reference to my educational development practice and scholarship, and my teaching. Some were kept intensively for short periods, while I was engaged in specific learning projects. These journals I approached differently than the journal noted above. In this case, I reviewed each chunk of journal (there were definite beginning and end points) as a whole, and then sat down and wrote my response to it — describing my sense of it, and noting important themes. As I continued through the analysis, I noted the ways that each of the journals were different and/or similar. This analysis, based on the recommendations of Rainer (1978), gave me a good sense of the changes in focus, interest, thinking, etc. over that period of nine years.

Also in April 1996, I reviewed all the documents produced in my ED work in 1994–95. This included letters and memos, short 'popular' articles, texts of presentations to a wide variety of groups, proposals for funding, descriptions and evaluations of programs and workshops, records of consultations with clients, agendas and minutes of meetings, reports and recommendations prepared as a consequence of committee work, etc. Concurrent with this review, I again re-read the (now-annotated) ED journal from the same period. At around that same time, I was asked to prepare a teaching dossier/portfolio, to articulate a vision of the role of educational development centres in universities, and to prepare my annual academic report. Shortly after I completed these tasks — all of which necessitated critical reflection on practice — I proceeded with the next step in my research, which was to make claims, on the basis of my own ED experiences, about the nature of educational development.

Process

I wish to comment on the process of learning through critical reflection. As I noted earlier, my perspective on educational development is shaped by the two roles I play: that of teacher/educator (in my case the educational developer who facilitates the development of other educators), and that of student/learner (in my case the educator who is engaged personally in the process of development). Barnett (1996) revealed some of the ways that 'becoming a student' is difficult; it included, for example, figuring out what it means to learn and be a learner, knowing how to interact with the educator, and establishing a relationship with the material. Analysis of my experiences as a beginning educator shows me that some of the difficulties in 'becoming an educator' are actually the same difficulties that any learner experiences in 'becoming a student'. The basic problem is that one cannot simply be a student or an educator — in both cases, the role is not a prescription to be adopted, rather one must construct a personal identity in relation to the desired role. In my situation, this process was further complicated by the fact that I want to see myself as educator and as learner; I had not fully anticipated the quandaries that this would pose. The feeling was one of wanting to be both closed and open at the same time — a paradox, which put me in the position of being a 'living contradiction', as Whitehead (1993) so aptly described it.

Generally, I think I am tolerant of my clients' sometimes slow and frequently indirect developmental path. Analyzing my own experiences meant that I had to learn to be equally patient with myself, and to drop some expectations about development that I did not know I still had. Eventually, unable to ignore my mounting frustration with my rather inefficient approach to development, I asked myself, 'Am I trying to arbitrarily shape the story of my development into something that it is not?' Bateson's (1990) *Composing a Life* served as a reminder that my journey may very well be emergent rather than goal-oriented and that improvization (rather than the traditional heroic quest) is probably the more meaningful metaphor for me; Bateson's legitimization of such a developmental pattern calmed me. I refocussed on my purpose, which is to understand what it truly means to become an educator, and looked carefully at the path I have taken. I was then able to uncover a prevailing theme in my development: that of actively and openly responding to people and to circumstances, and a propensity for imagining possibilities. I also discovered that I hunger for both a sense of coherence and a sense of competence. And I saw that all of this was overlaid on a recurring theme in my life as a whole: a desire for personal autonomy, particularly as a member of a community.

Claims

In this section I make and support some preliminary claims about educational development. My purpose in making these claims is to invite dialogue with others as I make sense of ED, and to learn from this dialogue so that I can deepen my understanding of educational development. My four claims look at educational development through four lenses; a claim is essentially a 'take' on the process of development, each from a different vantage point, which all together may illuminate the process as a whole. These claims address development as it occurs through:

- an educator's decision to think and act like a teacher in a particular setting;
- the presence of a developer as witness to the need for development;
- the educator–learner relationship (conventions of practice as relationship-forming rituals); and
- an educator's impersonal interest in the educational text of various situations.

1 For educational development to take place, individuals must choose to think and act like educators in particular settings and situations

My experience indicates that becoming an educator is an attitude (seeing learning possibilities and accepting responsibility for realizing them) in combination with circumstances, and the competencies that arise through action in those circumstances (acting to transform a situation into an educational experience). This leads to my claim that the process of educational development is initiated by individuals who, by posing and acting upon the question of 'What learning is possible?' in the context of their relationship with others, assume the role of educator.

Educational development happens in the spaces of possibility defined by intentions and constraints in local, specific and immediate situations. Constraints on individuals' educational intentions present problems that must be dealt with, and they provide a frame within which development can take place. An effective educator asks what learning is possible in a given context, pushes these limits as far as possible, and accepts the limits that can be changed.

There is a tension between the situatedness of teaching problems and the human capacity for transcending boundaries, that is, the ability to step outside frames and re-imagine. This tension creates an opening where development can take place. Humans are not defined by situations — this allows them to respond to the situation, but only to a certain extent. In fact, an educator's capacity for critical self-reflection is an important constraint on what is possible. When a person playing the role of educator chooses to respond from an educational perspective, educational development is set in motion.

I want to emphasize that educational problems can not be transferred to someone else. I have made the claim that for educational development to take place in a given situation, the educator must assume responsibility for transforming the situation into an educational setting; the educator must be prepared to develop as a teacher so that they can respond to the situation, and to develop their teaching so that it is effective in that situation. If they give the problem to someone else, the problem cannot actually be solved, because its very nature is defined by a context in which they are present, as teacher, in relationship with the students. If not taking responsibility for responding to a situation in an educational manner IS the problem, passing responsibility on never addresses it — instead, it reframes the problem in an inappropriate way, i.e. as a technical (instrumental) problem.

If development cannot be transferred to another person, the educator is faced with the reality of having to perform at their present level of competence, which may be inadequate (or else of finding assistance that is contextualized), and the developer is faced with the reality of not having the power to take direct action to improve instruction — the developer must work through and with the educator. This means that educators and developers must learn to live with the fact that what is feasible may not necessarily be what is needed or most desirable for the learners in a given situation.

I find that university faculty who are considering whether I (the developer) may help them to address their educational problems are constantly assessing the functional validity (Munby and Russell, 1995) of everything I do, say, and suggest the question: Is a proposed way of thinking, of viewing the situation, of responding, likely to get them where they want to go? And I am always asking myself: How will something I do, say, or suggest get a particular teacher where they want to go in a particular context? One challenge I have is in helping educators (myself and other faculty) to internalize this question, make it their own, and consider the functional validity of what they believe and what they do. A bigger challenge is in helping individuals to consider the educational validity of their goals, that is to question whether their goals focus on the realization of learning possibilities.

2 The presence of a witness to the need for educational development serves as a stimulus for the educational development process

My second claim concerns the role of the educational developer. The educational developer in higher education represents the educational mandate of the institution, challenging and stimulating faculty to take responsibility for the quality of teaching and the development of teaching and to approach situations from an educational perspective.

In effect, the developer acts as witness to the need for approaching situations from an educational perspective. It is often easier to ignore an idea (of teaching as essential, of caring as necessary, of development as requirement) than it is to ignore the presence of a person — especially a person who is grounded, held fast by conviction, experience, openness and authenticity. When faculty recognize parts of themselves in a person committed to the development of teaching, they can connect with the idea through the developer. Faculty are then more likely to reconsider their own perspective/approach and to search for a way to incorporate a new perspective into their own.

This claim about the role of developer is closely tied with my previous claim that development takes place when individuals choose to think and act like educators. Because the developer is witness to the fact that one can respond to limits through development, educators are not let off the hook, able to shrink to fit the constraints or to blame them on someone else. I challenge faculty to grow in the face of constraints, to respond as educators in the situations in which they find themselves. In helping faculty to see themselves as educators, my overriding goal (essence of my work) is for them to be self-directed, autonomous. They must CHOOSE to become educators — only then can they really learn the role.

In my journals, there is evidence of my efforts to maintain a unity of purpose ('what learning is possible here?') and seek out that same intention in my faculty colleagues. I step around and about, dancing through all their arguments to reach the place where it counts: that is, what faculty must do to call themselves educators. In effect, I ask them, 'Who are you as educators, and how does your practice reflect that commitment and identity?' I hope that faculty who aspire to being educators will hear me, and will choose to respond, when I express interest in them as educators and in the arguments they create for themselves as educators.

What kind of presence are faculty likely to respond to? What qualities enable a developer to 'bear witness'? Stephen Brookfield (1990) emphasized the need for trust between educators and learners, and said that educators must demonstrate authenticity and credibility if they wish to forge connections with students. The importance of credibility suggests that it may be worth considering the notion of authority. Authority identifies something (someone) as legitimate. But there are so many authorities, including, for example, the authority of gender, or of body size and different people respond to different authorities in different situations. It may seem that a developer has to always know when to use one authority over another, or actually has to be all of them.

O'Reilley (1993) reminded us to put authority where it belongs: in whatever is compelling, and speaks to the heart and intelligence. Munby and Russell (1994) talked about the various kinds of authority, including authority of position and of reason, that play a role in educational settings, and draw our attention to the special authority granted to experience — particularly among beginning teachers. Upitis (1996) added the authority of caring to the list of authorities that are compelling in educational settings.

Faculty, of course, are quite skilled at calling upon various authorities to dismiss that which insults them — and, that which challenges them. Although many can readily deny quite legitimate arguments of reason and of experience, developers can speak directly to them by embodying arguments of reason and experience in ways that are new, unfamiliar, challenging, and creative — and I can invite them to do the same. I do not always want to accept the responsibility of this particular educational development role. I have found that when I do (and when I am successful in it) my presence as developer becomes the holistic representation of authority — that which is compelling — and a form of caring educational leadership.

3 A relationship with learners is essential to the development of the educator (and thus, to educational development)

One of the most obvious and consuming roles I play as a developer is to help faculty make better connections with their students. These connections enable feedback from the student to the developing educator — feedback on student learning, and on instructional performance — so that the educator can improve the quality of instruction. In addition to this instrumental benefit of good educator–student relationships, there is, I believe, another very important communicative benefit. A relationship with students helps the educator to develop a personal identity as an educator; this burgeoning identity is the foundation for educational development.

My journals show how essential this connection is; I see, in the journals, the incoherence that was characteristic of my educational practice when I entered ED work full-time and no longer taught a regular course with a class of students. I lost the strand of my own development as an educator. What is an educator without learners? More specifically, how can I become an educator, without a relationship with students and without the boundaries provided by classrooms, terms, curricula and a designated area of subject expertise?

As a new developer I faced the need to establish my own educator–learner relationship with individuals and groups of faculty all over the university, in all sorts of situations. This need is ongoing; my journals and work documents indicate that I am constantly gauging faculty interest in a topic and their view of me, and adapting to circumstances so that a connection can be made. Searching for ways to improve the pattern of educational activity on the basis of their need and my interlocking with that need, I look for the opening, often waiting, responding to faculty concerns and interests, intuiting the starting points for learning relationships.

Conventions of practice can be seen as rituals for creating educator–learner relationships. One route to development is, therefore, to follow all the conventional ED rituals (workshops, newsletters, consultations), and I discovered that this did provide some shape for my work as I struggled to develop a more authentic coherence. Are current ED conventions the only possible rituals for establishing educator–student relationships between developers and faculty? My experience suggests that these conventions may be inadequate rituals for the growth of developers as educators. In many cases, it seems that they merely identify the developer as a technical expert or as program administrator, rather than as educator.

The irony of my situation is that I am committed to faculty as learners, but they don't know that; in fact, they may not see themselves as learners. I am constantly aware that faculty are sizing me up so that they can decide whether a relationship with me is likely to help them. If they do see me as an educator, what kind of educator do they expect me to be? Do they see me as their educator, or as the educator of others? What confusion results when I mix up my educator role with other institutional roles e.g. as administrator or as scholar, or as employee? I know, always, that faculty are assessing whether and how they should interact with me, and it is a challenge to present myself in a way that allows them to recognize me and communicate with me as an educator.

Still, just as they are assessing me, I am constantly assessing them: where are they on the path to thinking and responding like an educator? Some I prompt to get started with their learning, others to go one step further. I invite faculty to respond to bewilderment, boredom, anger, frustration, curiosity with learning. It is a challenge to present educational development in a way that allows faculty to see themselves as learners. I hope they will learn to be educators, and not just play the role of a 'professor who teaches'. This is the path my own development must take, as well as theirs. I must learn to be an educator, in the role of educational developer. To do that, for my own development as an educator, I need an educational relationship with faculty.

4 To sustain educational development, the educator needs an impersonal interest in teaching and learning beyond his or her personal commitment to the learner

Faculty centre their lives, their energies, and their interests on their disciplines, the 'text' of their work. They invite their students to engage with them in the pursuit of understanding through this text. This is scholarship. Similarly, educational development is also possible through interaction with a text, which allows faculty to separate themselves from a particular educational situation, to replay it and reflect upon its meaning. I believe that a videotape of teaching, for example, or a journal, or records of work (documents), or hypomnemata (notebooks in which there is a constitution of oneself, i.e. a collection of the already said, heard and done) . . . that each of these can describe the educational text of a situation, and that an interest in this text contributes to the process of educational development.

It is generally accepted that the disciplinary text provides the interest, mutual perhaps, around which the educator and learner may build a relationship — a relationship that I have already described as crucial to the development of the educator. My claim here is that sustained educational work requires that educators develop — in addition to their interest in the disciplinary text — an impersonal interest in the educational text. However, the 'impersonal interest' in this case is a human one, an academic interest in life learning.

I have already made the claim that the presence of a witness (i.e. the educational developer) to the need for educational development is of fundamental importance to the process of educational development. I wish to extend this to suggest that the presence of an educator is important to any learner, because that educator serves as witness to the need for learning. Therefore, anything that permits presence of the educator must be attended to.

An impersonal interest in the educational text allows the educator to maintain a useful presence while a student learns. Without the interest, the educator may have little that compels them to remain in the company of the learner beyond an expectation that they provide direct instruction; given that the adult learner has responsibility for their own learning, the educator might well feel that an ongoing relationship with the learner is unnecessary (even inappropriate). On the other hand, some educators tend to over-identify with the interests of particular learners, or try to control the learning process, which is really the responsibility of learners; an impersonal interest keeps the educator focused on understanding the nature of teaching and learning, reducing the likelihood that this will occur.

The learner needs the presence of the educator simply so that they are free to pursue their own development and own interests, knowing that the educator backs them, and that they are not alone as they pursue the study path that is most meaningful to them. The presence of the educator mirrors the learner as a person, allowing them to believe that they are worthwhile, and that their goals are worthwhile. This presence frees the learner to inquire into something of interest and to imagine what it may mean for their life. The educator is there for the learner when they need assistance, but meanwhile is busy pursuing their own interests in the disciplinary and the educational texts. This presence is similar to the presence of caring parents and teachers in the life of young children, but in the higher education setting the educator's interest in the educational text allows the relationship to be a mature one, and a mutually beneficial one. The educator's interest in understanding learning is an educationally legitimate reason for them to maintain a presence for the learner in the absence of a deep personal problem, which means that it is quite different from a therapeutic relationship. The value of the educational text is that it incorporates the developmental interests of both the learner and the educator.

An impersonal interest in the educational text balances the educator's personal interest in the development of learners. It acts as a bridge between educator and learner, though not necessarily a bridge in the sense of a mutual interest; rather, bridge in the sense that it allows the educator to maintain a presence that is powerful because it is focussed on the possibilities for learning. It allows growth of the educator to proceed (in the direction of a better understanding of what it means to learn), while at the same time fostering growth of the learner. Thus, a parallel process of growth — in educators and in learners, in teaching and in learning — is made possible, which I believe is the ultimate goal of educational development.

Conclusion

In summary, I conclude that educational developers and faculty together may broaden the possibilities for learning in higher education by responding to particular circumstances from an educational perspective. Educational development occurs when faculty develop as educators through interpersonal teaching–learning relationships with students, and is sustained through impersonal interest in the educational text of university teaching and learning situations; the same process of development occurs when developers become educators through interactive educational relationships with faculty and through interest in the educational text of educational development situations. The developer may help faculty and students forge better connections, and may highlight the educational text as a faculty agenda for learning.

References

BARNETT, R. (1996) 'Being and becoming: A student trajectory', *International Journal of Lifelong Education*, **15**, 2, pp. 72–84.

BATESON, M.C. (1990) *Composing a Life*, New York: Plume.

BROOKFIELD, S. (1990) *The Skillful Teacher*, San Francisco: Jossey-Bass.

CANDY, P. (1991) *Self-direction for Lifelong Learning: A Comprehensive Guide to Theory and Practice*, San Francisco: Jossey-Bass.

GARDNER, H. (1993) *Multiple Intelligences*, New York: Basic Books.

MOUSTAKAS, C. (1990) *Heuristic Research: Design, Methodology, and Applications*, Newbury Park: Sage.

MUNBY, H. and RUSSELL, T. (1994) 'The authority of experience in learning to teach: Messages from a physics methods class', *Journal of Teacher Education*, **45**, 2, pp. 86–95.

MUNBY, H. and RUSSELL, T. (1995) 'Towards rigour with relevance: How can teachers and teacher educators claim to know?' in RUSSELL, T. and KORTHAGEN, F. (eds) *Teachers Who Teach Teachers*, London: Falmer Press, pp. 172–86.

O'REILLEY, M.R. (1993) *The Peaceable Classroom*, Portsmouth, NH: Boynton/Cook.

RAINER, T. (1978) *The New Diary: How to use a Journal for Self-guidance and Expanded Creativity*, New York: G.P. Putnam's Sons.

UPITIS, R. (1996) 'On becoming a dean: Integrating multiple roles and authorities'. Paper presented at the Canadian Society for the Study of Education, St. Catharines, Ontario.

WHITEHEAD, J. (1993) *The Growth of Educational Knowledge: Creating Your Own Living Educational Theories*, Bournemouth: Hyde Publications.

6   Building a Teacher Education Community: Combining Electronic Mail with Face-to-face Interactions

Rena Upitis and Tom Russell

Introduction

The impact of electronic mail as a supplement to the familiar exchanges on paper and in meetings merits analysis and illustration for others who would foster the development of community in academic settings. This chapter describes the first year of a new dean's efforts to build a teacher education community through presentation and examination of electronic mail communication, including attention to its powerful effect in facilitating collective and one-to-one communication among academic and non-academic staff members. Our story is told from two perspectives, those of the new dean and one of her initially skeptical faculty members. We are both committed and experienced users of electronic mail, but neither of us was ready for the insights and understandings that would emerge as we reviewed the electronic 'trails' that were created.

When the news of Rena's appointment as Dean of the Faculty of Education at Queen's University was announced early in March of 1995, the announcement was received with mixed reviews. Many supported her appointment in the academic community and in wider community circles. Others, however, had significant concerns about her potential as a leader for our Faculty or about the closed process of her appointment. Also, there were many complex divisions among faculty members, some of which had been festering for two decades or more, that threatened to drive our fragile Faculty apart when we needed most to come together as a community.

Rena saw that her first and most important task was to help rebuild the community — a community that included tenured and tenure-stream faculty, adjunct instructors, secondees, staff members, and our student body, made up of beginning teachers, inservice teachers, and graduate students. One of Rena's early goals was to use electronic mail in new ways to enhance the community-building process.

In this chapter, we present a number of electronic messages. Our commentaries, on the re-building of our community told from two different points of view, are woven among the messages and examine the immediate and delayed impact of them. From her view, first as dean-in-waiting (from March, 1995) and then as dean (from September, 1995), Rena describes how she made changes to facilitate community-building. These included providing every member of staff and faculty with access to a Faculty of Education list-serve (EDNEWS-L) as a way of communicating with each other; centralizing administrative functions that had been decentralized and had served to enforce the divisions mentioned earlier; conducting open meetings at strategic times on difficult issues (beginning with the controversy surrounding her appointment); delivering carefully worded and passionate messages in large assemblies of faculty, staff, and student groups; and numerous face-to-face encounters with individuals. Rena also relates the turmoil that some of the events caused, and summarizes how, in working through such turmoil, she came to better understand her colleagues and herself as our community began to change.

From his point of view as a faculty member of 18 years who had some initial reservations about how her appointment was made, Tom discusses the changes Rena instigated and the messages she sent (both electronically and face-to-face). His comments, as he revisited the electronic trail of messages, indicate how Rena's *instinctive* moves to build community took advantage of the electronic medium, allowing her far more specific, frequent, and rapid responses to personal and collective concerns than would have been possible by face-to-face meetings or paper memoranda.

Related Literature

We explore literature from three areas: (1) research on educational applications of email; (2) Sarason's views on community building; and (3) examples of using email to build relationships within self-contained communities. In each case, we describe how the findings in a given study relate specifically to the research reported here.

Educational Applications of Electronic Mail

Educational research describing the use of email often includes situations where electronic means are used to supplement or augment class interactions. The main goal is to use email to enrich the curriculum while enhancing interactions within the community are often a by-product of the email exchanges. For example, a recent study by Anderson and Lee (1995) describes an application of email in a graduate course on reading education. In this case, the instructors used email to augment class discussions, reflect on their learning, and share ideas and resources. They describe how email played a major role in community building, because students who were more expert in technology were able to work with non-experts, and students were more willing to risk ideas on email than they might have been in class settings. One of the difficulties highlighted in the study, however, was that of accessibility: at times, students had difficulty getting access to computer equipment or found the software difficult to use.

Access is a significant issue in building community through email. Even assuring that everyone has a log-in account and a computer does not ensure access. When Rena's appointment was announced, it was clear to her that accessibility was an issue. While most faculty members had email access, only a few staff, adjuncts, and secondees had email accounts and/or computers. One of Rena's first decisions was to find the funding to ensure that every member of the academic and non-academic staff had access to email. Even during times when finances were tight, there were small pockets of contingency funds that, when combined, were enough to buy new computers or upgrade existing ones. A small number of faculty members resisted email as a form of communication; for those members, Rena made paper copies of all of her messages and had them distributed by surface mail. She was concerned that the move to email did not replace one marginalized group with another. Also, because these members of the community did not have the benefit of hearing all of the dialogue provided by other list users, she felt reasonably confident that the time would come when they would choose to use the system. Indeed, eight months after everyone had physical access to email, the last person indicated that she was now 'on-line' and would no longer require the paper versions of the messages. This professor recently proclaimed, 'Email is the most wonderful thing! I can't imagine not having it'.

Another way that electronic communication plays a central role is in linking educators and students who are not part of a physically self-contained community, but are bound by an academic interest. There are a number of examples where writers share and critique their work using electronic means (Fey, 1992; Hill and Whitaker, 1994). One of the best known examples of this is the work of Trevor Owen (1992, 1995) who developed a project called *Wired Writers*. Writers from high schools across Canada, including high school students and their teachers, link with one another and with 'electronic writers in residence' to comment on each other's work and share ideas about writing and culture. They built a substantial community of writers, linked solely by the electronic medium (1995). Some students who made considerable use of *Wired Writers* describe how the medium encouraged dialogue because they were able to remain anonymous as they wrote (Beckstead, 1992). This use of electronic communication as a means of building community is, however, markedly different from the one described here. Unlike the high school student who felt encouraged to write because he wore a cloak of anonymity, we are all known to one another, and electronic communication is but one way that we interact with each other. However, some features that make *Wired Writers* a success in building community are common to our situation: the opportunity to hear from many voices, the option to read but not respond to every message, and the ability to answer messages at one's convenience.

Sarason's Views on Community Building

When Rena and Tom first spoke with one another after the announcement of her appointment, one of the topics of conversation was about building community. The meeting took place in Tom's office, and Tom handed Rena a copy of Sarason's (1972) *The Creation of Settings and the Future Societies*. While it was one of many books that Rena was offered by colleagues or sought out herself, Sarason's book was the one most frequently cited, and Rena read most of it during the first few months after the announcement of her appointment. Many of the views expressed by Sarason were salient to our experiences over the past year. Sarason's book was written long before email was envisaged as a communication device. In some ways, this makes our experiences different than those that Sarason describes. Yet, in most of the fundamental ways, Sarason's analysis of the creation of settings is as timely now as it was nearly a quarter century ago.

Sarason's discussion of the creation of new settings out of old ones begins with the notion of 'confronting history' (p. 42). He claims that 'the very fact that the new setting reflects some preexisting conflict within and between existing settings suggests some potential support for the new setting' (p. 42). In our setting this meant that there was reason for our setting or community to evolve; we had experienced conflicts within, and the time was ripe for change in leadership. Sarason goes further: he argues that the more that the leader is aware of his or her relation to the proposed setting in terms of personal history, the more that the history of structured relationships is acknowledged, and the more that 'the individual given responsibility for the new setting utilizes this historical knowledge ... maximizes the chances that the new setting will be viable and in ways consistent with its values and goals' (p. 43). Throughout this chapter, Tom and Rena often cast their comments in light of historical patterns. Further, Rena, as the *individual given responsibility for the new setting*, acknowledged her personal history as she began to thrive in the leadership role.

Sarason (1972) discusses the act of choosing a new leader. He illustrates how, particularly in the university setting, the choice of a leader 'creates a morale problem regardless of whether they choose from within or without, and to choose as if this were not true is an example of the gulf that can exist between knowledge and action' (p. 52). As our email excerpts and comments will indicate, the choice of Rena as dean, and the way that choice was made, had considerable impact. Sarason, in analysing why published accounts of choices of leaders do not illuminate the difficulties in transition and fail to link early and later events, proposes these reasons: (a) attention to such issues 'would require description and discussion of touchy, conflictful, or downright messy events and relationships which writers would prefer to avoid' (p. 53); and (b) in the writing of a history of a new setting, particularly the kinds of settings devoted to service of some sort, evaluation of the setting tends to focus on the success of the mission of the setting, rather than on what happened to those who created the setting and were affected and changed by it. In this chapter, we deal directly with the issues surrounding the choice of leader and, as Sarason predicts, parts of our descriptions are indeed *touchy* and downright *messy*.

Sarason makes the statement that 'only those who have never created ... a setting can underestimate the myriad details which must be handled and the flow of problems which never ceases. Just as the growth of the human organism is greatest in the first two or three years, the earliest months or the first year or so of a setting are characterized by very speedy growth' (p. 87). He further argues how the need to focus on the demanding but narrow present makes it difficult to reflect on the patterns of change. Certainly one of the advantages of having an electronic trail was that Tom and Rena could examine some of the evidence of the changes that occurred when there was time to do so.

Email, while not quite conversational, is at least more dynamic than other forms of collected data might be — something that would not have been possible to do at the time that Sarason first wrote his book. Sarason discusses the issue of the pace at which the first year flies, and the lack of time to reflect on how the present impacts both the future and the past as he comments on the formation of core groups. One of the most important core groups formed during the first year comprised four of us, including Tom and Rena, who took on the task of steering the restructuring of the teacher education program (this group is referred to as C4 throughout the chapter). Partly because of the email culture, and partly because of our interest in self-study and teacher education, we were able to be both active and reflective as the year progressed.

In Sarason's final chapter, 'The New Setting as a Work of Art', he shows how successful settings are created with an artistic spirit. The emphasis is on the creative process, where the artist or leader requires a sense of purpose and a formulation that links feelings, values, and ideas with successful outcomes, informed by reflection throughout the process. We quote directly from Sarason:

> Like a work of art the creation of a setting requires of a group that it formulate and confront the task of how to deal with and change reality in ways that foster a shared sense of knowing and changing and allows it to regard its development as a necessary antecedent to and concomitant of its efforts to serve or please others. Like the artist, its problems are never solved once and for all, they are ever present and varyingly recalcitrant, they discourage and distract, but it knows that this is the way it is and has to be and there is no good alternative to trying and learning. It treasures feeling and reveres reflection and calculation; it knows that there is always a tension between the two from which something new may emerge. (Sarason, 1972, p. 283)

Rena had strong notions about community building as an artistic act based on her work as an inner-city music teacher in Boston, Massachusetts (Upitis, 1990), notions that clearly resonate with Sarason's work. In that context, she first confronted difficulties in being a member of a community and, over the course of several years, learned to lead without disenfranchising others in the group. The following excerpt is taken from her letter of application for the position of dean. Almost two years after writing the letter, Rena feels even more strongly that her music-related experience has had a profound role in shaping her views of leadership and community:

> I found those years . . . difficult and fulfilling. It is not easy, after a full day of teaching, to tentatively make your way to the school parking area, wondering if you will find your tires slashed or your windshield bashed in. It is not easy to plan music classes for Grade 1 students whose first unit in their homeroom class is titled 'Why I will not bring guns and knives to school'. . . . But . . . these challenges can be turned to one's advantage. I found that the Grade 1 children (who did not bring guns and knives to school) liked playing the piano just as much as the 6-year-old children I had taught, one-on-one, in the comfort of their rat-free-designer-decorated-living-room-piano-always-in-tune homes. I found that expecting significant achievements led to significant achievements (I once overheard a Grade 3 student say, 'Miss Upitis thinks you could write a symphony if you wanted to'.) . . . Producing a school musical became a goal of mine as the year progressed. There were many reasons for pursuing such a performance: the kids wanted to show what they could do . . . it was a way of building school community, and a way of providing these kids with a different view of themselves and their world. It is not easy to organize a school musical with 150 children along with a handful of teachers and parents . . . Fortunately, I have a great deal of energy and a love for detail. The musical took place, at a real theatre in Cambridge, and was a success in the eyes of the children and their parents. The musical was not a success in the eyes of the teachers, however. I had not yet learned to delegate, and I had not helped the teachers see that the musical was not an add-on . . . In the face of comments from teachers that included, 'That was all well and good, but next year there will be no musical' and 'These kids need to concentrate on their reading and math skills', it was difficult to suggest that we launch yet another musical . . . But I did. And the musical became important not only to the kids and their parents, but to the teachers and administrators and support staff in the school as well. I learned to delegate, to relinquish responsibility for portions of the production, to trust more, and to do less . . . We formed a strong community. By the third year, there was no question about whether a musical would be a part of the school

year. Indeed, the teachers had independently applied for and received funding to support school musicals as a regular part of their students' schooling . . .

Examples of how Rena's views about leadership are coloured by her work as a musician and teacher of music appear in the email exchanges related later in the chapter. For instance, one of the first messages she sent to the Faculty made use of a choral ensemble as a metaphor for community.

Self-contained Communities

The closest parallel we have found to the work described here is that of companies that have used email to transform their communities. One example, outlined in the premiere issue of the magazine *Fast Company* (1996), has similarities to our own situation. The VeriFone company, with 2500 employees world-wide, is led by CEO Hatim Tyabji, who conducts much of the company's business through email. All 2500 employees are linked with one another. While 2500 people is substantially more than the 110 of us who are on the EDNEWS-L list, this is not unlike the situation we will be in when our restructured program begins and all of us are in contact with associate teachers and teacher candidates through email list-serves. When teacher candidates (700 full-time and 660 part-time) and associate teachers (1000) are added to the teacher education community, the situation becomes remarkably like that of VeriFone's: a core group, linked with other members of the community who are dispersed geographically (our teacher candidates will be all over Ontario and, in some cases, in overseas placements) who come together for periods of time, but spend large chunks of time away from the Faculty of Education.

While we do not share all of Tyabji's goals, some of his statements ring true as they relate to our experiences in using email. For instance, Tyabji talks about the importance of authenticity (VeriFone is opposed to corporate perks — Tyabji claims that he 'can't have emotion if [he] behave[s] differently from [his] people' (Taylor, 1996, p. 120), the expectation that emotions and views can be freely expressed on email, and the goal of being both a 'results-oriented culture' and a culture of caring. Further, Tyabji claims that one of the reasons email is successful in his company is that everyone is connected. He states:

> E-mail is powerful in this company because there are no exceptions . . . I was interviewing someone recently from a very large bank. I told him about our e-mail system and he said, 'Oh yeah, no problem, we have e-mail at the bank.' And I asked, 'Is every man, woman, and child on the e-mail? Does everyone in the bank have the power to e-mail anyone in the bank, regardless of rank? Does anyone in the bank have the power to send a message to everyone in the bank world-wide, just by hitting the equivalent of I-Staff in our company?' He said, 'Oh no! The e-mail prerogative only goes from the CEO down three levels'. (Taylor, 1996, p. 118)

Rena had similar conversations with other administrators when she first began describing the use of email at the Faculty of Education. Most said, 'Sure, we use email', and then proceeded to describe how email was used to send memoranda about meetings to faculty members — the way that the list serve was used at the time Rena began to take on a leadership role. When questioned further, it also became apparent to Rena that very few large departments or faculties had every member on email — faculty, secretaries, adjuncts, mail-room delivery staff, technicians, and the like.

Some of the key issues that emerge from these three diverse areas of literature are accessibility, flattening of hierarchical structures, and authenticity in the interchanges amongst members of the community surface continually in the exchanges that follow.

Themes and Data

Our goal in this self-study is to understand how electronic mail, as a supplement to the usual face-to-face interactions, can influence community building. Our data are electronic mail messages sent during the period between March 1995 and March 1996. From March 1995 to March 1996, (one calendar year from the announcement of Rena's appointment), Rena initiated to EDNEWS-L a total of 186 messages which included announcements, issues, requests for help, philosophical tidbits, and general views and feelings. In addition, Rena and Tom exchanged 171 messages, 12 of which were initiated by Rena. Rena describes Tom as 'a medium-heavy to heavy, but welcome, email user'. Most people send fewer messages (from 0 to 2 or 3 a month). Tom sends about 11 messages a month to Rena, and she responds to all messages she receives.

In the initial analysis, Rena sifted through the messages stored on her office computer to construct over 30 themes that illustrate the wide range of electronic conversations within our Faculty of Education and between herself and Tom as two members of that community. She added comments about how each message appeared to her in March 1996, in terms of the community or hers and Tom's relationship, and Tom then added comments about how each message appeared to him. Then Rena and Tom re-examined the initial groupings of messages and responses, and grouped the themes into the broader categories that appear in this chapter. At that time, they also added another layer of commentary.

Our conclusions are almost self-evident, after going through this two-stage process of selection and annotation. Extensive use of electronic mail has enabled Rena, as a new dean, to communicate not just important information (which tended not to be available at all, under previous deans) but also to convey an image of herself as dean and of the community we are becoming. The data show that Rena and Tom have developed a relationship that is far more positive and productive than either could have hoped to develop in 12 months without electronic mail. In Tom's view, this self-study process of reviewing their messages and exchanging comments about them plays a central role in further developing their relationship. More specific implications are raised in the final section.

The first broad theme is that of how electronic mail was used to communicate with faculty and staff in the community building process. This is followed by an examination of ways that community was strengthened through Rena's active participation in non-administrative roles, where email played a supporting role. Finally, we end with a case study where we describe how, as a *new dean* and an *old teacher*, our relationship was fostered through the availability and use of email.

Rena Upitis and Tom Russell

Using Electronic Mail to Communicate with Faculty and Staff

Facilitating thought about issues

Electronic communication was initially used to post information about upcoming meetings or to forward information from other departments, such as research services. Rena's intent was to transform the existing EDNEWS-L list-serve into a medium that was also a *place* for thinking about issues affecting the Faculty, where responses could be made to individuals or to the group as a whole. Issues were as complex as discussions about the nature of our student body and the value of research, and as seemingly simple as whether a faculty pot-luck should replace the traditional wine-and-cheese reception. By discussing such issues on the list, face-to-face meetings were also enriched. Sometimes, use of the list-serve eliminated the need to meet. It certainly eliminated the need for paper memos. Other advantages of electronic mail became apparent, such as being able to respond at one's convenience, not having to wait to speak, and freeing up time to meet face-to-face on other issues.

We begin this section with an early discussion in which Tom publicly invited Rena to speak to the issue of whether she would welcome disagreement with her personal views in discussions on the EDNEWS-L list. This is followed by examples of ways in which the list helped us as a community to explore a range of issues. (Throughout the rest of the chapter we do not include the 'to' line from email when it is sent to the EDNEWS-L list. We include the 'to' line when the message is sent to a different group or person).

Can We Really Disagree with the Dean?

Date: Tue, 25 Apr 95
From: RUSSELLT@QUCDN.QueensU.CA
To: UPITISR@educ.QueensU.CA
Subject: Howard's message
I've already told Howard what a treat it was to find such a well-developed position on this new communication loop we all have. While minutes and meeting notices by this medium are very convenient tree-savers, the potential for discussion could breathe new life into our time-starved lives with so little space for meetings.

It may well be that people are taking time to respond to Howard, since his message did deserve thought and it is a very busy week. But then I remembered that there is a point at which Howard tackles the UBC model directly, and I also remembered that it was our new dean who put that model before us. It strikes me that as an organization we have a long tradition of not taking risks with our leader, who does have the ability to facilitate special requests and who does determine our merit pay each year. So it is not entirely ridiculous to think that people might prefer not to publicly engage Howard on his points, for statements of support for Howard's position might be seen as a way to disappoint our new dean.

Date: Wed, 26 Apr 95
From: UPITISR@educ.QueensU.CA
To: RUSSELLT@QUCDN.QueensU.CA
Subject: Howard's message

Thanks for your follow-up message to Howard's message — I also hadn't twigged to the significance of it being me, as you put it, who sent out the email on the UBC and UWO etc. models. But I also believe (I have to!) that past practices about dean-pleasing can and will shift, as long as people see me, time and time again, listening, considering, sorting, asking questions, stating my views, listening again, agreeing, disagreeing, . . . until that becomes the known practice. I figure the only way to change practice is to change practice. In some small ways, this is happening already.

Date: Wed, 26 Apr 95
From: RUSSELLT@QUCDN.QueensU.CA
To: UPITISR@educ.QueensU.CA
Subject: Howard's message

Of course you will state that you hope people will disagree with you, but I hope you will think long and hard about how you can say that so it is believable . . . I would be willing to predict that in the year 2000 you will find that the biggest challenge of your first 5 years has been getting people to tell you what they believe, rather than what they think you want to hear . . . it's only over time as people see you listening, shifting, accepting, and building, and see you not favoring those who work to stay squeaky-clean ('Yes, Rena; sure, Rena; you're right, Rena') that the image and attitude will start to shift . . . I really hadn't twigged to the significance of it being you (you're not 'just Rena' any more, you are the dean-designate for 1995–2000) sending out the UBC and UWO models.

Date: Wed, 26 Apr 95
From: UPITISR@educ.QueensU.CA
Subject: Howard's message

Hi everyone! OF COURSE YOU CAN DISAGREE WITH YOUR NEW DEAN!!! I say this with a RESOUNDING CHORUS (remember my choir metaphor???) — in fact, it would be unhealthy, unrealistic, and altogether weird if we didn't hold differences of opinion. As I stated at the open meetings, I welcome your views even if they are completely different from mine. And most of all, I welcome you telling me, directly, what those views are — that way we can talk about the issue and find some common ground (or live with the paradoxes and tensions, if there is no common ground to be had, other than mutual respect).

RENA: It never dawned on me that people would not disagree when they did not share my view. I am frustrated, but thankful to Tom for bringing this into the open. Thankful to have a chance to respond. I thought to myself, 'I can see why it is so hard to *report openly* — after all, I reported at great length what I heard at the various institutions I visited and openly gave my views about what I saw and heard.' It was hard to get 'Yeah, but we can't disagree with the dean'. '*Model*', I told myself, 'Model what you believe in'.

TOM: Notice Rena's opening and closing sentences above as she looks back over these exchanges. Two of the points I recall from my pre-tenure years in this faculty involved the dean at the time and my secretary at the time. I remember telling the dean 'X is happening' and he was unable to accept my point. Later I realized that, while everyone seemed to be talking about X, no one else was telling the dean about X — one did not tell deans that sort of thing. My secretary told me I saw things others did not seem to see. So here I was using the new list-serve technology to put those experiences from so long ago out before my colleagues. I do not know what price I paid personally, people probably know what to expect of me, but it was valuable for Rena to discuss this all publicly. And, of course, 'Model what you believe in' is still her motto and one of the many keys to her successful community-building.

Using the List to Explore Issues: Three Examples

The three examples presented here focus on a day-to-day operations issue, an invitation to reflect, and a request for input before an administrative decision is made.

Day-to-day operations issues

The first example, sent 2 May 1995, illustrates how the list enabled us to compare views on a possible change to a fundamental yet mundane aspect of our day-to-day operations, namely, the kind of paper we feed into our photocopiers and printers. While this may seem like an issue too trivial for extensive discussion, it served to illuminate various perspectives regarding the role that the Faculty should play in leading change. Also, it attracted comment from non-academic staff members who had not contributed to the list previously. This served to remind us that there are no issues on which people lack opinions, and that even 'simple' issues can be controversial.

Date: Tue, 02 May 95 11:10:33 EDT
From: UPITISR@educ.QueensU.CA
Subject: recycled paper

For a few years, I've been bothered by the fact that we use bleached white (cheap) paper for photocopying and laser printing. I've asked Margot to look into other kinds of paper possibilities — namely recycled, high post-consumer waste percentage, and non-bleached. We're starting to get information about the costs of these recycled papers. One is cheaper than what we use (a miracle); most (the better ones, i.e. higher post-consumer waste, etc.) are more expensive. They

---

are more expensive, in part, because there is relatively little demand for such paper.

I'd like to get a sense of how people feel about the 'paper issue'. If we went to a slightly more expensive paper, would changing our current 5 cents a photo-copy to 6 or 7 cents be acceptable? Cause riots on student street? Make you wish you didn't have a tree-hugger for a dean-in-waiting?

RENA: Part of the idea here was to see if this mail would attract some new voices, particularly those of staff. It did. Surprise to me was that some resisted the new paper if it was going to cost more. Most, however, said it was time to take the plunge. We ended up using a cheaper paper that is recycled. And now it is being used throughout the Queen's campus! The Vice Principal's and Principal's offices were among the first to switch over to 'earthwhite' recycled paper. This turned out to be a great example for change, and later it became a metaphor for me.

TOM: The date on this message is fascinating. It is the start of the second full month following the announcement that Rena would become Dean of Education at the beginning of September. She has raised a personal issue on email, engaged a wide range of responses, and ultimately lowered our photocopying costs while pleasing everyone (especially our teacher candidates) with our environmental sensitivity. Any administrator here at Queen's could have taken initiative and explored the cost-and-availability issues, but Rena made an early mark that influenced the entire university.

Invitations to reflect

The second example from 2 May 1995 and sent to EDNEWS-L is an invitation to reflect on the make-up of our student body. Rena's intent was to encourage widespread discussion several weeks before a planned Faculty retreat where this issue would be considered in the context of restructuring our teacher education program.

From: **UPITISR@educ.QueensU.CA**
Subject: **Concurrent/consecutive blend**
Sounds like coffee, doesn't it? At any rate, I'm concerned that we don't get 'roasted' in the following way. It is really important that, as we move towards designing a new two-year program, we carefully examine all of our concurrent programs as well (Queen's–Waterloo, Queen's–Trent, Queen's–Queen's). There are several issues at stake here (at least that I've identified so far . . . I'm sure there are plenty more!):
[A list of six issues follows]

RENA: I was aware that this was potentially a controversial issue. After the recent discussion about whether faculty and staff could disagree with the dean, I wanted to make every effort to signal that open discussion was what I was looking for. One way that I tried to do this was to use a coffee metaphor, making the invitation 'light' and with a touch of humour.

TOM: As a coffee lover, I had to appreciate this message! In hindsight, it really is a blend. Woven in with the specific issue of program balances, Rena signals her plan to spell out a view of our graduates by listing our view of what we want our graduates to be like as one of the issues. This is a powerful element of the new program document. There are issues for people to think about, but there are also signals of things to come, and she ends on a positive (and political) note by mentioning specifically one component of the faculty.

Asking for input before taking administrative decisions

The final example, sent to EDNEWS-L on 12 March 1996, typifies the way that Rena asks for input before taking administrative decisions. Rena used the list to ask for ideas and responses before she made administrative decisions about such topics as membership on university committees, changes to convocation procedures, or the availability of maintenance personnel within our building.

From: UPITISR@educ.QueensU.CA

Will it ever end? Yes — it's another IAR request! The Vice Principal's office has asked for names of staff who would be suitable nominees for the IAR internal committee that will be charged with reviewing our beautiful four volumes. Suggestions? If you have anyone in mind, please also include their phone number, department/faculty, and one or two sentences about them.

RENA: I hate cluttering up people's mailboxes with requests like this, but it is important to ask all community members these questions, rather than just asking a few people in the hallway. I remind myself, as I send messages like this, that it's worth the clutter in mailboxes — the alternative is relying on serendipity (whoever is around) or an 'in group' of advisors (or the perception of an 'in group'). I realized, when writing this paper, that I have developed a predictable method of asking for input, including the way I ask, the period of time I wait (usually just under a week), and the way I respond. I try to let the conversation unfold on the list, only adding my views if I feel strongly about something. Unless the 'answer' is crystal clear, I want to listen. And the answer is rarely crystal clear.

TOM: Rena's use of email for input from the community serves to remind us all of how many decisions were being made without general input, simply because in the absence of communal communication, it is so natural to go with the first suggestion one receives.

Revealing 'Rena's Take on the World'

Part of using electronic mail to communicate and build community includes situating oneself as a community member. In composing email messages, Rena deliberately revealed her views and feelings by using such devices as metaphors, humor, and including a quote in her signature. Two examples appear below the first from 13 March 1995 sent to the EDNEWS-L and the second comes from Tom in November of 1995.

A choral metaphor for leadership

From: UPITISR@educ.QueensU.CA

Yesterday afternoon I had a choir rehearsal for our Good Friday concert ('What?' I hear you asking . . .' is this what we get with an artist as dean-to-be???'). Since I am on a 'new planet' now as dean-to-be, I am seeing and hearing many things in terms of 'deaning metaphors'. So, there I was, in the soprano section, thinking how appropriate the choral experience is for signifying my hopes for us as a faculty. First, every voice matters, and all voices, while singing up to twelve different parts, sing in harmony (most of the time). Occasionally, some voices rise in solo above the group, still singing with the choir, nonetheless. And when the solo is over, the voice rejoins the ensemble, seamlessly. But for me, perhaps the most important thing of all is that, as a musician who plays solo music as well, I crave the choral experience because there are some kinds of music that can only be experienced in ensemble. Exciting and beautiful music at that. Music that is wonderful to perform but takes a lot of work to get there, to say nothing of the confusion as we learn the music, endless rehearsals, frequent misunderstandings, and so on. But we do it because we want to come together in ensemble.

By the way, if you're free on Good Friday, we're singing works by Purcell, Mendelssohn, Harris, Palestrina and others, at the Sydenham St. United Church, at 7:30 p.m. 'We' includes some of our current B.Ed. and M.Ed. students who can not only teach reading and math, but can sing a wicked alto line besides!

RENA: This was a risky message to send, but I figured it was time to let people know what I'm like, what I think about, what I feel about, what inspires me. It has been referred to, time and time again, since I first wrote it nearly eighteen months ago. It turns out to have been a risk well worth taking.

TOM: We have always associated Rena with music, but here we have some detail of how her musical interests play out and interact with her work as dean. *Self-disclosure* has not been a characteristic of former deans, and I found this very refreshing. Nor should the genuine invitation at the end pass unnoticed.

Quote of the week

From: RUSSELLT@QUCDN.QueensU.CA

. . . I've been forgetting to say that I really like your 'quote of the week' in your signature!!! It made a great way to start a class last Tuesday.

>Hey, thanks Tom. I'll look forward to some time during the Dec 4 week.
>Rena
>**

Students do not really listen well to the answers to questions they have not learned to ask. — Mary Rose O'Reilley

RENA: Some time in June of 1995, I started signing all of my emails with a quote of some sort — a way of telling people where my heart is without being blatant about it. In reply to a note of mine, Tom joined a growing chorus of people who commented on how much they look forward to the signature quotes. I usually change the quote about once a week. Not long ago, a colleague asked me if he could get a reference for the source. It was great to reply that I picked them up from books I'm reading, realising, as I made the comment, I still had time to read books!

TOM: I wondered where Rena found time to insert a new quotation every week? We are both drawn to this book by Mary Rose O'Reilley, but I had not noticed this quotation, a summary of my personal commitment to our new program design for pre-service teacher education; a design in which experience in the classroom will be used to generate questions to be addressed in education classes.

Meeting Face-to-Face on Issues that Really Matter

Rena's use of email enhanced face-to-face meetings. Three examples follow all were sent to the list. The first was dated 28 March 1995; the second 19 January 1995; and the third 5 Sept 1995. This range of dates reveals that such use is ongoing and continues to enhance community communication.

Planning gatherings of the community

From: UPITISR@educ.QueensU.CA

I am writing to inform everyone about plans for a Faculty Retreat. A number of people have expressed an interest in doing this, and I have cleared things with [the Acting Dean — Rena's immediate predecessor] so we can make some plans. Here's the plan so far — input welcome. [In the message, Rena asks faculty for ideas for the day and indicates she will meet on 20 April with Susan Wilcox from the Instructional Development Center who will act as a facilitator. Rena summarizes issues that have been suggested for the retreat] Obviously we can't do it all in one go! I see this first day as indeed just that — a first day of grappling with some of these things (outside of the building!) Sooo . . . let me know your thoughts. [Rena includes the date, place, time and asks for RSVP's] I'd also like to point out that there are funds available for this (no one is being 'robbed' for this event!!); . . . This promises to be an exciting (and probably hard) day/time to talk, and maybe even take a stroll in the woods.

RENA: Having used email to plan and carry out exit interviews, I decided to use the medium again to plan the Faculty Retreat. I allowed lots of lead time so that I could plan carefully and receive input, both electronically and in meetings with individuals. I began learning how to balance email talk with face-to-face talk. This worked. This meeting was the first large gathering where we seriously discussed the restructuring of the BEd/DipEd program.

TOM: The retreat worked. This message was the beginning. I wondered why we would invite someone to facilitate, but it was clear during the event. Susan Wilcox, now cross-appointed to our faculty, is a treasured colleague. The message and the retreat provided Rena (who showed she listens) with information about issues and general tendencies.

Meetings with individuals

> **From: UPITISR@educ.QueensU.CA**
> Hello all — Lynda [Secretary to the Dean] and I have just finished consulting one another (and reading all of the scribbles in my daybook!), and we think I will have had the luxury and pleasure of speaking with everyone come the end of July! If, by any chance, I have missed someone (that is, not talked personally with a member of our community even once!), please let one of us know and we will find a time that's mutually suitable.

RENA: This message was meant to make sure that no one was missed and reinforce the idea that I meant everyone when I said everyone! Initially, some of the traditionally marginalized groups wondered if they were included when I said *all*. Nevertheless, it took almost a year for the entire community to feel included.

TOM: This is one of the AMAZING ways in which Rena has made a difference, quickly. Talk about *carpe diem* — her ability to be inclusive will make a difference to our culture over time. Her willingness to put in the time required her incredible energy, and her ability to keep details of each person in her mind at all times. Rare, special, and new in our Dean's office.

Setting the tone for the community

> **From: RUSSELLT@QUCDN.QueensU.CA**
> I'd like to express publicly my admiration and gratitude to Katharine, Bill and Rena for the superb musical opening. Obviously, the times they are a-changing . . . for the better. I'm sure that the 650+ assembled will remember that opening far longer than any other first-day events they have attended.

RENA: We started the year with an address to teacher candidates and faculty/staff. Two colleagues and I played a song from the musical *Anne of Green Gables* called 'Learn Everything', and I talked about issues important to me — the profession, a passion for learning, broad issues of education. I did not believe Tom, that the opening would make

a difference, but I was pleased we had pulled it off with integrity and verve. I was wrong: people commented on that opening, and many teacher candidates described projects they had undertaken as a result, even while I was hooding them at convocation.
TOM: My prediction was correct. The teacher candidates in my own class were still talking about issues raised on the first day even in our last week of classes.

Strengthening Community through Participation and Information Sharing

In addition to communication through email and face-to-face meetings, other aspects of community building included Rena's participation in all aspects of teacher education. The issues here are availability of the dean (sent 26 May 1995), joining colleagues in a new self-study group (7 Sept. 1995), using administrative tasks to find out more about faculty members' work (5 Oct. 1995), and teaching both undergraduate and graduate students (5 Dec. 1995).

Availability of the dean

Rena decided early to notify faculty when she would be absent for extended periods of time with the assumption that she was a vital part of the community and as its leader members had the right to know when she was available.

From: UPITISR@educ.QueensU.CA
Subject: Rena away
[In her message Rena informs the faculty of the dates in May and June when she will be absent and where she will be during that time not to facilitate contact but as a point of information.]
****
Life begets life. Energy creates energy. It is by spending oneself that one becomes rich. — Sarah Berhardt

---

RENA: It seemed important, from the start, to let people know when I am away. I remember writing this note feeling glad about being away — not feeling the least bit guilty! I figured out, early on, that being available also means that one can be not available when needs be. I do not always take enough breaks, though, and I'm feeling it, especially now (July 1996); this is something I still need to learn to do for myself, and for our community.
TOM: It sounds simple, yet it's also new. The Dean's Office is now *where the action is* — a bright, cheerful place, door often open, Rena at work but welcoming anyone who drops in. The cynical person could say, 'Who cares whether Rena's available or not — just leave a phone or email message?' but Rena is saying that she cares whether she is available to her community. She wants people to know when she will be away, not available at a moment's notice. Notice as well the activities taking her away.

Participating in Faculty Groups

From: RUSSELLT@QUCDN.QueensU.CA
That was one of the most amazing hours I've ever spent in this building. [Another of our administrators] likes to talk about being an academic temporarily working 80% in administration, but you walk the talk. Your presence was as perfect as those of the other six, and I was fascinated by the way the conversation unfolded and expanded . . . I was truly unsuspecting when you asked if I'd look at the organizational data, but I love looking at data, particularly at that level, so it's quite impossible to decline — especially since I have a whole new sense of anticipation for the conference . . .

RENA: I started attending the self-study group meetings (I missed the first one, since I was not on the list — but when the group heard I was interested in the whole area, I was invited). At the outset, I did not mean for this to be a 'walk the talk' episode, but I came to realize how important it was for me to take part in this kind of activity. And — this paper is born! This was a day that I considered not coming to the group, since I was so busy (budget, or something — I can not remember now just what it was). But I do remember the group meeting, and Tom was right — even coming for 10 minutes was better than nothing.
TOM: It seemed important to tell Rena that I compared her positively to her predecessors. She did miss meetings occasionally, but her participation continues to be important.

And these notes are not coming just from Tom . . .

To: QS-STUDY_L@QUCDN.QueensU.CA
From: HUTCHINN@educ.QueensU.CA
Subject: Good Stuff
I'm like Tom, taking great pleasure in the out-to-lunch-bunch on Thursday. And I find thinking about how things are changing heartwarming.

Making the most of administrative tasks

To: UPITISR@educ.QueensU.CA
From: RUSSELLT@QUCDN.QueensU.CA
Subject: SSHRC proposal
Hugh reported his conversation with you — we certainly didn't mean to be as direct as our text stated, and it was great that you flagged it. Thanks. I'm still stunned that the occupant of the dean's office is actually reading rather than just scribbling. Feels like we have a real Dean, rather than an MC.

RENA: One of my deanly duties is to sign research proposals before they are forwarded to the Research Services office. Like a good lawyer, I do not sign anything I have not read! In reading Tom's and Hugh's proposal, I suggested, what was to me, an important but subtle change in wording.

TOM: This was not my only encounter with Rena's policy of reading what she signs. Where she finds the time remains a big puzzle.

A dean who teaches

> **From: UPITISR@educ.QueensU.CA**
> **Subject: quick! before it's gone . . .**
>   The Section F math class (P/J) constructed a lovely Sierpinski tetrahedron on the stage of the auditorium. It's there right now if you want to sneak a peek at it before the scissors wizards get at it.

RENA: One of the most important things to me has been working with teacher candidates. But it set me apart from other deans, and sometimes I feel the extra strain of carrying a teaching load that is equal to or greater than regular faculty members in other departments and faculties. But his was not one of those days — in fact, I could not resist sending a message to invite people to see a sculpture constructed by one of my classes.

TOM: One nice feature of this note is that it reminds us that Rena has taken on a substantial teaching load, quite unlike her predecessors or administrative colleagues. While it is not uncommon for a dean to teach a graduate seminar or supervise theses, few teach Monday morning undergraduate curriculum courses.

Openness and Valuing People

An issue permeating our community, whether through email communication, face-to-face meetings, or participation in a teacher education enterprise, is that we are committed to sharing information and acknowledging the work and ideas that people bring to our enterprise. In this section we highlight this aspect with four examples: explicit acknowledgment of people's achievements (sent 14 Sept. 1995), making minutes and reports widely available (the first two were exchanged on 5 April followed by another on 12 April 1995), linking our faculty with the rest of the university (3 Jan. 1996), and speaking openly about tensions and managing communication (the series of messages included were sent 4, 15, 16 and 24 Jan., 1996).

Acknowledgment of achievements

> **To: UPITISR@educ.QueensU.CA**
> **From: RUSSELLT@QUCDN.QueensU.CA**
>   Hi Rena — Here's the letter I'm planning to FAX to Bill [Principal William Leggett]. What do you think? [Attached is a copy of a letter to Bill Leggett, in

which Tom reasserts his concern about the standard process of the selection of Dean's at Queen's but in which he also indicates his respect and admiration for Rena's work as his dean.]

RENA: I realized that although Tom and I were working well together, this might not be obvious to *the outside* — and that it probably would not hurt if the Principal was made aware of the ways in which our situation was changing. Tom, after all, had made clear to the Principal his angst about how my appointment was made. But had either of them spoken with one another since? I posed this question to Tom, and in response he wrote a letter to the Principal, even though, as Tom put it, it was 'Bill's move'. We both learned the value of taking the first step. I learned that saying good things about people has far more weight than I realized. Also, my early impressions of the Principal were being reinforced: I respected him and admired him, and hoped that Tom would have a chance to develop similar views — something that would not happen without one of them starting the dialogue.

TOM: With no more promotions to seek, I felt I could afford to watch and wait, and see if the Principal would ever ask how things were unfolding. For whatever reason, that just does not seem to be part of his style, but when Rena made me aware of the potential value of writing and sending this message, I decided to take the first step.

Making reports available

This example begins with an interchange between Tom and Rena on 5 April 1995. Tom asks whether Rena has received reports from external consultants which the Principal had indicated would be sent to the college and which Rena had promised to forward. Rena indicates she has not heard further and agrees to follow up. (This note follows on 12 April 1995.)

> **From: UPITISR@educ.QueensU.CA**
> **Subject: Birch/Lacey reports**
>   Yes!!! They are finally available!!! I have placed copies of the external consultants' reports with Lynda Simpson in the Dean's office. If anyone has any comments to make after reading the reports, please share your comments with me and/or bring them up at the Faculty retreat on 25 May. Thanks for your patience,

RENA: I promised, at the open meeting, to see about getting the internal reports available for general distribution. I found out, unfortunately, that it took longer than I expected to get permission, and it also took lots of persistence. Tom's encouraging reply at the end of this task was important to me. It also made me realize how many iterations it would take to move forward in small ways.

TOM: It was important to make public the reports of the external consultants to the search committee that recommended Rena to the Principal. The Principal himself was new to Queen's in September 1994, and he had spoken of the importance of *transparency*.

Yet Queen's continues to search for and review deans using a committee that solicits views but usually has no more than one public discussion, early in its deliberations. The candidates being considered by the committee were never made public, but the rumor that Rena would be the next dean had first surfaced in December, 1994, when she resigned from the Search Committee in order to apply for the position of dean. The 'rumor mill' worked overtime, and eventually we did learn who the candidates were, but we were never told officially, there were no public presentations by candidates (Why would any external applicant accept a position without meeting the people in the organization??) and the gossip was itself very divisive — eventually leading a colleague and me to speak with the Principal on the day before the committee held its interviews. (We thought there were going to be three interviews, but the rumor mill was slow and one person had withdrawn a few days before, so there were only two.) By securing permission to make the reports of the two external consultants public, Rena made a crucial move in a personal practice of 'transparency' a practice that she continues consistently and to considerable advantage in the eyes of someone like me who values knowing what the big picture is.

Being an active faculty within the university

> **From: UPITISR@educ.QueensU.CA**
> Hi. I've just returned from a 7:30 a.m. emergency senate meeting, called by the Principal, to brief us on the impending budget cuts. You'll be able to get more details in the Senate minutes in the Gazette. The bottom line: cuts are coming, they're coming soon, they will be severe, we need to 'restructure'. The good news — the Principal held up the Faculty of Education as an example of 'willingness to move proactively to other models'. Something's working.

RENA: This was an exciting morning for me — it felt as if the Principal was paying attention to the Faculty of Education. It was important to share this, and to encourage whatever was happening to make it so. Also, I felt the need to warn people of the imminent budget crisis.
TOM: One of the appealing features of Rena's style involves her quick and clear communication of the details of meetings that we have not been told about in the past. Rena seems to sense intuitively that information shared freely and clearly is a major step in making her work as Dean easier.

Acknowledging tension and maintaining communication

> **From: UPITISR@educ.QueensU.CA**
> **Subject: BUDGET NEWS (long message — Don't shoot the messenger!)**
> This afternoon I received the figures for our budget cuts for the upcoming (1996–97) budget year. [Rena outlines what the cuts will be both in per cent figures and dollar amounts. She then outlines what her initial budget cut expecta-

tions had been, her plan to meet that cut and a contingency plan for deeper cuts. She reveals the amount by which the cuts were deeper than even the contingency plan. She tells the community that there will be staffing cuts. She outlines the options of making the cuts initially or incurring debt and trying to make the deficit up later. She outlines her decision to not incur debt. She then outlines the current financial status of the college. She indicates ways the faculty could help with some of the voluntary programs. She notifies them that her strategy for considering budget reduction is not an across the board cut but a program by program consideration. She indicates which cases programs might make suggestions for cuts themselves, when she will act independently on behalf of the faculty, and when she will ask for external input about how to manage the needed reduction. She ends with this comment] The point here is that I will seek advice broadly, and deal with the cut as fairly, openly, and honestly as I possibly can. To this end, I would like to call a series of open meetings so that we can talk. No agenda — just questions, dialogue, and maybe a few innovative answers! [She lists three meeting times]

I would also like to stress the importance of the work that we have already done, not only insofar as this work has served to 'protect' us from a much deeper cut, but in that our entrepreneurial efforts and program revisions will make these cuts possible — and make our programs better. We are moving forward in many ways; I fully expect that some time in 1997 we will begin hiring once again . . . Cuts do not mean total freeze. They mean shuffling, rethinking, changing our views, and, above all, remaining open and energetic. I'll try and practice what I've just preached!

RENA: Here's where the email medium really shines. I was able to give people real information about our budget cuts immediately after receiving it. This was an uncharacteristically long message for me, but an important one. I spent a long time phrasing the words and tone. There is not much humor here in contrast to most of the messages I send, but much encouragement and a willingness to be open with information. I thought this would be of utmost importance, because of the staffing implications.
TOM: This illustrates Rena's superb use of email. The detail included in the message speaks volumes about Rena's awareness that people can contribute if they understand rationales.

From: UPITISR@educ.QueensU.CA
It has come to my attention that I may have offended a few people by my comment about 'maybe we can get more than four academic staff on the WWW page' — sorry, no offence intended. I need to remember to use the universal sign :-) when I mean humour, not a barb.

From: UPITISR@educ.QueensU.CA
Subject: this is REALLY bugging me!(message for academic staff)
Margot and I are looking at the list of CVs outstanding (there are 18), performance appraisals outstanding, blah, blah, blah (you fill in the blank) out-

standing — PLEASE GET THESE ITEMS IN IF YOU HAVEN'T DONE THIS ALREADY!!!!!!!!!! I'm afraid it's the same people who aren't responding to all of these requests. The CVs are important. Very important. We cannot prepare the reviews for OCGS and IAR without CVs! OK? Rena

From: **UPITISR@educ.QueensU.CA**
Subject: jewelry workshop
     A few months ago, some of the secretarial staff asked if I could host a paper jewelry-making workshop — JUST FOR FUN! (fun sounds good right now, especially since I've been dreaming bout spreadsheets lately.) So, I have arranged a date for just such an event (of course, faculty members are welcome too — this invitation is to any and all on the list-serve!) The workshop will be Wednesday, 21 February at 12–1, in the Dungeon. No cost, no prep, just come (and maybe bring your lunch).

RENA: January is a tough month, and our January was awful. As noted earlier we had a 16.5 per cent budget cut (over $1 million), and people were scared about losing jobs. There was a lot of uncertainty and tension (see above). As I wrote my apology, I thought about how much easier it has become for me to apologize for my mistakes. (I make them more often as dean than I did as professor — or maybe I'm more aware of them.) And I was impatient (see note about CVs); I and others were working around the clock and I felt as if some people were not pulling their weight. This was particularly true as we prepared the Internal Academic Review (IAR) — or the Eternal Academic Review, as I've come to think of it.
     Part of keeping sane, for me, is making things — building furniture, painting water-colors, playing music. It seemed like a good time to offer a workshop to staff and faculty. This was a nice case, by the way, of staff being the 'main' group and faculty on the 'margins'! Nearly every non-academic staff person showed up for this — a great way to see that they all read email, even if they do not always respond (electronically at least). *TOM*: This makes the point again — Rena offers many different and unusual alterna-tives to typical or expected behavior from a dean. And she has a keen intuition for community building. This collection of email also makes me aware of the range of responsibilities that Rena is attending to from the seriousness of budget cuts to needs to include staff as part of the community.

Building Teams for Projects

Rena quickly moved herself apart from previous deans by asking individuals to be members of small teams to work on specific projects, and having those small teams draw wide and overlapping circles of consultation as they proceeded with their work. One of the first of such teams came to be known simply as 'C4', for 'Committee of Four'. This team, which included Rena and Tom, served to oversee the gathering of ideas from faculty, staff, students, teachers, federation representatives, other professors and administrators at the university, and members of the community as we began to think about changing the nature and structure of our teacher education program. There were well over 100 meetings of various kinds with representatives from the above-named groups, including open meetings, small group discussions, focus groups, and meetings with individuals. There were also several rounds of requests for written input from faculty, staff, students, and associate teachers over the ten-month period during which the restructuring was conceived. The effects of this work were impressive, leading to approval of the new program design at a Faculty Board meeting on 13 December 1995. Soon after the new program structure was approved, Rena developed a large number of sub-committees (with 4–6 members each, including a student), with a view to involving every single individual on the faculty in some aspect of program change. This series of memos outlines the difficulties of initiating program change and how Rena used email as a way to build, strengthen and maintain community during this period. It begins with approval of the new program (sent 13 Dec 1995), working out the details (20 March 1996), and celebrating tasks completed (1 May 1996).

Approving a new program design

> **To: UPITISR@educ.QueensU.CA**
> **From: RUSSELLT@QUCDN.QueensU.CA: WOW!!**
> Well done, Rena — as always, you were superb. And didn't we learn a lot about students today!! I truly hope this brings even more excitement and energy to your work at the Fort Richardson level. Again, I hope it looks like Education is leading the way forward. I sure think we are . . . and it matters so much to have a dean who cares and UNDERSTANDS what we are doing (perhaps better than most of us!!!). JOY to the world!

RENA: I remember this day very clearly. Much was at stake: we had invested an enormous amount of time, energy, and love into designing a new program, and I hoped for the program not just to be passed by Faculty Board, but to be passed with joy. There was no doubt that the faculty would vote in favor (in fact, they did so unanimously), but I was unsure about the student votes. The students, it turned out, resisted the first of the six motions, but by the end of the meeting, were in favor of the changes. It became clear to me that they had not felt involved in the decision-making up to that point: I resolved to include them in formal ways as I developed the sub-committee structure, even though I realized that this would make some of the sub-committees quite cumbersome (I am convinced that more than four people in a committee makes for slow deliberations!).
TOM: Like Rena, I remember this date and day very clearly. There were some potential tensions, and as so often happens, my commitment to the new design as a profound improvement over the old was *too close to the surface*. Rena's behavior in the meeting was superb, always measured and positive. We had anticipated some reservations from colleagues, but I had not been alerted to reservations from the six student representatives, who all voted against the first motion. This taught me an important lesson about the fact that students IN a program cannot be expected to be objective about alternatives. Despite their reservations about the design of the program they are following, they seem to assume that any other design is flawed in fundamental ways.

Working through the details

To: UPITISR@educ.QueensU.CA
From: RUSSELLT@QUCDN.QueensU.CA
   Hi Rena. I wound up feeling rather 'hung out to dry' after that meeting. I guess it's a way of saying C4 'isn't what it used to be' but it also touches on what the subcommittees are and are not. I'm feeling some 'gaps in the process.'

To: RUSSELLT@QUCDN.QueensU.CA
From: UPITISR@educ.QueensU.CA
   Yes — me too. And you're right — it's time that we are all lacking. I, for one, am having trouble holding all of the pieces together right now. The end of March looms, and the University is suffering deeply. So are we. How about starting with a C4 meeting, next week? We need a 'take stock' meeting, if nothing else! We could also have a tete-a-tete if you like — maybe over the paper that we are writing! Thanks for your note — as always, the feedback you send is worth reading.

From: UPITISR@educ.QueensU.CA
Subject: parting words
   Well, everyone, it is difficult to leave for the next two days, [but] I am at the end of my rope, and I need to restore my energy for myself and for us as a Faculty. There are a couple of items I'd like to leave you with. First, I think we are doing a splendid job in moving forward with both the pilot and the new program, but that we are now in a position where there are simply so many moving parts that things are getting clogged up. I realize (clever woman that I am!) that I can't be everywhere at once, so I propose a concentrated meeting with only one representative from each of the subcommittees and C4 to unclog the system and help the parts move in synchrony . . . 9:00 11:00 on Wednesday March 27. . . . Second, I am not deaf to the pain that many of us are expressing these days in terms of changes in our community. I can't remember the last time I hurt this much. And, while I am not at liberty to divulge information about personal situations with faculty and staff, I can tell you that I have spoken with all of the non-academic staff who will be directly affected by staffing changes. My view, right or wrong, was to inform people with the information that I had about position closures rather than being faced with the infamous 'pink slip' in April.
   Finally, I want to thank everyone for their support these past few weeks. I am proud to be a member of this community, and this University, and I thank you for making this — even now — the most wonderful job I've ever had.

RENA: Tom's note came at a difficult time for me; I was tired and I felt the pain of the people who were suffering directly as a result of budget cuts. And Tom was right; I was finding it hard to keep C4 going along with the 11 sub-committees. In retrospect, it was still worth having the complex sub-committee structure, though; for about eight months, the sub-committees toiled madly, and as a result, a well-planned pilot of the new program will begin in August, 1996. After receiving the message from Tom, much later the same day, I wrote the 'parting words' message to faculty and staff.

TOM: I do not remember this one clearly, but at the time, I obviously found the process lacking. Seeing the interpretation Rena gives it in hindsight, it might better have been dealt with by phone than by email, even though we have developed a significant email relationship. Aches and pains work both ways. When Rena feels aches and pains, does she tell all of us, or just pick one person? Notice the power of the long message Rena sent to everyone in the community. Did my note prompt that, or would she have sent it anyway? Was it a useful message for everyone to hear? I have to assume so. The one thing Rena has not done yet is told me to slow down on the email. Her ability to listen, despite her own pressures that none of us can really appreciate, continues to impress me.

The Faculty of Education self-study

From: UPITISR@educ.QueensU.CA

Last night, not so very late, Hugh, Pat Deir, Bonnie, and I finished the final volume of the IAR. We could have partied at that point, but it would be even more fun to invite everyone to a celebration. So, here it is:

FRIDAY March 8, 4:00 p.m., Location TBA

I will have extra copies available at the 'launching'. And let me thank, once again, all of the people who put countless hours into this — Hugh, Nancy, Eva, Sandy, Lynne, Pat, Bonnie, Heather. . . .. .and the list goes on.

With great relief and glee,

RENA: I feel real kinship with the community as this work unfolds. The self-study was fun to assemble because there was a good deal of *above and beyond the call of duty* commitment from both faculty and staff (pizza, popcorn, coffee, music — a summer-camp-don't-ever-want-it-to-end-shared-experience feeling). I remember thinking this was a real breakthrough when I typed this message. And I was tired.

TOM: This message points to an extremely significant event and says much about Rena's personal style. The Faculty of Education produced a four-volume report on itself ('self-study'!!) and delivered it on time. The quality of the presentation and the completion on time owe more than many may realize to Rena's ability to mobilize a committed group and then to join that group herself to ensure that the work was done. I marvel at her energy. Her high standards are music to our ears.

New Dean/Old Teacher: Case Study of Electronic Mail in Building a Relationship

Although we have already revealed a good deal about the relationship between Rena and Tom, we turn here to an analysis of specific exchanges that contribute to our understanding of how their own relationship began to change through email and face-to-face interactions. There are three sections, beginning with initial exchanges (sent 7, 8, and 10 March 1995), followed by instances of tension (sent 12 Sept., 9 Nov. and 9 Dec. 1997), and ending with examples of ongoing support (two of only many sent 20 June 1995 and 7 Feb. 1996).

Initial exchanges

> **From: RUSSELLT@QUCDN.QueensU.CA**
> **To: UPITISR@educ.QueensU.CA**
> Hi Rena! Just heard the news that you have been offered the deanship. That fits well with your comments in the corridor about liking what you see of Bill Leggett [Principal of Queen's University]. Rumors abound, I'm told, but in time the dust will settle. I'm also told that there is a rumor that Bob and I went to Leggett last week 'to stab you in the back'. Well, it was just a little different than that, and I have no more control over rumors than you do. But when you get a moment, let me know, so that I can give you my 'take' on that meeting. I'd like to keep the slate as clean as possible and let you know how I saw that meeting.

RENA: This was a difficult message for me to receive (the first ever from Tom), but as I swallowed hard, I also realized this was an opportunity to practice what I preach — listen, pay attention, respond honestly, follow through, be courageous, trust . . . and then hope like hell! In his office, Tom also shared a fax he'd sent to the Principal; this really hurt. And I did not mind my hurt showing. A tough but important conversation. The most difficult part was listening to Tom's feelings about who I should not consult as dean. I made an important reply, I think, which was that I would listen to those individuals as well as everyone else. It was, in my view, as wrong to listen to only two or three particular voices as to exclude two or three particular voices.

TOM: I was pedaling fast as I sent that note to Rena. Email got us talking, face-to-face in my office, far faster than we would have by waiting for an appointment. I was wondering if I had managed to poison my relationships with my dean and the university principal for the next five years! If I suggested Rena should not consult certain individuals, then I expect it emerged from my sense that certain individuals had extensive *influence* in Rena's appointment. Because some of us have never been appointed to Dean's Review or Search Committees and others have been appointed several times, I was adjusting to the close of yet another chapter in which Queen's central administration makes some voices much more equal than others. There can be no doubt that one of Rena's key community-building strategies involves listening to everyone and to drawing people into engagement with issues we must address as a community.

> **To: UPITISR@educ.QueensU.CA**
> **From: RUSSELLT@QUCDN.QueensU.CA**
> Thanks for responding so quickly, stopping in so quickly, and listening with care . . . Finally found your memo and look forward to hearing your presentation on Friday.

[In the week after her appointment was announced, Rena scheduled two presentations of a version of her presentation to the Search Committee, so that everyone in the Faculty of Education could begin to learn her vision for the future. Tom attended the presentation scheduled from 12:30 to 2:00 on March 10, and shortly afterward [Fri, 10 Mar 95 14:39:19 EST] sent a long email message to Rena, to which she replied later that afternoon. We present her reply, which contains Tom's message, using the conventional '>' symbol indicating an original message within an email reply.]

>**From: UPITISR@educ.QueensU.CA**
>**To: RUSSELLT@QUCDN.QueensU.CA**
>Sorry I was late to your talk — a class ran until 1:00 . . . 'You and some others'
>are going off to Western and U of T to see what they are doing. Another nice
>junket with money we don't have?? It will look that way unless we all receive
>soon after a copy of a substantial report — not just to the committee but to
>everyone . . . I'd worry less about who doesn't have email and do more about
>getting good stuff to those of us who do. Then those who don't will want to get
>on email??

A good point; I am a great fan of email, as you can see, and I plan to use email to communicate with as many people as I possibly can, both one-on-one as we're doing now, and to the group that receives email . . . As to the trip to Western/U of T [Toronto]; it is critical that we understand what other faculties are doing. I volunteered to go on that road trip (don't worry, it will be cheap — my truck is good on gas!) because I need to meet those folks anyway. You can bet I'll be reporting, in great detail, what we find out.

>I had a dreadful thought as you were recounting the many challenges ahead of
>us — program coherence, relations with schools, etc. Weren't [previous deans]
>hired to help put this place on the research map? Help fix our relations with
>schools? What can we learn from the past by asking such questions? They had
>the best of intentions and the 'power of the office' but we still seem to have the
>problems. What water are you going to walk on so that we can see some
>change? Better still, how will we know when we have changed??

And I guess I've been appointed to do it all. Well, I'm going to try. I'll start by talking with colleagues, and by finding out what worked and what didn't work for [other deans]. I must say, that I think I have two advantages (1) people expect change now and I'm going to harness all the goodwill I can muster to move our energy in good directions, and (2) I have a ton of energy and lots of credibility (at least outside the building, and some inside), and those two things can only help. Oh yes — one more thing — I believe research and field stuff are important; that's what I've been doing myself for the past 14 years!

>Energy and credibility certainly help, but they still don't make change easy,
>even if people expect it . . . Passion for teaching . . . that was obvious on Friday

>. . . yet I would defy you to convince me that 'learning to teach' is part of our
>institutional fabric. It's hard enough for curriculum people to focus on it.

No need to 'defy' me on this one. If it is part of our institutional fabric, it
probably isn't one of the biggest squares in the patchwork quilt. I, myself, have a
great deal of difficulty focussing on the 'learning to teach' aspects of the math
curriculum course, even though I want to — partly because I have students who
say, 'We didn't mean that we wanted you to teach us how to teach long division.
We wanted you to teach us how to DO long division'. Arrrggh.

>I too spent a long time not calling what I was doing action research. I've never
>assumed we did not have a lot of common ground — I simply didn't have any
>evidence either way. That's the state most of us are in with respect of most of
>our colleagues, because the front office has never been used as a resource for
>getting us together. It's going to take years, Rena, not months, to begin to
>change that reality here. The doubts and mistrusts are very deep-seated. Count
>yourself lucky if you can see significant change in four years, not one.

I know it's going to take more than a year to do all of this (thank goodness it's a
five-year term). I think we've made a small start with respect to sharing research
. . . but we're talking about changing a culture, and this is long work (and not solo
work).

>I've gone on far too long but do appreciate knowing that someone is listening,
>and I hope you are getting lots from lots of sources, and that you will give us all
>(email etc) your updates on our institutional fabric as you come to know it better
>and better.

Thanks Tom — I am getting lots of views from lots of sources, and not only will
I share what I find out, but I'm asking others to share as well. Stay tuned to your
favorite internet channel!!!

RENA: I was glad that Tom was sending lots of email, and willing to speak openly
about his frustrations. This gave me the chance to show that I'm serious about reporting
to the community. But it was hard. I phrased my replies carefully — with strength and
humor. We started here what would be a long-term pattern: talking about research and
teaching in the middle of all the other issues at hand. I was disturbed by Tom's comment that I would be lucky to see change in four years, not one. I wondered, to myself,
if he was right. I still believed, though, that in six months it would be possible to turn
this place into a community. And I told myself that if I could not make some significant
change in six months, it could not be done. Four years is too long. We did not have that
kind of time.
TOM: What an awful set of messages to send to a new dean! What a jaded view of
reality I had acquired from her predecessors. This message is a treasure for the discomfort it creates. It's certainly not my job to tell her what she should be doing. I certainly
was not in a community-building mood, and in some ways I suppose I was feeling

excluded from any sense of community. In hindsight, a year later, I feel differently. I can not help but notice the combination of confidence and openness in this exchange with Rena, who clearly knows herself and knows her base of support. She is not one to duck critical comments. Her positive and constructive tone is like nothing I've ever seen at Queen's. Her implication that something will change when she does 'assume the position' masks the reality that she became the dean as soon as her appointment was announced. She did not have the official responsibility, but she took on all the actions of a dean, actions that I had been waiting to see for 18 years, and had come to assume would never happen. An interesting thought occurs as I look back over the evidence of what we said to each other. In a university community, it is easy to identify 'the new and the vulnerable' in the form of those who are working for tenure. Often these people are young, but this is not necessarily the case. Having been awarded tenure after six years, now nearly 13 years ago, I have to accept the fact that I am not new here. Yet I remember those early years very clearly, and felt *new here* far longer than most people seemed to credit me with being new. We who are *older* are easily painted with a single brush, when in fact we vary enormously in our relationships to whatever community exists around us. We who are *older* are not a homogeneous community in any sense beyond mere 'been around a long time'. Although much has changed in Rena's first year on the job, we are still a community with disparate views about the relevance of research in a Faculty of Education that, some say, should first and foremost be known for good teaching. We have still not resolved the *common sense notion* that doing research means *neglecting teaching*.

Tensions

To: RUSSELLT@QUCDN.QueensU.CA,WHITEHEA@QUCDN.QueensU.CA
FROM: UPITISR@educ.QueensU.CA
Subject: C4 — Remember? you bums!!!
(I'm sure you had a good excuse).
Nancy and I met and discussed five things. We've resolved them . . . for now; if there are any objections, let us know. I'm going to speak with M this afternoon. Nancy will give a short 10 minutes presentation at the open meeting tomorrow to bring visitors up to speed. She says, 'Be there'.

To: UPITISR@educ.QueensU.CA
From: RUSSELLT@QUCDN.QueensU.CA
Subject: C4 bum reporting in
Well, sort of . . . [responses to the five issues, then:] Don't ever hesitate to prowl the halls for me . . . Being lunch hour, Jan was away and of no help either . . . Really sorry . . . but after-class discussion was so powerful and helpful. Still, not an excuse.

RENA: When I wrote this message, Tom, Nancy, LeRoy, and I had been hard at work for close to four months as members of C4, working on program revision. Tom and LeRoy both missed a meeting. I was angry. But humor, I tell myself, humor. And move forward. Tell them what they missed and move on. But register angst! Tom responds with humor and humility and encouragement (phew). He encourages us to look for him when he misses meetings — I do not respond to this, since it bugs me that I should be spending time to do this. Even 45 seconds is too much for me to spend this way. (I can answer two phone calls or three short emails in that time!) And I do understand that he gets wrapped up with class discussions — so do I!

To: UPITISR@educ.QueensU.CA
FROM: RUSSELLT@QUCDN.QueensU.CA
Subject: The breaking point
        To make a long story short . . . maybe it's time for a wake-up call. Could we be getting to the point that too many good people are being asked to do too many crucial things? I didn't intend to get into this, but it seems to be part of the package. I could have described my Waterloo duties as far more elaborate . . . by the time you had said several times that my Waterloo work isn't very onerous, I was ready to hand it back to you on a platter (and it's yours for the asking, but until I hear otherwise, I carry on). . . . Everything's important, but we may be on the verge of destroying ourselves??? I applaud our efforts to bring order to the chaos you met. Somehow, the organization was surviving on 1/3(or less?) of the time and energy you are putting in. I know it's eating you up too. How do we stand back, smell the coffee and see the forest, and stop self-destructing? . . . I thought I should warn you that some of your best 'troops' may be nearing burnout.

RENA: Bang! A difficult message arrives from Tom. But, unlike when I responded to similar messages in March and April, I know this will be worked through. And I truly welcome it. I would be suspicious if all was good. (No one can be pleased all the time about the decisions we take and the ways in which we operate — not colleagues, not friends, not partners — no one with whom we have serious relationships.) Again, much to think about. And I was afraid, because I knew that the next three months would be even more difficult than the last three, with major budget issues looming. It was around this time that I decided to spend every weekend at the cabin!

TOM: In hindsight, it is interesting that Rena calls this a 'difficult' message. As I look back over it, I was trying to protect myself. More than anything else, I was probably trying to signal to Rena my concern that some people may be 'padding' their administrative duties as a way of making themselves look better in her eyes. I try to see administrative work as essential but also inevitable, while every organization will always have people who see it as something to be seen as self-important. In hindsight, I'm sure I could have sent a 'clearer' message. It was nearing the end of the week.

To: UPITISR@educ.QueensU.CA
From: RUSSELLT@QUCDN.QueensU.CA
Subject: Sharing my letter
I thought I'd risk sharing my efforts at PR in writing to tell B.F. that D.L. has had his assignment shifted. Rena, I hope you don't mind my implying that it was at

your request. I'm trying to keep B. on our associate list! This is partly a way of letting you know, Rena, that I've succeeded . . . in getting D. into SHS for Round 2.

To: RUSSELLT@QUCDN.QueensU.CA
From: UPITISR@educ.QueensU.CA
Subject: Sharing my letter
   Yikes! I do mind — but what's done is done. In any case, I'm sure D. will be an asset at SHS. But please, check with me before you say I've done something I haven't.

To: UPITISR@educ.QueensU.CA
From: RUSSELLT@QUCDN.QueensU.CA
Subject: Sharing my letter
Apologies, Rena. At least I was open about it?

RENA: I get mad when Tom writes a letter saying that I did something I did not. This was an important time to set out my views — in a way that I hope is not too serious or 'end of the worldish', but serious, just the same.
TOM: This was an interesting *skirmish* because I was reverting to behavior that made no sense in terms of Rena's style but would have not phased other deans I have worked with. The good part of it was that the letter was still sitting on my desk when Rena replied, so the letter to which she objected was never sent. It does help that Rena uses email so easily and frequently.

Support

To: UPITISR@educ.QueensU.CA
From: RUSSELLT@QUCDN.QueensU.CA
   WELL DONE, Rena! It's about time someone had the courage to say that we don't need more people earning tenure through exemplary service . . . There may be many takes on what you sent, but I think you got the sense of 'balance' perfectly!

RENA: This was one of the first, if not the first, message from Tom that started to appear in my mailbox at regular intervals, praising me for something I had done (this was four months after my appointment was announced — I was not even the dean yet!). What a surprise — and shock! I was not sure what to expect with the heading 'service', and realized, only after reading the message, that I had been bracing myself. I chuckled to myself after reading this one, remembering the earlier prediction that it would take years for anything to change! Small victories.
TOM: Here's a place where this shared paper becomes uncomfortable. Of course Rena would be aware that I could 'go either way' in my reactions to her early efforts, given

the 'welcome to your new appointment' that I had given her. But I still see myself as 'new around here', just because most people have been here longer than I have. I can not have it both ways — but I am very glad that I was 'open to the evidence' — Rena is a very compelling personality, as well as a very powerful one. I've always known that 'charisma' is a significant element in leadership, but knowing and working with Rena gives new meaning to charisma. Perhaps most amazing of all has been Rena's ability to move beyond the close friendships she had within the faculty before becoming dean, to showing everyone that she values his or her presence in the community.

> **To:** UPITISR@educ.QueensU.CA
> **From:** RUSSELLT@QUCDN.QueensU.CA
> **Subject:** THANKS again
>
> Your presence made such a difference. And we got into some fabulous issues after you left — all on tape . . . Nancy and I said to each other afterwards, we are so unaccustomed to support and understanding from the front office . . . Gee, we might soon start counting on it!!! Don't ever let us take you for granted — just as I know you never will let us.

RENA: So it did not take four years! Partly, I'm sure, because of the crises we face as an institution, but partly because we have formed a community.

TOM: Am I sending too much email to Rena? It's entirely possible, as I review all this, even though she says I am not the most frequent person. Does she tire of these thanks? Probably not, but there is so much we should not take for granted.

Summary

The store of messages and our interpretations have taught us that, indeed, electronic mail can serve to foster and strengthen community. But in order for email to serve such a function, we are convinced that everyone in the community must have the opportunity to read and respond to messages. Further, however good the email medium might be, it must be supplemented by face-to-face interactions of various kinds. In addition, if email is to work in the ways that we have described, it is essential to acknowledge the tensions that are a natural part of any complex organization of relationships. Even as we were completing this chapter, there were tensions between us as we navigated our way through a new relationship — that of co-authorship. Because of our extended experience with email, and our growing trust in one another, we were able to resolve those tensions with minimum disruption. And the resolution of that tension occurred through email and a phone call — illustrating, once again, that email is an invaluable supporting actor, but can never take the place of the sound of a human voice.

References

ANDERSON, J. and LEE, F. (1995) 'Literacy teachers learning a new literacy: A study of the use of electronic mail in a reading education class', *Reading Research on Instruction*, **34**, 3, pp. 222–38.

BECKSTEAD, D. (1992) '"I detest school, but I love to learn": Wired writers and their views on writing, teachers, and the writers in electronic residence program'. Unpublished M.Ed. thesis, Queen's University, Kingston, Ontario.

FEY, M.H. (1992) 'Building community through computer conferencing and feminist collaboration'. Paper presented at the annual Computers and Writing Conference, Indianapolis.

HILL, E. and WHITAKER, E. (1994) 'The multi-cultural e-mail of high school–college collaboration'. Paper presented at the annual meeting of the Conference on College Composition and Communication, Nashville.

OWEN, T. (1992) 'Wired writing', in MASON, R. (ed.) *Computer Conferencing: The Last Word*, Victoria, BC: Beach Holme.

OWEN, T. (1995) 'Poems that change the world: Canada's wired writers', *English Journal*, **84**, 6, pp. 48–52.

SARASON, S.B. (1972) *The Creation of Settings and the Future Societies*, San Francisco: Jossey-Bass.

TAYLOR, W.C. (1996) 'At VeriFone it's a dog's life (and they love it). Fast company: How smart business works', *Fast Company*, **1**, 1, pp. 115–21.

UPITIS, R. (1990) *This Too is Music*, Portsmouth, NH: Heinemann.

Part III

Case Studies of Individual Self-study

Introduction

Mary Lynn Hamilton

We selected the chapters in this section to provide examples of individual self-study that best illustrate how self-study can help us, as teacher educators, to reconceptualize our notion of teacher education. Thus far in this text, we have presented ways to think about self-study and approaches for undertaking self-study; this section offers individual examples of self-study in practice. For the scholars in these particular studies, self-study was an individual undertaking. Importantly, while there are similarities among the examples offered here, there are also apparent differences in style and research approach.

As the title 'individual self-study' suggests, scholars who undertake this research operate alone, studying their own teaching practice. Within this context scholars can focus on what occurs in their classrooms, can pursue a selected problem or issue in the classroom, or can focus on issues beyond the classroom to produce a change, either as a part of a classroom or within an academic setting. Scholars engaged in self-study are not simply navel-gazing — a frequent, but inaccurate characterization of this work. Instead, they systematically bring to bear all of their past experiences, understandings, scholarly perspectives, and theoretical frames to make sense of the experiences within which they are engaged. Critical reflection becomes an essential tool in this form of study. Uniquely, the data collected are from self about self, to promote self-development and understanding. The forms of data collection — such as journaling — utilize individual reflection on the landscape of practice for a particular solution. The examples here present a range of diverse purposes and possibilities within individual self-study: (1) a simple look at what occurs within a selected classroom; (2) an investigation of how to generate change within a classroom experience; and (3) an examination of a way an individual can prompt reform within her institution by attempting to alter how members of a teacher education program view teaching.

Oda's chapter explores her desire to document whether and how her cultural background influences her teaching. This chapter presents one teacher educator's self-study of her own classroom and her own teaching experience. She saw her study as the initial step toward a better understanding of her teaching practice. Her main findings suggest that her cultural heritage strongly influences her classroom teaching and that her students, mostly white, middle-class, females, appreciate her diverse perspective. This chapter is important because it offers an example of a strong first step in self-study — identifying what occurs within a selected classroom and the practices used there.

In the second chapter, Hutchinson examines and considers the ways in which she might improve her practice using critical reflection and case studies. In this chapter, using her own journal entries and students' responses to her work, Hutchinson briefly sets the context at Queen's (her institution), defines her approach to case work and critical reflection, relates her experiences while teaching her Critical Issues course, as well as shares her students' responses to the work. She systematically utilizes a variety of data and provides clear evidence that she takes her students seriously and works carefully toward a course structure that suits her students' needs and her own concerns. More importantly, we are artfully drawn into her reflective trials as we come to understand the ways in which a reflective teacher educator attempts to make changes in her classroom. Her major findings suggest that critical reflection helps uncover what we take for granted in the classroom and that understanding the practical knowledge of teaching and teacher education facilitates our fostering stronger, more thoughtful teachers and teacher educators.

In the third chapter, Gipe explores the potential of the course portfolio as a way to examine one's teaching and as a tool to heighten the University's interest in teaching. She asserts that the university does not recognize or reward teaching excellence and promotes the use of the teaching portfolio and self-study as one provocative way to document the scholarly value of teaching. The teaching portfolio can also help create a context within which an education scholar can force the University to recognize the value of teaching as a part of rank and status politics. After providing a context with which to understand Gipe's experience, a description of the portfolio process is presented. In addition, she offers a discussion of her portfolio, her own teaching, and her students' responses to tools she used when she attempts to make changes. Her major findings suggest that course portfolios help explicate the implicit theories of teaching and learning as well as reveal dilemmas and inconsistencies in one's teaching that a teacher can then not only address and overcome but through which the academic can systematically reveal that process within the political structure of the university. This chapter is important because it takes self-study beyond the consideration of one's place within the classroom to the broader context of the institution, where it might be used to demonstrate the vital role of improving teaching within an educational institution.

7   Harmony, Conflict and Respect: An Asian-American Educator's Self-study

Linda K. Oda

As I prepared for the beginning of the school year, I pondered the ways in which I could better prepare my pre-service teachers to meet the needs of the diverse students in the public schools. Of course, my twenty years of experience as a teacher, supervisor, and administrator in the public schools and my seven years of experience as a teacher educator informed my process. Indeed, as a teacher I had worked in the most diverse school in an inner city school district which fit well with my background and experiences as an Asian-American. In this new year, I wanted to explore the ways in which my Asian-American heritage influenced my work with students to foster equitable and humane environments within their future classrooms. I wanted to discover in what ways, if any, my cultural background affected my teaching.

When I considered this exploration, a self-study using a life history framework seemed like an appropriate approach. Life history research methods have gained credence in psychology (White, 1963), sociology (Denzin, 1989; Plummer, 1983) and anthropology (Langness, 1965; Watson and Watson-Franke, 1985). In education, Goodson (1992) asserts that studying teachers' lives provides valuable insights and assists educational reform and restructuring. Furthermore, Cole and Knowles (1995) maintained:

> that the exploration of our own lives and the lives of others around us, in the context of institutional and societal influences, will provide important insights into elements of professional socialization and career development in academe. (p. 142)

Plummer (1983) argues that the use of life history research promotes the importance of life experiences as people interpret their own lives and the lives of others. Finally, as I began this study, I believed that the life history method would lend itself to giving perspective to my experiences as they influenced and informed my professional practices.

The purpose of this study was two-fold: first, to undertake a self-study that explored the effects of my own Asian-American cultural influences on my teacher education classes, and second, to establish a foundation from which I could develop ways to help my students address multicultural issues. This self-study centers on analyzing key experiences in my personal and professional history that are unique to my cultural heritage in an effort to determine how my culture has affected my role as a teacher educator. I hope to translate what I learned from this study to assist my students in sifting through issues of diversity they will confront when they begin their teaching.

What I Did and Where I Did It

I am an Asian-American teacher educator at Weber State University (WSU). This institution has approximately 15,000 students and within the WSU Teacher Education Department there are mostly female students with a less than 10 per cent ethnic minority representation. In contrast, the surrounding school district has more than a 40 per cent minority representation, suggesting that our students will be working with students different from themselves. As a result of this difference, our students will need assistance in dealing with issues of diversity.

The theme within the WSU Department of Teacher Education is 'Teacher as Reflective Practitioner'. This focus on reflection demonstrates our commitment to nurturing practitioners who evaluate relevant choices for teaching, decide and act on the preferred choices, and continually reevaluate their choices in light of their effectiveness. My self-study models the work expected of our students because I examined how my cultural background influences the ways in which I evaluate, decide, act upon and reevaluate my choices for teaching.

Throughout the Teacher Education Program, strands of competencies are integrated into the courses. One of these strands includes the knowledge and understanding of the characteristics of culturally and linguistically diverse populations. Within this context I am responsible for organizing, developing and teaching the following courses: reading methods, language arts methods, multicultural and bilingual education, diagnosis and remediation of reading difficulties, and primary reading methods. In addition, I integrate experiences with multicultural and bilingual issues and practices into my planning.

How and When I Did the Study

To best explore the ways in which my cultural background influenced my teaching, I audio taped teaching sessions in my undergraduate and graduate language arts and multicultural and bilingual education courses throughout two quarters (winter and spring, 1996). This allowed me to capture both my own words and the words of my students. I selected these courses because they emphasized the need for employing a multicultural perspective when teaching.

I also distributed a questionnaire to all of my spring quarter students as well as many of my former winter quarter students. In addition, the following school year questionnaires were also distributed and returned. Although the questionnaire was not originally planned, I realized that I needed students' perspectives to understand whether my cultural background was apparent to students in our interactions. Evidence of cultural influences on my practice was sought from the audio transcriptions and questionnaire responses. Instruction, verbal and written responses were scrutinized and interpreted to determine whether there was evidence that my own culture was evident in our interactions and whether these cultural influences were helpful for my pre-service students' understanding of multicultural issues. The questionnaire responses helped me decide if my background was helpful to their understanding multicultural issues.

Memories and Personal Images

During my research I examined my personal and professional growth over my life, particularly, my 25 years in the education profession. As a youngster, I grew up as an Asian-American living in a challenging neighborhood with a lower socio-economic status. My achievement as an Asian-American woman not affiliated with the dominant religion of the region made me unique.

When I reflected on my experiences as a youngster, I remembered the difficulties of growing up as an Asian-American in an at-risk neighborhood. Asian-Americans were considered the minorities among African Americans, Latinos and Native American minority groups. Our family lived in and owned a grocery store on 25th Street (affectionately known as 'two-bit street'). On this street you could find many vices, including gambling, drinking, prostitution, drugs, murder and robbery. In the 1940s, 1950s and 1960s most minority populations were relegated to lower social-economic areas and our neighborhood was as multicultural as you could get.

To maintain our cultural heritage, Japanese-American youths were sheltered from the outside influences by our community members including parents, elders and the Buddhist Church, each of whom wielded an iron hand in maintaining the expected values and behaviors. These values and behaviors included: maintaining a reverence for the family, attaining a good education, working hard, being frugal, being honest, achieving harmony with others, and maintaining dignity.

In my experience, maintaining harmony and dignity were problematic both as a youngster and an educator. Balancing these values with the realities of the world was difficult. For me, the tension between wanting to maintain harmony, but fearing a loss of dignity has been heart rending. I did not realize that under certain circumstances you can maintain both values. For instance, an elementary school was not a haven of safety, but a challenge to survival. In order to survive in this environment I had to fight which, over time, allowed me to achieve harmony. I remember in second grade being called out to fight Estell, a giant of a girl. I stood my ground. Although battered and bruised, I maintained my dignity and later achieved harmony with my adversaries. While at a high price, these acts of bravado somehow bought the respect of my adversaries. They aligned with me and created a protection for me in future situations. Indeed, I did not align myself with them but when they understood that I was brave enough to meet their challenge, they left me alone. My dignity remained intact and a kind of harmony was achieved.

More than ten years later I taught my first class in the same elementary school that I attended. My childhood experiences influenced how I responded to my students — with harmony and dignity. I tried diligently to create an atmosphere where students were winners, not losers. I created plays where everyone participated in cooperation with each other. In my classroom, cooperation was more coveted than competition. My students learned Japanese festival dances, that promoted togetherness and fostered co-operation. Conflict was dealt with honestly and openly. A master teacher taught me to intellectualize conflict. As I learned these skills, harmony with dignity was promoted.

As an adult in a profession that was predominantly white, female (as a teacher), male (as an administrator) and middle class, I continued to seek harmony. As an elementary principal, situations with disruptive students, demanding parents, and unhappy teachers were not unusual. For example, in my role as a principal I attempted to develop trust and harmony with a parent who instigated many of the neighborhood's problems. As I was informed, her children were constantly in trouble for breaking and entering, stealing, and intimidating the neighborhood children. Consequently, never a kind word was uttered in the school or neighborhood about her or her children. After many efforts to involve her in the school activities and sending her positive reports about her children, she became one of the prime advocates of the school. She actually gave me information about the sources of some of our vandalism problems around the school. She told me herself that her last three children in the school were behaving themselves and keeping out of trouble. However long this lasted, in this case, creating a base for her to have dignity worked to create harmony.

Emergent Theme: Japanese-American Upbringing

My reflection on my Japanese upbringing promoted insights into the foundation that under girds my teaching and provided insights into teaching practice. Exploring the ways in which my Japanese upbringing influenced my role as a teacher educator helped raise my awareness and my reflection about my own teaching, while also supporting my teacher education students.

Harry Kitano (1969), a Japanese-American anthropologist who has studied Japanese immigrants and Japanese-Americans, highlighted the following values traced to Japanese upbringing:

(a) Promote harmony among others and avoid conflict. These values stemmed from the Confucian and Tao view of a hero. The hero is the gentle person who finds her/him self in the background — unnoticed, suffering for virtue's sake, and leading without others knowing. He/she gives recognition to others not her/himself. Propriety is observed with consideration and appreciation expressed in verbal and non-verbal manners. Words that you choose to say reflect what you really feel. In other words, the outer self reflects the inner self.

(b) The Japanese family was characterized by strong solidarity, mutual helpfulness and a patriarchal structure. Cohesion and harmony were valued above individual achievement. Hard work, duty, obligation and responsibility were emphasized. Desirable behavior was strongly reinforced both within the family and by the community as a whole.

(c) A respect for education was stressed by the Japanese immigrants (Issei — first generation) and their offspring (Nisei — second generation). The Isseis had an understanding of, familiarity with, and respect for the educational process even before they arrived on American soil. The perfect student was passive, accommodating, conforming, unquestioning but competitive. The Japanese child must be a model student. Every element of the Japanese-American students' society sanctioned conforming behavior and school success.

(d) Language and culture are important differences. Any outsider can be spotted as soon as he/she opens her/his mouth and speaks. Sometimes cultural actions point out differences. A Japanese person had language and cultural differences, as well as differences in appearance that marked her/him as an outsider if he/she wanted to integrate and assimilate in the mainstream of society. The Isseis and Niseis stressed the importance of learning the dominant language and culture as quickly and expediently as possible. But also the Isseis and Niseis promoted the continuance of the Japanese language and culture by having their children attend Japanese language schools and religious services at the Buddhist Church on Saturdays and Sundays.

Using Kitano's ideas as markers, I reviewed the students' tapes and questionnaires. From this data, I could begin to glean the ways in which my cultural background affected my teaching practice, particularly in regard to promotion of harmony and avoidance of conflict. The following excerpts capture the tone and the tenor of the responses.

Harmony and Conflict

Evidence of the theme of the balance between harmony and conflict is found in the transcription of various classroom interactions. This is one such transcript of a conversation held between a student and myself:

Student: Even though some of our students will not be exposed to a diverse population, they need to broaden their horizons and see how other people view things.

Instructor (ME):   You are absolutely right. For example, a Jr. High principal said that the teachers don't need to celebrate Martin Luther King Day because they had very few Blacks in the school. That doesn't mean that we don't need to try to understand others. We live in such a global world. (Transcription, Education 418: Language Arts Methods, 12 January, 1996).

As I reviewed this interaction I had insight into the ways that I promote harmony. First of all, honoring a person who has been a great teacher is unquestioned in the Japanese culture. Martin Luther King is considered a great leader and teacher. In Japanese, a teacher is called sensei, which means 'the one who has gone before us', thus designating that he has gone before us in knowledge, wisdom and/or years. Also, consideration and appreciation of diverse populations can be promoted without having a large representation of particular ethnic minority groups. I wished that my own elementary teachers would have taken the time to know and appreciate the Japanese culture. I wished they would have recognized how important the Japanese language, customs and ethics were to us, who were so few in numbers. Another classroom interaction that illustrates the theme of the balance of harmony and conflict emerged in this conversation.

Student: Chapter 2 in the (reading diagnosis) book disagreed with breaking things apart and keeping things as a whole. If the child understood the ideas then the parts are not as important.

Instructor: I don't disagree with that, but you need to examine the child and his needs. In some cases you may want to tell the child the word and move on, but if the student has not stopped in the past when he obviously made an error and continuously makes the same mistakes then we need to stop him and help him learn to problem solve immediately and on the spot. (Transcription, Education 465: Diagnosis and Remediation of Reading Difficulties, 16 January, 1996)

Again, after reading this interaction, I was easily able to make connections between my cultural background and my classroom teaching practice. As a child, I was brought up to avoid disagreements or conflicts. I was taught that the gentle hero is

117

revered in Taoism. The hero would not bring attention to themselves and cast asper-
sions on someone else. They are a figure in the background — unnoticed, suffering for
virtue's sake and leading without others knowing. They give recognition to others not
themselves. On the other hand, stating another way of thinking about a situation is
appropriate to allow the other person to 'save face' or maintain their dignity. Another
viewpoint came to mind. Frequently as a Japanese person meets, greets, and or extends
good wishes to another, the receiver of the message will use the expression, *okagede*.
Okagede means 'because of you'. Someone might say, 'How are you?' The person
replies, 'I am fine *okagede* (because of you)'. Or someone else might say, 'Happy New
Year!' The other person responds, 'The new year will be wonderful *okagede* (because
of you)!' Credit is given to the other person for all of the good fortune and outcomes. In
this interaction credit and recognition were given to the person for the thoughts that
were expressed. The idea that this person had contributed to a better understanding was
important.

In my class, I read a passage from *In the Year of the Boar and Jackie Robinson* by
Bette Bao Lord that recounts where Shirley Temple Wong humiliates herself in front of
the class. I commented:

> I read this passage to illustrate to you how a real child might feel the humiliation
> and responsibility of a child whose first language is not English. A child like
> Shirley may be in your class. How should we teach to help this child? (Transcrip-
> tion, Education 307: Multicultural and Bilingual Education, 21 February, 1996).

This example illustrates how I use the experience of others to help my students
think about what they will experience as teachers. In addition, this particular event is
important because of its connection to my own cultural experience. I hope such experiences help make connections for my students. Trying to *save face* or maintain dignity
for the other person is an important part of my culture and a value I hope my students
incorporate into their classroom behaviors. I also use examples from books and movies
to illustrate my point. For instance, 'Shogun', the television mini-series about the Japanese culture, has a character, Mariko, who contemplates taking her life because she wants
to save her leader's dignity. From her perspective, her life was not worth living if her
leader was humiliated. Sometimes, issues of humility and responsibility are critical
issues. Indeed, in my experience, asking our students to think about ways of avoiding
humiliating situations with their students as in this case Shirley Temple Wong or Mariko
is important. Sometimes I find I must also practice avoiding humiliating my own students. One day in class, a student asserted that:

> There is also something about letting go of these historical wrong doings like the
> internment of the Japanese-Americans. As an American, I am appalled at what had
> happened. But at the same time I am tired of being punished for what happened. The
> people must let go of the past. I think Japanese-Americans are doing better at that.

> *Instructor*: There are individual reasons why people hold on to the past. It takes
> empathy and understanding for all of us. Some of you have had hardships. You
> may have had reasons that you feel you have been wronged. When the Japanese
> were interned you heard very little about resistance. The culture says that if in fact

you are being punished, there is a reason why you are being punished. So therefore, you must be patient and withstand your punishment. You must be tolerant and be that much better. . . . It is totally wrong for the Japanese-American to feel this way. They will never be able to face this if they don't face the fact that they did not do anything wrong. (Transcription, Education 685: Improving Language Arts, 22 May, 1996)

In this interaction I tried to diminish the student's guilt ('tired of being punished . . .') by generalizing that many people have hardships and that they may feel they have been wronged. But I also tried to help the students gain a deeper insight into the issue of how a student in a class might feel humiliated by providing further information about the situation and issue the student chose. My comment on the event the student raised provided a deeper more complex example of possible humiliation. It also caused me to reflect deeper on what I knew about the Japanese-American internment camp experience and the Japanese-American response to it. Only good things are credited to individuals as in the saying, 'okagede' not making someone feel he is at fault. When the Japanese and Japanese-Americans were incarcerated during the war they did not resist or blame the government. They looked to themselves for blame. I remembered hearing the words, *shikataganai* (cannot be helped), *gaman* (endure), *shiumbo* (be patient) and *hazukashe* (embarrassing). These words were often used when discussing the internment experience. The internees expressed that the internment cannot be helped. They must endure these hardships and be patient. This was an embarrassing event in their history. I never heard expressions like, 'We are not to be blamed'; 'We didn't do anything'; and 'The government is wrong.'

Examples from Questionnaire Responses

In response to Question 3 (*In your perspective, did Dr. Oda exhibit any traits/behaviors/ actions that seem to correlate with your perception about an Asian-American?*) students responded that I exhibited humility, fairness, and exactness. Further, the students felt that I exhibited an ability of 'Getting along well with others'. Another student said that I always exhibited tolerance and acceptance. In addition, students found me to be soft-spoken, respectful, and reverent to students that I encountered, very polite, as well as thoughtful and reflective: 'Dr. Oda was very reflective in her teaching practices'. These comments informed me about the range of my influence. On the basis of the Japanese culture, the following traits would be praised and recognized overtly: humility, fairness, tolerance, acceptance, soft-spoken, respectful, reverent, polite and reflective. A Tao hero would emulate these traits.

In response to Question 5: (*Did Dr. Oda tell/relate/share stories about her Asian upbringing/experiences?*) the students stated that my stories were helpful. For example, the students repeated a story I told about myself as a guest speaker describing

a group of adults that disagreed with her feelings (about the gentle nature of the Japanese as they related to the cruelty of the Japanese soldiers in W.W.II) and how she responded to them with a statement: 'No one has a corner on all good and no one has a corner on all bad!

Further, other students claimed they appreciated hearing about my struggle to fit in at school and to gain social acceptance. It also helped for them to learn words in another language.

The students mention of the specific experience provided me with further insight into how my behavior in responding and teaching others reflects my cultural heritage. I found myself reflecting on the experience mentioned by the students.

When I presented to these school district teachers and administrators, I was greatly surprised that I was lambasted with derogatory remarks about the Japanese. As I recall, there were many older participants in the audience. They referred to World War 2 many times and the atrocities that the Japanese army had perpetrated on the American soldiers. In order to avoid conflict and at the same time give them food for thought, I referred to humanity as a whole. Trying to get them to see that not one race of people has a monopoly of humanitarianism nor cruelty. In a time of war people react in very instinctual manners.

I also talked about how important it was to assist ethnic minority students to fit in and be socially accepted. I related stories about how difficult it was for me to be a minority among minorities. I talked about having to fight often to show that I was unafraid and what happened to some of my Japanese-American peers who did not fight — they were intimidated relentlessly. I, also, talked about how teachers made distinctions of the more able students to the less. The Japanese-American children were usually deemed the model student. The distinctions made it difficult for both. The less able felt inadequate. The more able were sometimes categorized as different and socially unacceptable. Disharmony resulted.

My students commented on appreciating that I taught a few Japanese words. I taught them the sounds of the syllables, how to blend them together to make words and the definitions of the words. My objective was two-fold: first, to model the technique of teaching a new word with unfamiliar symbols and words and, second, to illustrate the need for pre-service teachers to empathize with students who are learning new and unfamiliar words, especially language different students. I was hopeful that this would assist pre-service teachers to create ways to avoid problems that can be alleviated by understanding the students' difficulties in learning a new language.

Findings

Disagreement and disharmony are natural occurrences in interaction among people, yet Kitano's (1969) research showed that the Japanese and Japanese-Americans avoid conflict and promote harmony. As shown in transcriptions from Education 465 and 685 and student questionnaire comments, I used techniques to avoid conflict. The data illustrated that I used agreement with and also disagreement paired with reasoning targeted to other ways of looking at the problem. Traits such as humility, fairness, tolerance, acceptance, soft-spoken, respectful, reverent seemed to fit into a pattern of promotion of harmony and avoidance of conflict. The comments made by students and the ways in which I dealt with conflict informed me that my Asian-American background does influence my role as a teacher educator.

Evidence of the influences of my Japanese-American upbringing was subtle. While the transcriptions and questionnaire responses alluded to certain behaviors, values and beliefs of mine that had been evidenced through discussions, assignments, and examples given in class. I realized the evidence was not just inherent in action and events in my classroom and in my personal interaction with students. More difficult to pin point was the evidence inherent in the intent and purposes for my instruction. Since I could relate these to my life history, I recognized that I was able to connect the information from the transcriptions and questionnaires to values and expected behaviors of the Japanese culture.

Conclusions

Korthagen and Russell (1995) state:

> ... teacher educators who are able to create real innovations in their field are highly reflective. They are able to analyze and challenge the basic assumptions in their work. They use their ideals as the compass that guides them on their route, and they reflect on this route repeatedly and discuss it with colleagues. (pp. 191–2)

Reflecting on where my ideals originated and how I use them as a compass has been fascinating to me and, also disturbing. How I deal with conflict and maintain harmony has led me to reflect on my Japanese-American background. After gathering and analyzing data from audio tapes and questionnaires, I recognized some basic assumptions that informed my interaction and teaching in my courses. These assumptions led to questions about my practices. What does it mean to me to live in harmony? How does this contradict with living in a competitive world?

Living in harmony means that I consider and appreciate others. I give deference and credence to other people's thoughts, ideas and actions. I learn from others as they relate their thoughts, ideas and actions. I assist them to move through the path of resistance. I give them credit where credit is due. I understand blame and guilt. I respect the great teachers who have gone before me and their teachings. I recognize others and avoid bringing recognition to myself. I try to maintain someone else's dignity without giving my own away. I try to defuse anger by imposing thoughtful reasoning. I try to reconcile differences and look for ways of capitalizing on the differences.

Attempting to maintain harmony and avoid conflict does create difficulties. Harmony and kindness may be mistaken for weakness. For example, would it have been better to force the student, who felt responsible because of the Japanese internment, to face these feelings? Would it have been better to confront the educators that were so derogatory against the Japanese? Am I causing more conflict in the future if I do not have them face their feelings? As Bullough (1996) indicated as one of his principles that arose from his experience and work: 'Teacher education must be powerful enough to challenge beliefs that potentially might be miseducative in their effects' (p. 21). I have learned that showing bravado helped me gain respect, harmony and peace of mind as I stood up to the challenges of fighting. Fighting and harmony did not seem to match at the time. In this competitive world, is it a good idea to avoid being aggressive or assertive? These are disquieting questions for many Japanese-Americans.

After team-teaching a multicultural class, I compared and contrasted myself with another colleague. I thought about how my approach to maintaining harmony would make a difference to pre-service students seeking solutions to multicultural issues. I would like to cite a statement by a former student who responded to a take home examination from Education 462 and chose to discuss her transfer of learning in a joint class taught by a colleague (Dr. Graciela Italiano-Thomas) and myself. Dr. Italiano-Thomas is a Uruguayan-American. Born and raised in Uruguay, Dr. Italiano-Thomas studied and received her higher degrees in the United States. She received her doctorate within the University of California system and also instructed there. As a colleague, she would relate often to me comments from her students about her assertive and straight forward teaching. This statement from one of our students illustrated the influence my cultural background has on my teaching as well as how this potentially can affect a pre-service student.

> . . . Dr. Graciela Italiano-Thomas and Dr. Linda Oda taught a multiculturalism class I had Winter quarter. For me, this class invoked a desire to teach to and for all children who may enter the classroom. It was also a chance to open myself to several cultures with which I am not very familiar. The reason why these two instructors benefitted my transfer learning stems from their personal connection to the class. Both of these ladies have a strong tie to cultures I have no real knowledge about. It was a wonderful opportunity to learn from them and be able to experience from them those things that cannot be captured in books or from mere instruction. . . . I find it interesting that both of them taught me so much in such different ways. Dr. Italiano-Thomas is a very strong individual who showed to me a sense of pride for who she was and the culture from which she came. It is obvious in her attitude and behaviors that she is proud of her heritage and feels it to be a strength in her overall character. As a student in her class, I couldn't help but appreciate this confidence and respect her for it. Dr. Oda taught with a quiet assurance that made you trust her words and respect her message. She is an example of an individual who seeks to honor her heritage and appreciates the several cultures that surround her. It was fascinating to watch her speak of her Japanese-American heritage and appreciate both her sincere desire to reflect her culture and her feelings of respect for her family.

Obviously to the student, Dr. Italiano-Thomas and I had different approaches to the issues of multiculturalism. Dr. Italiano-Thomas taught with confidence and strength. I did so with quiet assurance and pride. Both invoked a desire to teach to and for all students, which is exactly what I would like to have the pre-service student learn from the class. In this case, maintaining the values and the integrity that I brought to my teaching produced the desired outcome. I have become aware of the benefits and problems of infusing my values and beliefs into my teaching and how to enhance or diminish them. As the Arizona Group (1996) discovered:

> I am learning how to address some of the issues I encounter, and realizing there are others that will continue to be problematic because of my experience, beliefs, theories, and commitment to demonstrate practice that promotes justice and equality for all. (p. 45)

However subtle or direct the evidence of how my Asian-American background influences my teaching, understanding and examining important experiences in my life history have provided insight into my current practices. I could relate to what Guilfoyle et al. (The Arizona Group, 1996) stated:

> Our past experiences gave us insight into our current experiences, and this brought new understanding, an enrichment of the meaning of being a teacher educator and greater commitment to the development of teachers. (p. 45)

This self-study can facilitate the next steps to my professional development and, in the process, facilitate my students' own journeys toward becoming professional teachers. Teacher education students need to start with their experiences and background to be able to understand other cultures and diversities. They can use their reflections to guide them on their journey to teaching multiculturally. As Bullough (1996) stated, 'To teach is to enable boundary crossing while seeking to build a sense of belonging to a wider and ethically grounded community' (p. 22). At least one student felt that a teacher could include her culture without being imposing. The student responded to Question 2 on the questionnaire (*If Dr. Oda reflected on her Asian-American background, how helpful was this reflection to understanding multicultural issues in class?*) with the following reply: 'It [Dr. Oda's reflection] gave a good example of how a teacher's culture can be included naturally in a classroom without being imposing'.

My self-study using a life history framework has helped me understand that in trying to create an environment to support all learners, I strive to maintain harmony. The value of maintaining harmony is a cultural influence. Yet, I also have to reconcile the conflicts created in maintaining harmony. I hope to extend what I discover to support pre-service teachers in understanding how to reflect on what influences them and to reconcile the conflicts of these influences.

References

ARIZONA GROUP (GUILFOYLE, K., HAMILTON, M., PINNEGAR, S. and PLACIER, P.) (1996) 'Becoming teachers of teachers: The paths of four beginners', *Teacher Education Quarterly*, **23**, 3, pp. 35–55.

BANKS, J.A. (1991) *Teaching Strategies for Ethnic Studies*, Needham Heights, MA: Allyn Bacon.

BULLOUGH, JR., R.V. (1996) 'Practicing theory and theorizing practice in teacher education', *Teacher Education Quarterly*, **23**, 3, pp. 13–31.

COLE, A.L. and KNOWLES, J.G. (1995) 'Methods and issue in a life history approach to self-study', in RUSSELL, T. and KORTHAGEN, F. (eds) *Teachers Who Teach Teachers: Reflections on Teacher Education*, London: Falmer Press, pp. 130–51.

DENZIN, N. (1989) *Interpretive biography*, Newbury Park, CA: Sage.

GOODSON, I.F. (1992) *Studying teachers' lives*, London: Routledge.

KITANO, H.H. (1969) *Japanese Americans: The Evolution of a Subculture*, NJ: Prentice Hall.

KORTHHAGEN, F. and RUSSELL, T. (eds) (1995) *Teachers Who Teach Teachers*, London: Falmer Press.

LANGNESS, L.L. (1965) *The Life History in Anthropological Science*, London: Holt, Rinehart and Winston.

PLUMMER, K. (1983) *Documents of Life: An Introduction to the Problems and Literature of a Humanistic Method*, London: George Allen and Unwin.

WATSON, L.C. and WATSON-FRANKE, M. (1985) *Interpreting Life Histories: An Anthropological Inquiry*, New Brunswick, NJ: Rutgers University Press.

WHITE, R.W. (ed.) (1963) *The Study of Lives*, New York: Atherton Press.

8   Reflecting Critically on Teaching to Encourage Critical Reflection

Nancy L. Hutchinson

Introduction

This chapter is a teacher educator's account of her study of her own teaching through critical reflection and action research. Personal data were supplemented by the reflections of those she was teaching — pre-service candidates who were expected to demonstrate critical reflection. I examined my motives, as well as the pedagogical issues I have faced, in using cases to teach pre-service candidates about teaching exceptional learners in their classrooms. My reflections showed that I had many starting points for the research. In addition to focusing more class discussion on critical reflection, I asked students to analyze complex dilemmas and bring case notes to class. To increase my awareness of student concerns, I instituted periodic meetings of a Student Advisory Committee (SAC). I listened in SAC, responded to student concerns, and reported in subsequent classes the responsive actions I had taken. Students led the case discussions in many classes, and some questioned our assumptions and critiqued our analyses. I found contradictions among the teaching actions I took, even when the actions seemed consistent with experience, my reading, and each other before enactment. Action research reveals ongoing agendas for teachers who are students of teaching. Case-based learning ventures a response to the critics who argue that teacher education undermines developing teachers who are criticality reflective in their work.

I wonder how long I've been staring out the window without seeing anything. It's dark now, and snow is falling. My watch says 5:30. Maybe I'll write my notes before I leave. For three afternoons I have interviewed students in my exceptional children course, individually, about their self-assessments. Did they think self-assessment was valuable? Would they recommend I use self-assessment in the future? My immediate reaction is that maybe the interview about self-assessment was too indirect to be an indicator of critical reflection. I wonder why I thought it might be [an indicator]. I think they understand that we are dealing with dilemmas in learning from cases, that we focus on specifics, that every solution has an up-side and a down-side, and that it is important we question our assumptions. They just don't articulate it very well. Lots of comments about cases. Interestingly, not one person said, 'You should have taught us more'. I wonder why. I probably should have. (5 December, 1995)

This account grows from a research direction that I have followed over the past five years. During that time, I have documented my efforts to improve my teaching of pre-service candidates by adopting case methodology, and I have studied the critical reflection that candidates demonstrate in written case analyses. I joined a group of colleagues in self-study, in September 1995, to work more systematically on improving my teaching. In this chapter, I first present the background to my efforts in autumn 1995, and then I focus on my critical reflections about encouraging critical reflection, examining briefly reflections of class members from autumn 1995.

Looking Back: Providing a Context

Since my arrival at Queen's in 1987, my teaching responsibilities have included a one-semester, elective course intended to help elementary and secondary teacher candidates include exceptional learners in their classrooms. Gradually, cases have assumed a more prominent role in the course. From 1987 to 1990, I used short cases to help candidates identify the nature of students' learning difficulties. From 1990 to 1992, case discussions constituted about half the course. I recognized that case discussions were the richest part of my classes, but I knew little about teaching with cases. I began reading the classic books (e.g. Christensen and Hansen, 1987) and papers on case methodology (e.g. Harrington, 1991; Kleinfeld, 1991a).

In summer 1992, I began writing longer, more detailed cases based on puzzles that had arisen in my practice, and I modelled on cases appearing in case books, such as Silverman, Welty and Lyon (1992). Unfortunately, case writing took much longer than I anticipated. Recently I recorded recollections about 8:30 a.m. classes in autumn 1992 and winter 1993:

How did I do it? Staying up most of the night to write the case for the next day, and praying a photocopier would be free at 8:00 when I rushed in. The students who arrived early expected to collate the day's case. The amazing thing was that the students were as excited as I was about each new case. They knew I was writing them as we went. The first thing they said every class was, 'Did you get the case written for today?' (recollected 1 October, 1995).

About half the candidates chose the assignment that required them to write a case based on experience (Florio-Ruane, 1990; Kleinfeld, 1991b). Now I can see that, in our excitement, the candidates and I forgot to be critical. In 1994, I reflected on these experiences:

> I have found teaching with cases demanding. There are few Canadian resources, so I have written my own cases . . . Some of my cases gave only a slightly elaborated version of a theoretical or textbook issue. This lack of authenticity undermined the approach. Sometimes students expected right answers, and this may have reduced their confidence in learning by the discussion of cases. . . . Some of my cases generated too much agreement among the students. On these occasions there was too little of people giving reasons, looking at sources, drawing from personal experiences, and trying to convince others — the things that make small groups productive (Cohen, 1994). Occasionally I found too much disagreement . . . I came up against my own limitations more frequently when using case discussions than [with] other teaching approaches. (Hutchinson, 1994, pp. 86–7)

The months between autumn 1992 and summer 1994 were a time of constant change in my teaching. I revised the cases I had already written and sought dilemmas from student-authored cases to form the basis for new cases. I used cases to stimulate discussion whenever I could. These ranged from my original two-paragraph vignettes about individual students to dilemmas faced by teachers who were including children with severe disabilities in the social fabric and the learning communities in their classrooms.

What is a Case?

Early on, what constituted a case was unquestioned in my teaching. Half-page cases in textbook chapters about exceptional learners described individuals with disabilities, their characteristics, and some of their learning needs. In their casebook, Greenwood and Parkay (1989) focused on frequently occurring incidents that required 'teacher decision making' and provided sample analyses to demonstrate the application of particular theoretical frameworks. They assumed that when teachers make decisions, they should explicitly apply theoretical knowledge to the facts of the case. Working with contrasting assumptions, Judith Shulman (1988, Foreword) described *The Intern Teacher Casebook* as an example of 'commitment to building and using practitioner knowledge'. The vignettes, which were authored by interning teachers, contained reflections in addition to the narrative of a classroom event or interaction.

In all the above instances of cases, the reader is confronted by a vignette that describes a critical incident that can elicit teachers' immediate reactions. In a critical incident, a right or wrong choice can be made and there may be a series of well-remembered events, but vignettes do not contain puzzles of professional practice (Carter, 1991). Teaching dilemmas, on the other hand, by their very nature, do not lend themselves to direct and decisive courses of action. Rather, they present puzzles in the form of paradoxes where a chosen course of action may simultaneously ameliorate one problem and prompt another.

The dilemma case is an instance of the case as a problematic situation. Dewey (1929), Schwab (1978), and Rorty (1982) have argued for 'practical deliberations' on particular problematic situations that reconnect moral arguments with theoretical ways of knowing. Within this pragmatic stance, the emphasis in case deliberations is on acting and reflecting on problematic situations. 'The flow of practical deliberation moves back and forth, revealing aspects of the case from the perspective of theory and exposing the limits, lacunae, biases, and interconnections of theory in its encounter with cases' (Sykes and Bird, 1992, p. 471). The implications are that cases become the focal point of curriculum, and that constructing and arranging cases is central to curriculum development.

In this Deweyan perspective, cases can be conceived as instances of vicarious experience that initiate shared inquiry. Harrington and Garrison (1992) propose a dialogical model of case-based teaching that helps prospective teachers see teaching as shared inquiry that incorporates cognitive, practical, and normative components. One implication of this model of shared inquiry is that case-based teaching must involve communication, communities and dialogue (Dewey, 1916/1961). Case discussion is necessary. It is also important to examine the quality of thinking that characterizes the deliberations.

What is Critical Reflection?

The cases I first presented to students for discussion were brief vignettes much like those found in texts. Then I wrote longer vignettes in the style of Greenwood-Parkay (1989), sometimes containing principles to apply in making decisions. From 1992 to 1994, I moved inexorably toward cases as problematic situations and case deliberations as focal in the exceptional children course. My students were grappling with dilemma cases I had written or adapted, and the discussions were intense. Because of the situated nature of the knowledge of teaching, I encouraged teacher candidates to use what they had learned from classroom experience in discussing others' cases and in authoring their own. My goal was that the candidate-authored cases be genuine — a question within some situation or personal experience of the prospective teacher. These cases ventured a response to Dewey's question, 'Is the experience a personal thing of such a nature as inherently to stimulate and direct observation of the connections involved, and to lead to inference and its testing?' (1916/1961, p. 155). Although I was excited by the case deliberations, I was unhappy with my attempts to discern the quality of those deliberations and of the experience-based written case analyses.

In April 1994, I heard Harrington argue at AERA that not only was Dewey's view of cases as problematic situations essential for teacher education, but that Dewey's construct of critical reflection provided a lens for gauging the quality of written case analyses.

> Reflecting our conceptual and theoretical framework, critical reflection has, for the purposes of our study, been operationalized as (1) recognizing and acknowledging the validity in other perspectives (open-mindedness); (2) considering the moral and ethical consequences of choices (responsibility), and identifying and addressing limitations in one's assumptions (wholeheartedness) when making decisions. Whereas, the concepts of open-mindedness and responsibility illuminate reflection on the other and on obligations to the other, the concept of wholeheartedness illuminates self-reflection on the assumptions that may limit our ability to hear others and meet our obligations to them. (Harrington, Quinn-Leering and Hodson, 1994, p. 3)

I resolved that when I returned to the classroom, after sabbatical leave, I would refine my teaching to provoke critical reflection in teacher candidates, and I would reflect critically on my own teaching. I would also try to discern how much critical reflection was shown in case analyses written by teacher candidates in my classes when I had been tacitly, rather than explicitly, aware of the need to emphasize critical reflection.

Critical Reflection in Candidates' Case Studies

I analyzed 48 candidate-authored cases (written prior to my sabbatical leave) for evidence of critical reflection — open-mindedness, responsibility and wholeheartedness (Hutchinson, 1996). Using the framework developed by Harrington, Quinn-Leer and Hodson (1996), I found that, on open-mindedness, most of the cases revealed the middle of three levels, that is, multiple perspectives, rather than author-only perspectives or comprehensive perspectives. What was most interesting was that when I analyzed whether the candidates had authored vignettes or dilemmas, I found that no candidate who had authored a vignette took comprehensive perspectives on open-mindedness. There were similar findings for responsibility — only two candidates who authored a vignette discussed consequences at the highest level, broad consequences for society, while twelve who had authored dilemmas considered consequences in such a 'broad' way. Similarly for wholeheartedness, four who wrote vignettes showed complex questioning of taken-for-granted assumptions, while twenty who wrote dilemmas reached the complex level on wholeheartedness.

I asked myself why these candidate-authors did not write dilemmas, did not question their taken-for-granted assumptions, and did not critique their case analyses. I also thought about my teaching when these cases had been written. Some of the cases we discussed in class were not dilemmas, and rarely did I remind myself in my teaching notes to model questioning assumptions or critiquing analyses. Questioning of assumptions was implicit, not explicit, in my instructions for writing and analyzing cases. Changes in these aspects of my teaching are explained in the next section of this chapter.

In hindsight, these data on critical reflection of candidates suggest that when teacher candidates framed an experienced classroom problem in a simple manner, they were unlikely to engage in high levels of critical reflection about the experience. The implication is that it may be vital to help teacher candidates pose and frame experienced problems in a complex manner. Otherwise, the benefits of case analysis for understanding experience may be lost. Examination of the candidates' recommendations for including exceptional children in the classroom suggested that half the candidates made recommendations that were 'intense enough to make a difference' in the classroom; however, all but one of these candidates had written a dilemma rather than a vignette. I learned that almost half the candidates showed high levels of critical reflection, and I could see ways to make my teaching more consistent with my aims. However, the more challenging finding was that the influence of framing experience, on critical reflection, may be extensive. These became starting points for my efforts to teach differently.

Changing the Course . . . and Getting 'SACked'

In autumn 1995, I made many changes in assignments, course organization and teaching. The assignments required all candidates to submit both a written case analysis of a prepared case that I believed to be a dilemma case, and to submit a case they had authored and analyzed based on teaching experience. The organization of the course changed too. I gave the cases to the students before the class session in which they were to be discussed and distributed preparation notes at each class suggesting ways in which candidates could prepare for the next case discussion. Below is an excerpt from the notes distributed at the fifth class.

LERN-476A Fall 1995 Preparation Notes for Session #6
1. Our topic for session #6 will be program planning for exceptional learners.
2. Continue to work on the case we started in session #5. It provides detailed suggestions. Look back to the notes on case analysis in the course outline. Also, ask hard questions, assume a variety of perspectives, and consider the consequences of adopting various solutions. I don't ask you to do these things because I

want you to give up on inclusion, but because teaching is an ambiguous activity and a moral activity. Cases are dilemmas in which each solution often generates other complications. This is one of the ways in which they are like life. However, they go more slowly than real time, so we have more time to think than is often the case when the clock is running in life.

The excerpt from the preparation notes refers to 'the notes on case analysis in the course outline'. The course outline contained detailed guidelines for preparing for a case discussion, that is, for analyzing a case. The course outline also included the steps we followed in class for case discussion and the rationale for learning from cases. I tried to use case discussion in most classes.

Other aspects of the organization changed as well, as noted by candidates themselves in the following observation recorded at the third class.

'Oh, we're separated. She put us in all the groups around the class. Look at that!' Seven girls who sat together in the first two classes voiced their concerns loudly about the composition of the home groups as they entered class on the third day. (19 September, 1995)

Students sat in 'home groups' at seven tables of five or six per table. I created the home groups by trying to maximize diversity within groups based on the information students provided about themselves on the first day — the level at which they hoped to teach, previous experience with persons with disabilities, and previous experience in psychology. In order to get ongoing feedback from students, I instituted another new organizational structure. I asked each of the seven tables to select a representative to attend occasional Student Advisory Committee meetings, which I called 'sacks.' The SAC met after class on 19 September. During that first meeting, I wrote the essence of the students' advice in point form. It was not until three days later that I brought myself to write the following reflective note. The students were engaging in critical reflection already, and that was supposed to be my emphasis for the course. But I was not as ready as they were.

'19 September, first SAC' I wrote at the top of my page. The students started by saying they liked the preparation notes and the agenda on the board, because 'these help with organization'. But they want the readings to 'tie in more'. That comment stimulated an avalanche of criticism: 'I'm overwhelmed, and it's not just me; so are the other people at my table. The readings are in too much depth'. 'Could we have one instead of two readings?' Next concern was 'Thursday's assignment [personal learning goals for the course, unmarked but required early in the course] is too soon. We're not ready. We don't have a concrete sense of what we should be doing'. [Later,] they returned to the positive, [for example] 'I took this course because it was using cases, and my friend who was here two years told me I'd love the case discussions . . .' Why is it so hard to accept their criticisms when I asked for them? (22 September, 1995)

I fashioned a response to demonstrate that I appreciated their advice, and to be responsive to their concerns. At the next class, I began with my response. It was essentially 'Thank you, we are listening. We will retain the prep notes and agenda and . . .' The easy ones first. Then I tackled the tougher criticisms. I said I had engaged in some critical reflection about the amount of reading and had decided to cut the reading assignments for the next two classes in half. There was spontaneous applause. I suggested they pair up, each do half the reading, and then conference. Three teacher candidates stayed at the end of class to thank me for paying attention to their concerns and for making a public response. Five others stood around and listened. I felt we had begun our shared critical reflections.

Changing Everything (and Nothing, Yet): Planning a New Program

While I was busy changing everything in the course outline and organization of the course, I was also one of four members of the Faculty of Education working on restructuring the pre-service teacher education program. We had decided to take a risk by proposing a structure that placed candidates in schools for experience first (the entire first term, after a brief orientation), followed by an extended term of courses on campus and two short practica. The plan we were evolving would see candidates return to the Faculty for one two-week period during the autumn term's intensive teaching. They would also complete two 'field-based' courses during that term. The second draft of the restructuring plan included the following:

> Consistent with the extended practica is the notion of project-based or experienced-based learning. Pre-service teachers seek answers to their own questions through carrying out projects, engaging in discussions with peers about cases they have encountered in their practice, and other 'hands-on, heads-on' ways of learning. (UPITIS, RUSSELL, WHITEHEAD AND HUTCHINSON, 1995, p. 5)

I emphasized the aspect of the field-based term that was on my mind. It seemed to me that in the autumn term, while they were completing field-based courses in schools, candidates would be expected to lead their own case discussions. We needed some indication that candidate-led case discussions were feasible and productive. I am not certain when this issue began to weigh on my mind, but by early October it was always with me.

The first two case discussions had moved slowly. I wondered if my pacing was off after my sabbatical leave. Perhaps it was because I had shifted from using specific probe questions unique to each case to providing general guidelines for case discussion. Then, beginning with the third case discussion, the students analyzed the case and discussed it vigorously without so many furtive glances at the posted guidelines. Minutes before the eighth class, I told my teaching assistant, Nicole, that I thought we should try asking the student groups to lead the discussion. Nicole had led part of a case discussion the previous week, and she remarked, 'It isn't easy'. I argued that this would force members of the class to take more ownership. We did it, and, for the first time that fall, I couldn't wait to write my reflective notes.

> Today was session 8 of [course] 476. I gave the students some new opportunities. The main part of the class involved them preparing in groups and then the groups presenting [I wanted them to lead, but like them, I focused on presenting] the various steps in case analysis. Faye presented for the first group [rather than draw-

ing out the facts of the case from the class members]. She asked for more input and got one idea from me and one from someone else. The second group did the issues — Joanne reported — she didn't say enough [about] why. I realize now, I didn't ask why . . . The third group was represented by Kirsten. She did, orally, adaptations to the morning schedule [for a severely disabled student included in a primary classroom] . . . All very inclusive. Matt was the only one who really led a discussion [for the fourth group]; he said nervously, 'I'm going to try the discussion thing'. He asked people to comment on the consequences, and was aware of the time. Eventually, I cut him off, although he was doing well. The fifth group had everyone in the group talk . . . I like it when everyone takes part, but I didn't want to mandate it the first time. (5 October, 1995)

The sixth and seventh groups had little time to lead the class, but both groups had one male candidate do the talking. I summarized the discussion at the end and, even while I was still talking, I wished I hadn't. It seemed to me that I had tried to hand over ownership for orchestrating the case discussion but then I contradicted myself by proceeding to explain what the symphony meant. My intentions had been good — to relate the readings to the case — something the students had requested in the first SAC meeting. My poor judgment at the closing of the session did not undo what had happened — the class had 'caught fire' that day.

After class, it seemed that half the group stayed, and the room was buzzing. The most interesting comment was Ron's: 'Other people around here don't know all these things'. When I asked what he meant, he answered that this course with its cases about teachers making adaptations for exceptional learners was 'causing people in this class to expect more of themselves, and if this is going to happen to us, it should happen to everyone'. My first interpretation was that he thought these heightened expectations were a good thing. I told him I agreed. He looked so surprised that I knew I must have misunderstood. He didn't clarify the issue much for me, but the gist was that it wasn't fair to make some teacher candidates think they had to do these difficult things 'when teachers aren't all doing inclusion' and 'there's a big difference between ideal and reality'. There was also a vague reference to 'tired teachers'. Ron was engaging in critical reflection about the whole premise of the course — inclusive education for students with disabilities. He was questioning my taken-for-granted assumption that grappling with the ambiguities and high expectations that accompany inclusive education is valuable for teacher candidates. He seemed to be fearing the prospect of higher expectations for himself. I tried to understand it. Was he saying, 'Because of this course, I will expect more of myself. Maybe I won't be able to do it. Teachers in the field can't always do it. So I might think I've failed, while others who are ignorant of the ideas in this course will think they've done fine'. For the next few days, I asked myself, 'What is wrong with this picture?' because I tend to agree with McIntyre and O'Hair (1996) that 'a feeling of dissatisfaction may help improve rather than hinder your teaching performance' (p. 4).

'Sometimes I'm Not Thinking, I'm Just Teaching'

When I asked Nicole how she thought the students had done while leading the discussion, her reaction was much like mine: 'They were great!' Mark had told her that this was a good idea; students should be leading class discussions before their first teaching practicum. I could see that I had not provided enough direction to get every group to lead discussion; perhaps they all knew that was expected, but were not ready to try 'the discussion thing'. I found myself trying to take the perspective of someone who has been a teacher candidate for less than a month. Yes, maybe they weren't ready to lead a discussion in front of Nicole and me and a room full of peers. I reminded myself, 'If case discussion was easy, it probably would have featured prominently in my courses a decade earlier'. I still asked the question about how we would make this work 'in the new program'.

I wrote field notes and some direct quotations while the students led and discussed the case. That evening I reflected on whether my willingness to write was entirely a function of my excitement about the class. I came to think that talking with the self-study group had helped me to open up on paper. The morning of 5 October, I had told my colleagues about the second SAC meeting. The students had raised two issues, especially focusing on the written case analysis of a dilemma case that they had to submit soon. At the beginning of class on 3 October, I discussed both issues. We took a break that day, and spent time with their questions about the assignment. One student spoke out in class:

> You changed what you're doing. According to what we said. That made me think, I can change things too. She [referring to me] told us 'I'm changing this', and I thought, hmm, I could change things too. And tell my students. I always thought once I started something, I'd have to keep going that way. (3 October 1995)

I talked with John Loughran, who was visiting our Faculty from Monash University and was a member of our self-study group. John reminded me, 'Modelling is powerful'. But, as we agreed, this means we have to tell our students what we are thinking. Later I wrote, 'Sometimes I forget to tell them what I am thinking; sometimes I remember and don't have enough energy. Sometimes I don't know what I am thinking. Sometimes I'm not thinking, I'm just teaching'.

5 October seemed to be a watershed day. I bared my soul in our self-study group. The candidates led the case discussion in class. I wrote reflective notes eagerly right after class. That evening Tom Russell sent me a copy of an email message he had received as part of a student's reflective journal in his physics curriculum course. The student, Dan, was also in my 476 class. Dan was describing in his journal the similarities between the teaching, and the reflection expected, in Tom's course and my course. This mature student came to the pre-service program with considerable experience teaching internationally, and I valued his critical reflections on the course. It encouraged me that he was positive in his evaluation after thinking through the way the course delivery supported the course aims. Very late and very tired, I sent a semi-literate email message to Tom:

> That really helps me. I find all of this stuff about our teaching fascinating. There are so many dimensions to what we each do. Sometimes I think two parts of what I do are contradicting each other, but I choose to do each because I see it encouraging the students to take ownership of their own learning. But on some other dimension entirely, or through another lens, they contradict. I am puzzled by my

own teaching, let alone someone else's. Oh, I see I called them students [instead of teacher candidates]. More contradictions. (5 October, 1995)

We had been trying, in the restructuring committee, to provide leadership in the Faculty by thinking and speaking of our 'students' as fellow teachers, beginning teachers. The term that was gaining consensus was 'teacher candidates', the term I have tried to use throughout this chapter. This was consistent with the notion that the year of teacher education is the first year as a professional, not the last year as a university student. But again in my email message, I wasn't thinking. It is hard to escape the risks that accompany uncovering new knowledge about yourself (Brookfield, 1995; McIntyre and O'Hair, 1996) — 'Sometimes I'm not thinking, I'm just teaching'.

Candidates' Reflections on Learning from Cases

I wondered what the candidates thought they were learning from cases and what critical reflections they had to supplement mine. Twenty-eight teacher candidates wrote 'reflections on learning from cases' at the mid-term informal course evaluations. Because I wanted quantitative data about the relative numbers of positive and negative reflections, I parsed the written comments into 41 idea units — 35 that expressed the value of learning by case study and 6 that described negative aspects of learning from cases. Of the 35 ideas expressing the value of learning from cases, 16 referred to the epistemology or the nature of case learning as decision making or problem solving. Many used positive statements such as '. . . you think how best to approach a problem' and 'Cases help to internalize the thinking process required for problem solving', and '. . . give hands-on experience'. Others referred to the nature of the knowledge through negative comparisons like 'I find this useful because it relates the info to the real life situation, rather than just getting the facts from a textbook'. In nine idea units, candidates valued the 'specifics' they were learning 'about various exceptionalities' and 'the process of learning', while five focused on the value of learning about inclusive classrooms: 'how to modify my teaching' and 'the relevance of adaptations'. Only five used the Deweyan terminology of critical reflection, with three referring to perspective, 'seeing the importance of info from a variety of sources, i.e. teacher's perspective, students', parents' and two referring to consequences, 'the possible outcomes of your actions'.

The six references to negative aspects of learning from cases included one reference to the student's lack of confidence ('I am hesitant about my reflections'), one about the way the cases had been written ('sort of long winded'), and four about the way cases were used ('sometimes there seems like too much to cover in class', 'never learn about what is being done'). Two of the six started off by saying they liked working on cases, but gave no reason; these were not judged as valuing cases. The other four negative references to cases gave valuing openings that were coded positively.

In summary, while the majority of candidates put positive value on learning from cases, only a few referred directly to the aspects of Deweyan critical reflection (Harrington et al., 1996) while almost half referred to epistemological reasons. Learning from cases was valued because it was seen as the kind of knowledge that is 'probably the best way to learn' to teach; 'very real and practical'. Without the opportunity to follow the open-ended written reflections with interviews, it is impossible to ascertain whether or not the paucity of spontaneous references to critical reflection meant the candidates did not value critical reflection. It could be that few thought to use this language on their own, but would have responded to Dewey's (1916/1961) aspects of critical reflection — taking perspectives, considering consequences, and questioning assumptions — if prompted.

'You Profs Can't Win': Experience and Epistemology

After the candidates returned from their first three-week practicum, I found it easier to keep the focus on the case discussions. Prior to the practicum, Marnie had asked, 'How are we supposed to know what a teacher should do when we haven't been teaching yet?' After the practicum, I asked her whether she found the case discussions easier. Her response was thoughtful, and essentially said that once you know how complicated the classroom is, the cases look like oversimplifications. She thought that perhaps it was a situation where 'you profs [teacher educators] can't win; either we know too little or we think we know too much [about how complex teaching is]'. Because she made her comments while I was circulating during small group discussion of a case, I did not write a field note until two hours later, and the only words of hers that I remembered verbatim were the most insightful ones about how teacher educators 'can't win'.

The emphasis, in the group's mid-term reflections, on epistemology, and the above comments of one reflective teacher candidate came to mind when I read Kessels and Korthagen (1996). They argue that when understanding a case of teaching, it is much more important to know the concrete details in the situation than to know general rules. For even if the general rules are applicable, 'the question is still how exactly they should be handled in a reasonable and practical way that is appropriate to the situation' (p. 20). Phronesis (from Aristotle, *cited* in Kessels and Korthagen, p. 20), practical wisdom (Richardson, 1994), or moral perception (Dewey, 1929) uses rules only as summaries and guides. Nussbaum (1986) says, 'It must itself be flexible, ready for surprise, prepared to see, resourceful at improvization' (p. 305).

> In all these cases [of decision making in teaching], however, perceptual knowledge is the basis for a proper judgment of the situation and for an appropriate choice of behavior. Mind you, the perception that Aristotle speaks of is not just the normal sensory perception, it is the 'eye' that one develops for paradigmatic or type cases. . . . Given such perception, no further proof or theoretical justification is needed. (Kessels and Korthagen, 1996, p. 20)

The question remains for teacher educators, 'What learning experiences will support teacher candidates in their quest for such perception?' Nussbaum argues that the person of practical wisdom inhabits the human world and does not try to rise above it (1986, p. 314). I take him to mean by this trying to rise into the conceptual world, and substituting theory for experience. Kessels and Korthagen answer my question with the following:

> An important prerequisite of this type of knowledge is that someone has enough proper experience. For particulars only become familiar with experience, with a long process of perceiving, assessing situations, judging, choosing courses of action and being con-

fronted with their consequences. This generates a sort of insight that is altogether different from scientific knowledge. . . . Such knowledge cannot be transferred to him [a student described in their opening paragraph] (or induced, provoked, elicited) through the use of purely conceptual knowledge. The appropriate criterion for correct choice in an example like ours is not its correspondence or consistency with an abstract rule or principle . . . but instead what a concrete person would do, the person of practical wisdom. (1996, p. 21)

Kessels and Korthagen's analysis leaves me with many questions about the role of the teacher educator. These are the same kinds of questions prompted by our newly restructured pre-service teacher education program. Their attempts to answer these questions leave me exhilarated and, simultaneously, terrified. They suggest that our task is to help candidates become aware of the salient features of their experiences, to help them see and refine their perceptions. They continue by suggesting that the task is 'to help the student capture the singularities of the experience, to find the rightness of tone and the sureness of touch that only holds good for the particular situation' (p. 21). This is a tall order for teacher educators and for teaching with cases. I hope I am up to it. And I hope I learn how to communicate more clearly with teacher candidates about the nature of the enterprise on which we are embarked.

Candidates' Perceptions of Self-assessment

In the third class of the course, candidates submitted written personal learning goals for the course and the actions they intended to take to reach these goals. Near the end of the course, they submitted a written self-assessment, grading themselves out of thirty, and this was 30 per cent of their course grade. I thought that the candidates' views on self-assessment might tell me something about their critical reflection. With this in mind, I invited (but did not require) the students to meet me individually to discuss their self-assessment in the week after the course ended. Twenty-nine of the thirty-seven came to interviews over a three-day span. Three themes emerged from my analysis of the notes I recorded during these meetings. Although I asked specifically about the students' perspectives on self-assessment, most also commented on the use of cases in the course. I did not ask for these comments, but I had told the candidates that I was involved in self-study and that I was placing more emphasis on cases.

   With reference to the self-assessment, most candidates remarked on the benefits to them personally and professionally, and then cited drawbacks or made recommendations for improvement. They rarely commented on only the benefits or only the drawbacks. In terms of benefits, many thought the experience was 'useful for the long term'. Reasons included because it 'helped me to realize what life-long learning means', 'helped me to reaffirm what is really important in education', 'it promotes awareness that we can and should continue learning and assessing ourselves'. One candidate said that because the learning goals for the course were not prescribed, she felt 'as if I was a professional', and another described the process of setting and assessing goals as development in 'trusting ourselves'. The theme permeating the interviews was that professionals who will be responsible for their own learning for the rest of their lives can learn much about this process during pre-service teacher education. One candidate who often criticized practicing teachers suggested that many teachers in the field need to engage in such an exercise to refresh their commitment to ongoing professional development.

Short-term benefits included: 'helped me with my professional development portfolio', and 'when I was teaching, I had goals in mind'. Many cited the advantages as influencing their thinking about the course: 'forces you to think at the beginning about what you want to get out of the course', or 'focuses you'. Others emphasized how it changed the amount and kind of work they did for the course: 'I wouldn't have done that extra work', 'I might not have gone to that workshop', 'I was challenging myself all the time to meet the goals I set', and 'because someone had seen it, that pushed the issue, accountability'. Many referred to the affective benefits, in comments such as these: 'I realized how many things I could do', and 'it was a highlight of the course, the fulfillment in doing it'.

Four candidates described critical reflection explicitly in their interviews. One stated 'self-assessment made you reflect on your progress, question how appropriate your goals were and how far you had come'. Another described how 'difficult it was to meet my idealistic goals, and the negative feelings I had to deal with about not reaching my own goals'. The third described a process in which she came to 'get so much more' from the course because of the goals, after feeling at the mid-point of the course 'a little sense of guilt, letting you down, letting myself down'. She described her feelings early in the course: 'This course made me think, [and] I don't know if I can do all this, if I can be a teacher'. The fourth candidate finished her interview with the comment, 'This is a challenging year and this course concentrated my self-development and my self-criticism'.

About half the candidates also critiqued the practice of self-assessment, many making constructive suggestions for its improvement. The theme debated throughout was whether or not more structure and clearer criteria were needed to make the process work better. Those strongly recommending structure said 'half-way through we should have re-capped', and what was needed was 'in the middle, a brief activity, which goals you've achieved and which you need to work on; in a pair, say what you are planning to do'. One simply asked 'what criteria?' and another recommended 'a list of things to rate yourself at the beginning and the end'. Many suggested that I should have prompted discussions at regular intervals throughout the course so the reflection on goals was ongoing and so the members of the class could 'hear each other and learn from each other like we do with cases'. On the other side, there were suggestions of a 'qualitative assessment' with no mark assigned, and the candidate who said, 'It was not a point system. I liked it much more that way; it was a better indication because you were doing it because you wanted to learn'.

There were also comments on cases. Although I did not explicitly ask students to comment on learning with cases, many took the opportunity to reiterate their views on this subject. Many focused on the ambiguity inherent in teaching exceptional learners in inclusive classrooms: a simple statement of this was 'cases were hard initially', while more complex comments included 'it's scary, all the unanswered questions in this field'. One candidate with considerable experience outside educational settings with individuals with severe disabilities said, 'I knew what disabilities were, but this is much more philosophical than I thought; it was not as clear cut as I thought it would be'. Another said, 'I came with a fair bit of experience, but the course challenged me to think, how do I adapt teaching?' One stated explicitly that she 'liked the write-up part of cases because it helped to organize my thinking'. Despite the ambiguities, many suggested that the case discussions influenced them in their autumn practicum: 'I had a different feeling when I went to my school for practice teaching; I included a student who was totally blind'. 'How many students are [exceptionally] challenged was the first thing I thought of when I walked into a classroom'. 'The case studies were based on teaching, and then we used them when we taught'. 'I was aware of myself and others interacting with and effectively including these children'. One student remarked with pride, 'My awareness of a girl with disabilities was noted on my summative report by the associate teacher'.

The teacher candidates knew that I was studying my own teaching with cases as a member of a self-study group. Sometimes I felt that some of them were joining me in self-study. Many seemed to see the time that Nicole and I stayed after class to chat, the SAC meetings, informal assessment, and the interviews as opportunities to question their actions as well as mine. I think that about half the class members viewed these 'critical conversations about teaching' (Brookfield, 1995, p. 140) as opportunities to recognize how much they were taking for granted in their own teaching, while pointing out to me what I took for granted in my teaching with them.

What I've Learned: 'The Knowledge is in the Experience, Not in the Story'

As I write these reflections I cannot help but question whether I have learned what I will need to know to work effectively in the Critical Issues course, in fall 1996, when we pilot our restructured BEd program. Learning from experience is an ongoing and demanding process. I recently told two of my self-study colleagues that 'the knowledge is in the experience, not in the story' while discussing the storied way we talk about our experience. Placing 'the authority of experience' (Munby and Russell, 1995) and case learning at the centre of teacher education makes sense, but only experience will teach us what we need to know to do this well. And reflecting critically will help us to ferret out what we are taking for granted (6 May 1996).

Now, in May, 1997, I can look back. I have piloted the Critical Issues course and helped two school groups to lead case discussions with their peers. I have been impressed by the cases written by candidates reflecting on four months' experience (Hutchinson and Martin, 1997; Munby and Hutchinson, 1997). And I have learned that I have much to learn if I am to support my colleagues who will join me in Critical Issues in 1997–1998.

What did I learn in this action research intended to improve my teaching with cases? Looking back, I see that I have used the term 'critical reflection' loosely and inconsistently. When I applied it to my students' written cases, I looked for explicit perspective-taking, consideration of consequences, and questioning of assumptions. However, most other times, I accepted implicit indications of what Brookfield (1995) describes as recognizing what we take for granted about teaching. Sometimes I considered all critical comments to be critically reflective.

I think I have tried to learn from many aspects of my teaching simultaneously. Because I experienced all these aspects in context, the multiplicity of foci makes sense to me. However, I am wondering whether my account will prove helpful to others. Perhaps I can only contribute to others' learning from self-study by providing encouragement. For me, self-study has enabled a focus on my teaching that has led teacher candidates and me to question our assumptions about teaching, wholeheartedly and together. If my account encourages other teacher educators to embark on this process, perhaps that is all I can expect. It seems inconsistent to extol learning from experience while assuming we can learn from others' self-study without conducting our own.

Inconsistencies appear in my learning in other ways. Sometimes I took two actions in my teaching, and both seemed to me consistent with my experience and with my reading. But these actions, when taken in a specific context, were contradictory. Back and forth I go, it seems, between the experienced and the theoretical and the experienced in a disjointed, recurrent and gradually enlightening way. Perhaps this is what it means to learn to teach — to learn to perceive and act by tacitly experiencing the specifics in a situation and in another situation and in another.

Critics have argued that the dominant rhetoric in teaching and teacher education undermines the aim of developing teachers who are critically reflective in their work (Garrison and Rud, 1995). Studies like this one move beyond rhetoric about critical reflection to practical knowledge of teacher educators and teacher candidates. This is practical knowledge in the education of teachers who can deal with teaching's ambiguity in the particularly vexing area of inclusive education.

References

BROOKFIELD, S.D. (1995) *Becoming a Critically Reflective Teacher*, San Francisco: Jossey-Bass.

CARTER, K. (1991) 'Conveying classroom knowledge through case methods', in HARRINGTON, H. and THOMPSON, M. (eds) *Student Motivation and Case Study Manual*, Chapel Hill, NC: University of North Carolina.

CHRISTENSEN, C.R. and HANSEN, A.J. (1987) *Teaching and the Case Method: Text, Cases, and Readings*, Boston: Harvard Business School.

COHEN, E.G. (1994) 'Restructuring the classroom: Conditions for productive small groups, *Review of Educational Research*, **64**, 1–36.

DEWEY, J. (1929) *The Quest for Certainty: A Study of the Relation of Knowledge and Action*, New York: Minton, Blach.

DEWEY, J. (1916/1961) *Democracy and Education*, New York: Macmillan.

FLORIO-RUANE, S. (1990) Creating your own case studies: A guide for early field experience', *Teacher Education Quarterly*, **17**, 1, 29–42.

GARRISON, J. and RUD, A.G. (1995) *The Educational Conversation: Closing the Gap*, Albany, NY: State University of New York Press.

GREENWOOD, G.E. and PARKAY, F.W. (1989) *Case Studies for Teacher Decision Making*, New York: Random House.

HARRINGTON, H.L. (1991) 'The case as method', *Action in Teacher Education*, **12**, pp. 1–10.

HARRINGTON, H. and GARRISON, J. (1992) 'Cases as shared inquiry: A dialogical model of teacher preparation', *American Educational Research Journal*, **29**, pp. 715–35.

HARRINGTON, H., QUINN-LEERING, K. and HODSON, L. (1994) 'Written case analyses and critical reflection'. Paper presented at the Annual Meeting of the American Educational Research Association, New Orleans.

HARRINGTON, H., QUINN-LEERING, K. and HODSON, L. (1996) 'Written case analyses and critical reflection', *Teaching and Teacher Education*, **12**, pp. 25–37.

HUTCHINSON, N.L. (1994) 'Preparing teachers for inclusive classrooms: Reflections on teaching with cases', *Exceptionality Education Canada*, **4**, 3&4, pp. 75–89.

HUTCHINSON, N.L. (1996) 'Student-authored case studies and critical reflection in a course on inclusive education'. Paper presented at the Annual Meeting of the American Educational Research Association, New York.

HUTCHINSON, N.L. and MARTIN, A.K. (1997) 'The challenges of creating inclusive classrooms: Experiences of teacher candidates in a field-based program'. Paper presented at the Annual Meeting of the American Educational Research Association, Chicago.

KESSELS, J.P.A.M. and KORTHAGEN, F.A.J. (1996) 'The relationship between theory and practice: Back to the classics', *Educational Researcher*, **25**, 3, pp. 17–22.

KLEINFELD, J. (1991a) 'Changes in problem-solving abilities of students taught through case methods'. Paper presented at the Annual Meeting of the American Educational Research Association, Chicago.

KLEINFELD, J. (1991b) 'Wrestling with the angel: What student teachers learn from writing cases'. Paper presented at the Annual Meeting of the American Educational Research Association, Chicago.

McINTYRE, D.J. and O'HAIR, M.J. (1996) *The Reflective Roles of the Classroom Teacher*, Belmont, CA: Wadsworth.

MUNBY, H. and HUTCHINSON, N. (1997) 'Using experience to prepare teachers for inclusive classrooms: Teacher education and the epistemology of practice', *Teacher Education and Special Education* (submitted).

MUNBY, H. and RUSSELL, T. (1995) 'The authority of experience in learning to teach: Messages from a physics methods class', *Journal of Teacher Education*, **45**, pp. 86–95.

NUSSBAUM, M.C. (1986) *The Fragility of Goodness*, Cambridge, MA: Cambridge University Press.

RICHARDSON, V. (1994) 'Conducting research on practice', *Educational Researcher*, **23**, 5, pp. 5–10.

RORTY, R. (1982) 'Method, social science, and social hope', in *Consequences of Pragmatism*, Minneapolis: University of Minnesota Press, pp. 191–216.

SCHWAB, J. (1978) *Science, Curriculum, and Liberal Education: Selected Essays*, Chicago: University of Chicago Press.

SHULMAN, J. (ed.) (1988) *The Intern Teacher Casebook*, San Francisco: Far West Laboratory for Educational Research and Development.

SILVERMAN, R., WELTY, W.M. and LYON, S. (1992) *Case Studies for Teacher Problem Solving*, Toronto: McGraw-Hill.

SYKES, G. and BIRD, T. (1992) 'Teacher education and the case idea', *Review of Research in Education*, **18**, pp. 457–521.

UPITIS, R., RUSSELL, T., WHITEHEAD, L. and HUTCHINSON, N. (1995) *BEd Program Revision*, (draft 2). Kingston, ON: Queen's University, Faculty of Education.

9 Self-study of Teacher Education Practices Through the Use of the Faculty Course Portfolio

Joan P. Gipe

I first became interested in exploring the potential of the course portfolio as a methodology for self-study during the Fall of 1994. I had been awarded a sabbatical to develop a teaching portfolio[2] as a possible means for faculty evaluation, and through that process learned of the course portfolio as a model for teaching evaluation being explored at the University of Wisconsin–La Crosse (Cerbin, 1993). Educators interested in self-study and in the documentation of effective teaching practices for purposes of promotion, tenure, and/or merit may find the course portfolio to be an efficient means to achieve both endeavors.

Background and Theoretical Framework

My interest in self-study began rather abruptly in December 1992. I can state this unequivocally because it was during the National Reading Conference that year, when I chose to attend an alternative session entitled *Creating Communities of Inquiry: Teacher Educators Exploring Together Who We Are*, that I realized I both wanted and needed to study my own teaching practices. At that very first meeting each participant identified a personal teaching dilemma. My dilemma focused on a perception of my role as a course instructor to mean that I alone was in control of the course; that is, I alone must determine the goals, the readings, the assignments, the grading, the agenda, and the flow of each class. However, my teaching beliefs were in conflict with this perceived role. I believe that learning occurs best when learners are actively involved in deciding what they will learn and how they will demonstrate that learning. I also believe learners share a social need to communicate their learning with others. Therefore, I made a commitment to that group of colleagues to address my personal dilemma of 'control' by turning

---

[1] 'A course portfolio contains material that documents the nature and quality of teaching and learning in one course — reflecting the range and scope of the course, the goals, methods and outcomes' (Cerbin, 1993, p. 92).

[2] 'The teaching portfolio is . . . a careful, thoughtful gathering of documents and materials that judiciously and honestly reflect a professor's teaching effectiveness' (Seldin, Annis and Zubizarreta, 1995, p. 238).

over more responsibility to students for their own learning. I was to report back at next year's conference on my progress in confronting this dilemma. This, then, was my formal introduction to the study of my teaching practices (cf. Richards, Moore and Gipe, 1996).

As I began reading the various literatures related to self-study, I recognized self-study research to be research grounded in the knowledge and questions held by the practitioner, or practitioner inquiry (Drennon, 1994). This led me to learn more about the area of action research that seeks to directly link theory and practice. In other words, if I agree with a social constructivist theory of learning that describes knowledge as being constructed by the individual learner through social interactions with other people, then my teaching practices must reflect that orientation. Upon using teaching practices in my classroom that align with my chosen theory, I can then 'test' their effectiveness by evaluating how well my students learn under those conditions. The results could lead to a change in teaching practices or a reconsideration of the chosen theory. 'The purpose of action research, then, is to make teaching, and the inquiry process that is part of it, explicit, which enables improvement' (Bullough and Gitlin, 1995, p. 180). Whitehead (1995, p. 122) summarizes this action planning process: 'I experience a problem because some of my educational values are negated; I imagine a solution; I act in the direction of the imagined solution; I evaluate the actions; and I modify my actions/ideas in the light of my evaluations'.

Since I am a teacher educator, I work with adult learners. Menges (1994) discusses several theoretical perspectives that are appropriate for study of post-secondary teaching. I have found the social perspective (i.e. conceives of the classroom as a group situation and conversation as the means for learning) and the integrated cognitive/ motivation perspective (i.e. for learning to last, both cognitive and motivation variables must be considered) to be two theoretical perspectives that most closely align with my own views about teaching and learning. Thus, these are the theories that I find myself testing in my self-study research efforts. It was not until I investigated various theoretical frameworks for self-study that I realized I had engaged in aspects of self-study research for some time. For example, I have always sought feedback from students about my teaching practices. Often this feedback took the form of a journal, or narrative statements written by students to discuss their learning in the course. I would then use this information to make changes in the course syllabus for the next semester. This overdue realization points out the recursive nature of our professional development. In going forward we also look back.

Self-study research, then, contains elements of life history as well as narrative and reflection (Clandinin and Connelly, 1991; Connelly and Clandinin, 1990, 1994). Cole and Knowles (1995) view self-study research as grounded in a life history perspective and describe self-study 'as an opportunity to explore our personal professional practice' (p. 2). It was not until I read someone else's narrative of her professional development (Beattie, 1995) that I realized from where my own dilemma over control in the classroom originated.

In her book *Constructing Professional Knowledge in Teaching: A Narrative of Change and Development*, Mary Beattie (1995) relates a story (or a re-story as she puts it) of her first year as a teacher. It is a story of her experience as a fifth grade teacher across the hall from Miss Doak's sixth grade classroom. As Mary Beattie's fifth graders got noisy, which was often, Miss Doak would appear at her door and glower at those fifth graders. They would immediately become quiet, with order and control restored. Soon Mary 'decided that I could not begin to think of myself as successful until I 'got things under control'' (p. 17). While I was reading Mary's words it suddenly occurred to me that it was my own similar episode as a first-year fifth grade teacher that had stayed with me for so many years and had kept me from trusting my students to take responsibility for their own learning.

Mary Beattie has described her development (and my development!) so well that I will repeat her words here:

> 'Classroom management' for me then was associated with control, and when I was successful I understood it as 'being in control'. I have since come to understand 'class-room management' in the context of relationships and acceptable classroom behavior as those behaviors present in relationships where people know and respect each other. As my relationships with students grew and strengthened, my expectations for classroom behavior and interactions were being met. What I had then thought of as my 'good classroom management skills' and 'being in control', I now understand as my growing understandings of relationships and my ability to make this knowledge work for me in the classroom. (p. 18)

Meanwhile, I had made a commitment to a group of fellow teacher educators to report back on my efforts to come to terms with my dilemma of control; that is, giving more responsibility for learning to my students. I needed to develop a way of presenting and sharing my work in this regard. Although I had been pursuing ways to demonstrate the scholarly essence of teaching to university administrators, I had never before written about my own teaching.

I found that the literature on teaching portfolios, teaching cases, and case methods in the study of teaching provided potential formats for presentation of self-study ex-plorations (Anderson, 1993; Shulman, 1992; Wassermann, 1993; Wolf, Whinery and Hagerty, 1995). Additionally, the notion of self-study as assisting in the 'creation of living educational theory' (Pinnegar and Russell, 1995, pp. 5–6; Whitehead, 1993) demands representation that is also living. I submit that a course portfolio can serve as documentation of one's own living educational theory, at least as it relates to the life of one course. It enabled me to show my colleagues how I had relinquished control and allowed my students to take control of their own learning.

Description of the Course Portfolio and Illustrative Action Research Projects

I constructed a course portfolio using the guidelines and suggested elements set forth by William Cerbin (in Anderson, 1993). These elements are:

- A Teaching Statement that explains what the instructor wants to accomplish and how his or her teaching is intended to bring this about. The statement explains the relationship between intended outcomes and teaching practices.
- A course syllabus that offers an example of the primary nature of the course as explained to students.

- A copy of key assignments and learning activities, two or three assignments, that suffice as representatives of the types of academic work students engage in during the course. The assignments should address one or more of the course goals in substantive ways.
- Examples or summaries of students' performance on the key assignments.
- A summary of student perceptions of teaching and learning that are collected during the semester.
- A self-assessment that summarizes the extent to which students attained the course objectives, and students' perceptions of their experience, and given the outcomes, what the instructor might do differently next time. (p. 92)

During the development of my course portfolio it became clear to me that the process itself of compiling the portfolio is the essence of self-study. The attempt to explain specific teaching practices in relation to what one hopes to accomplish in a course is certainly one aspect of self-study. This very first element of a course portfolio can reveal contradictions between what one believes and what one does in a course. Likewise, issues of student learning as a result of the particular course activities gives impetus to action research studies to support, or not support, those teaching practices.

Within my first course portfolio effort I can point to two such action research projects that probably would not have come about if I had not developed the portfolio. One of these has to do with the issue of peer evaluation and my dissatisfaction with the way peers were evaluating each other (see self-study case in Appendix A). The second has to do with asking students to rank course activities, representing my teaching practices, as to each activity's impact on their learning (see item #3 in Appendix B). Thus, the development of a course portfolio can, in itself, be viewed as a methodology for self-study. From the process of development will come a clearer understanding of one's educational values, contradictions between these values and teaching practices, and ideas for pursuing a greater degree of agreement between values and practices.

Results of Action Research Projects

The first effort on peer evaluation remains ongoing, but results over a three semester period indicate the need for the students themselves to develop specific and objective criteria for use during peer evaluation. The evolution of ways to assist peer evaluation reflects this understanding as my initial peer evaluation form was too general and far too subjective in terms of criteria. Items from the first peer evaluation form and from the most recent form can be seen in Appendix C. As an instructor in control, I had developed the initial form that, with hindsight, provided no specific criteria for students to objectively evaluate a peer's presentation. The current form, which I only facilitated as an instructor giving control for learning to her students, shows specific and objective criteria developed by the students themselves prior to making their presentations.

The second effort of students ranking the effectiveness of course activities on their learning, again with three phases completed, indicates that the use of collaborative learning groups, specifically triad groupings (Q 3.3 in Appendix B) was clearly the most effective teaching practice with 28 per cent of all students ($n = 67$) ranking this activity first. Investigating topics of personal interest (Q 3.9, with 19 per cent ranking this activity first), weekly summary sheets (Q 3.5, with 18 per cent ranking this activity first), demonstration lessons presented by others (Q 3.2, with 16 per cent ranking this activity first); and preparing a demonstration strategy lesson for others to observe (Q 3.1, with 8 per cent ranking this activity first) are the most effective course/teaching practices for assisting student learning, with this last followed closely by students' self-examination of pre and post questionnaires regarding teaching beliefs and philosophies (Q 3.7, with 7.5 per cent ranking this activity first). (Refer to Appendix B for Question-naire items.)

Discussion of the Results

The results of both of these self-study action research projects support the theoretical perspectives that I hold about the teaching and learning relationship. In keeping with the social perspective that learning, specifically for adults, occurs in a social context, conceptual frameworks such as collaborative learning and group process theory provide characteristics that should assist student learning. Efforts to structure my course to further these characteristics (e.g. collaborative group work (triads), demonstrating instructional strategies to others) proved to be positive elements for assisting student learning. These teaching practices both encourage dialogue with peers that follows individual study and preparation.

Similarly, the integrated cognitive/motivation perspective requires that both learning, or cognitive, strategies (e.g. elaboration strategies, peer learning) and the motivation of the learner (e.g. self-efficacy, intrinsic/extrinsic goal orientation) must be addressed if learning is to be lasting. I believe the responses, reflections, and connections that students were required to write in order to complete weekly summary sheets of their assigned readings comprise an elaboration strategy that demonstrates clearly to students the importance of writing in the acquisition and clarification of knowledge. The follow-up collaborative group (triads) discussions then allowed for increased opportunities for individuals to verbalize and clarify their understandings of course content with their peers and the instructor. Self-evaluation and peer evaluation also helped students realize it is their own behavior that accounts for their grades (i.e. self-efficacy). Being able to choose a topic of personal interest or concern provided each student the opportunity to achieve a personal benefit, such as learning more about multiple intelligences theory or developing a literature-based thematic unit for third grade students (i.e. intrinsic/extrinsic goal orientation).

Conclusion

To develop the course portfolio I first had to state my teaching beliefs as clearly as I could at the time. Next, I tried to match learning experiences assigned for my course to those stated beliefs. In so doing, dilemmas, consistencies, and inconsistencies emerged in my own teaching. In response, I addressed those issues directly through action research. The results of the action research projects further informed my beliefs, strengthening some and causing me to question others. If improvement of teaching through self-study of teaching practices is a desirable endeavor for educators, then I can state emphatically that the course portfolio is a viable means of promoting inquiry into one's own teaching.

At the beginning of this chapter I also mentioned the course portfolio as useful for documenting the scholarship of teaching toward purposes of faculty evaluation for promotion, tenure and/or merit. The process of developing a course portfolio helps take implicit, personal theories about teaching and learning and make them explicit so they can be examined, tested, and clarified. Such a process should lead to improved teaching. Improved teaching is what colleges and universities say they want. Therefore, another reason to embrace the course portfolio is its effectiveness in documenting the scholarly essence of studying and reporting on one's own teaching practices.

Until recent years I had never considered myself a political person. However, after too many years in the university community of being recognized as an outstanding teacher but not rewarded in the ways that contribute to one's financial security, I reached a point that demanded that I try to affect change in the policies of the university regarding the recognition and reward of teaching excellence. I agree with Jack Whitehead when he points out the significance of economic and political relationships as they relate to educational inquiry. I, too, 'want to see the educational knowledge [that is] embodied in such educative relationships legitimated with as high a value as possible within the Academy and Society' (Laidlaw and Whitehead, 1995). So, in addition to recommending the course portfolio as a way of studying and reporting on one's own teaching practices, I recommend it as a way to document teaching as a research endeavor, worthy of the same consideration as other research effort, for evaluation purposes within the university setting.

References

ANDERSON, E. (ed.) (1993) *Campus Use of the Teaching Portfolio: Twenty-five Profiles*, Washington D.C.: American Association for Higher Education, pp. 92–6.

BEATTIE, M. (1995) *Constructing Professional Knowledge in Teaching: A Narrative of Change and Development*, New York: Teachers College Press.

BULLOUGH, R.V. and GITLIN, A. (1995) *Becoming a Student of Teaching: Methodologies for Exploring Self and School Context*, New York: Garland.

BURKE, R.J. (1969) 'Some preliminary data on the use of self-evaluations and peer ratings in assigning university course grades', *Journal of Educational Research*, **62**, pp. 444–8.

CERBIN, W. (1993) 'University of Wisconsin-La Crosse', in ANDERSON, E. (ed.) *Campus Use of the Teaching Portfolio: Twenty-five Profiles*, Washington, DC: American Association for Higher Education, pp. 88–96.

CLANDININ, D.G. and CONNELLY, F.M. (1991) 'Narrative and story in practice and research', SCHON, D. (ed.) *The Reflective Turn: Case Studies in and of Educational Practice*, New York: Teachers College Press, pp. 258–81.

COLE, A.L. and KNOWLES, J.G. (1995) 'Methods and issues in a life history approach to self-study', RUSSELL, T. and KORTHAGEN, F. (eds) *Teachers Who Teach Teachers: Reflections on Teacher Education*, London: Falmer Press, pp. 130–51.

CONNELLY, F.M. and CLANDININ, D.J. (1990) 'Stories of experience and narrative inquiry', *Educational Researcher*, **19**, 5, pp. 2–14.

CONNELLY, F.M. and CLANDININ, D.J. (1994) 'Telling teaching stories', *Teacher Education Quarterly*, **21**, 2, pp. 145–58.

DRENNON, C. (1994) 'Adult literacy practitioners as researchers', *ERIC Digest*. Washington, DC (ERIC Document Reproduction Service No. ED 372 663).

LAIDLAW, M. and WHITEHEAD, J. (1995) *An Educational Epistemology of Practice*, [On-line paper]. Available: http://www.bath.ac.uk/~edsajw/home.html.

MENGES, R.J. (1994) 'Promoting inquiry into one's own teaching', in HOWEY, K.R. and ZIMPHER, N.L. (eds) *Informing Faculty Development for Teacher Educators*, Norwood, NJ: Ablex, pp. 51–97.

PINNEGAR, S. and RUSSELL, T. (1995) 'Self-study and living educational theory', *Teacher Education Quarterly*, **22**, 3, pp. 5–9.

RICHARDS, J., MOORE, R. and GIPE, J. (1996) 'Inward journey: Putting our stories next to yours', *Teaching Education*, **8**, 1, pp. 65–73.

SELDIN, P., ANNIS, L. and ZUBIZARRETA, J. (1995) 'Using the teaching portfolio to improve instruction', WRIGHT, W. ALAN (ed.) *Teaching Improvement Practices*, Bolton, MA: Anker Publishing, pp. 237–54.

SHULMAN, J.H. (ed.) (1992) *Case Methods in Teacher Education*, NY: Teachers College Press.

WASSERMAN, S. (1993) *Getting Down to Cases: Learning to Teach with Case Studies*, New York: Teachers College Press.

WHITEHEAD, J. (1993) *The Growth of Educational Knowledge: Creating Your Own Living Educational Theories*, Bournemouth: Hyde Publications.

WHITEHEAD, J. (1995) 'Educative relationships with the writings of others', in RUSSELL, T. and KORTHAGEN, F. (eds) *Teachers Who Teach Teachers: Reflections on Teacher Education*, London: Falmer Press, pp. 113–29.

WOLF, K., WHINERY, B. and HAGERTY, P. (1995) 'Teaching portfolios and portfolio conversations for teacher educators and teachers', *Action in Teacher Education*, **17**, 1, pp. 30–9.

Appendix A: Self-study Case: Peer Evaluation

By Joan P. Gipe, Course Instructor

Over the past few semesters I have been working to involve my students more as participants in their own learning. A natural consequence of placing responsibility for learning with the students is that they also have more input into assessment and evaluation, and ultimately, their final grades. My students are now asked to participate in both self and peer evaluation. Both of these alternate types of assessment provide me with information that I use to determine students' final grades. While the limited research available on this issue (Burke, 1969) indicates that peer evaluation is more accurate than self evaluation, I have not been pleased with the results of my peer evaluation efforts.

One night in my graduate level Developmental Reading course stands out. One of the assignments in this course is to become an 'expert' on a topic of choice and prepare a 10–15 minute oral presentation, accompanied by a one-page summary handout for all classmates. This assignment is to be peer evaluated immediately following the presentation using a form, prepared with student input, that provides evaluation criteria.

My expectations, stated orally, were that students listen critically and be prepared to ask questions of presenters. I also expected students to write comments about various aspects of the presentation on the evaluation sheet. Maximum points to be earned was 15. The average of the individual scores was the grade for this presentation (i.e. with 29 students in class, each student's presentation score would be the average of 28 peer's evaluations).

Prior to this particular class session, several presentations had already been given the week before so I had calculated those scores. They were all very high (14–15), and most were higher scores than I would have given. So I decided I needed to do more modeling of the rigor I expected from students. I began to ask questions of the presenters. I thought I asked questions that weren't particularly difficult, just clarification of some point in the presentation — questions the presenter should have been able to answer if well-prepared to do the presentation. However, the mood of the presentations began to change until finally, following one presentation, Patty, a very bright student and one I admire and respect, said 'Now Dr. Gipe, go easy'. Her comment was followed by a few nods and 'yeses' from other students so I felt as if I was being viewed as the 'Grand Inquisitor.' I smiled and said in a light-hearted way, 'Well, if the rest of you would ask some questions, I wouldn't have to'. The students did begin to ask more questions, but the peer evaluations remained very high with very few written comments being made. As I looked back on it, it seemed to me that the students were simply trying to be supportive of their peers in a situation that causes anxiety for many of them (the oral presentation). It was almost like they were evaluating based on the difficulty of the situation rather than the quality of the presentation. I say almost because in one instance students *did* give a poor evaluation to a student who truly deserved a poor evaluation, but this was a most obvious case of someone being under-prepared.

My questions are these: Are my students taking peer evaluation seriously and how can I help them to do so? Is peer evaluation viable when the evaluation will influence a student's final grade? Can peer evaluation be more discriminating? How can I help students engage in peer evaluation and still feel supportive of their peers?

Appendix B: Final Exit Sheet

PLEASE COMPLETE ANONYMOUSLY, BUT PROVIDE TODAY'S DATE

DATE: _____

1. On a 1 (low) to 10 (high) scale, how would you rate the overall value of this course to your professional goals?
2. On a 1 (low) to 10 (high) scale, how would you rate the instructor's effectiveness in assisting your learning?
3. Read the following list of course activities. Then rank EACH ONE in numerical order (1 = most helpful, 2 = second most helpful, 3 = third most helpful, etc.) according to how helpful that experience was in facilitating your learning of the course content.

Q 3.1_____ Preparing for and demonstrating one literacy instructional strategy
Q 3.2_____ Demonstration of instructional strategies by others
Q 3.3_____ Triad/small group discussions
Q 3.4_____ Whole class discussions
Q 3.5_____ Weekly summary sheets (check all that were helpful)

_____ a. responding to chapter questions
_____ b. identifying a 'muddiest point' for group discussion
_____ c. participating in specified chapter activities
_____ d. reflecting and making connections on chapter content
_____ e. relating a personal story relevant to chapter content

Q 3.6_____ Self-evaluation of work

Q 3.7_____ Examining pre-post questionnaires/teaching case on educational beliefs and teaching orientation
Q 3.8_____ Preparing an autobiographical sketch for literacy
Q 3.9_____ Investigating a question/concern of personal interest
Q 4.0_____ Maintaining a reading log of professional readings
Q 4.1_____ Peer evaluation of class report
Q 4.2_____ Feedback from instructor on weekly summary sheets
Q 4.3_____ Preparing the Final Reflective Statement
_____ Other (please indicate activity) _____

Please place your final exit sheet in the large, brown envelope available on the front table.

Appendix C: Initial Peer Evaluation Criteria

1. On a scale of 1 (low) to 15 (high), how would you rate the overall value of this presentation?
2. What did you like best about the presentation?
3. What would have made this presentation even better?
4. What additional comments would you like to make?

Current Peer Evaluation Criteria

Directions: For each item answer the question using the scale provided. Comments are encouraged in order to supply more detailed feedback for the presenter. Your efforts in this peer evaluation process are greatly appreciated.

1.	Did the presenter clearly state her/his objective(s)?	yes	somewhat	no
2.	Was the topic's relevance to literacy clear or explained?	yes	somewhat	no
3.	Was the presentation clear and easy to follow?	yes	somewhat	no
4.	Is the presenter knowledgeable about the topic?	yes	somewhat	no
5.	Was the information shared reflective of a strong research effort?	yes	somewhat	no
6.	Were plans or ideas for applications or implementation provided?	yes	somewhat	no
7.	Did the presenter manage time wisely?	yes	somewhat	no

Comments:

Part IV

Case Studies of Collaborative Self-study

Introduction

Vicki Kubler LaBoskey

This section of the book is designed to contribute to our understanding of what self-study in teacher education is and what role it can and does play in the education of teachers by providing more examples of self-study work. The previous sub-section included samples of individual self-study; this sub-section contains samples of collaborative self-study. Collaborative research is not uncommon in the field of education. Indeed, much research, even if it is written by a single individual, involves more than one researcher, particularly in the data collection and analysis phases. However, there are distinct differences between typical collaborative research and collaborative self-study, as the three samples in this section will demonstrate.

Collaboration in educational research usually means that two or more researchers work together on an investigation. The nature of the study is not fundamentally different from one that an individual researcher would do alone. The primary benefits of this kind of collaboration can be captured by the following sayings: 'Many hands make light work'. and 'Two heads are better than one'. The workload can be shared and more ideas about all phases of the study are likely to be generated. Concerning the latter, it is important to note that the ultimate goal is consensus; the final product is usually written with one voice and does not include a place for 'dissenting opinions'. Traditional collaborative researchers are looking outward together at the same data set; they are, in a sense, facing in the same direction. In contrast, those involved in collaborative self-study are facing one another; they are interacting. Indeed, 'interactive' may be a more apropos referent for multi-party self-study than 'collaborative', especially because, in many cases, the researchers are not just interacting around an external data set; the interactions are the data set, or at least a part of it. This is true of all three self-studies included in this section, to an ascending degree.

The first chapter by Vicki LaBoskey, Katharine Davies-Samway and Sara Garcia documents the impact participation in a cross-institutional teacher educator group had on their individual efforts to improve their practice through action research. This chapter contains a brief history of the teacher educator group, a synopsis of each of the author's action research projects, and a discussion of their self-study on group influence. The data for their research included the three cases of individual action research and the authors' responses to a whole-group questionnaire. The focus of the study was, therefore, more on the outcomes of the participants' interactions with one another and with the group than on the interactions themselves. Their main findings were that group dialogue not only provided the motivation for action research, it also helped in problem clarification and in strategy development. This chapter is important because it shows how group interactions can improve individual self-study, and because it demonstrates how such collective inquiry might make a powerful contribution to the kind of educational reform being called for in the current literature.

The collaborative self-study presented in the second chapter by Pam Lomax, Moyra Evans, and Zoe Parker is also a self-study of individual action research projects and the impact of both the projects and their interactions around those projects on their practice. In this case, however, the focus is much more upon the latter. Unlike LaBoskey, Davies-Samway and Garcia, these teacher educators are working in the same institution with the same group of students — special education teachers. They have their students engage in action research that includes frequent group discussions of those projects. One of the techniques they used to facilitate these interactions is 'memory work' that they describe as 'a collective investigation of experience' often triggered by an individual story. This chapter begins with an example of a student story and a brief description of both the means and outcomes of the group's processing of that story. The authors then proceeded to describe how they used the same technique to explore their practice. They shared two personal pieces, a story and a poem, and transcriptions of some of their responsive interchanges, woven together with interpretive reactions to both. In the process, they not only presented individual lessons learned, they also demonstrated how such a technique might result in the revelation and perhaps transformation of a teacher educator's fundamental values. The chapter is important for its form as well as its content. The benefits of and indeed need for alternative means of reporting on the results of self-study research are apparent in this presentation.

The final chapter in this section, written by Carola Conle, William Louden and Denis Mildon, is a study of group inquiry. The intent of their self-study is to examine what and how they learned from a study group they had while they were doctoral candidates at the same university. To do so, they analyzed a series of taped conversations concerning both content and process; they studied their interactions. They discovered several 'dialectical tensions' implicit in their conversations, one of which is explored in depth in the chapter — free will versus determinism. In the process of this examination, they developed a characterization of joint inquiry that may be particularly well-suited to learning activities or self-study research 'without specific objectives' or 'preordained methodology'. They described their process as having a particular line of development: lived 'tensions with a history' and 'implicit telos' made possible by such group dynamics as mutual respect and frequent reference to personal experience. They stressed that they are not trying to provide a recipe for constructive group inquiry. Instead, they examined a particular instance of what they considered to be successful collaborative self-study in order 'to shed light on the transition period we and many of our colleagues are experiencing as we move toward new paradigms of research and toward new forms of inquiry'. The authors also pointed out how similar types of joint exploration might be helpful to our students in their efforts to learn from their practice. Thus, the study has implications for the curricular choices we make. Such connections between our learning and teaching are the essence of self-study.

10 Cross-institutional Action Research: A Collaborative Self-study

Vicki Kubler LaBoskey, Katharine Davies-Samway and Sara Garcia

We are teacher educators who strive hard to improve on our practice. We have found that it is often hard to focus systematically on one's own practice at the higher education level simply because so little attention is paid in the teaching profession to college and university teaching. We have found that membership in an informal, local group for teacher educators has been very helpful to us as we reflect upon and make changes to our practice. In this paper, we will provide a brief history of the teacher educator group that has supported us; discuss ways that this group has influenced our practice, particularly through teacher inquiry projects that we each embarked on; and examine our efforts in light of current trends in the areas of professional development and school reform.

Effective Teaching at the IHE Level

It is interesting to note the limited nature of the literature devoted to the professional development of teacher educators, key players in both pre-service and inservice teacher education programs. This is particularly disturbing when one considers that no specialized teaching preparation is required of teachers in most institutions of higher education. Knowing how to teach is not a priority at this level of education, despite periodic reports that point out the sorry state of classroom teaching on the IHE (Institutions for Higher Education) level (e.g. Policy Perspectives, 1989). The situation is not much different in teacher preparation programs, where one might expect to find a different state of affairs. It is true that teacher preparation programs often require some K-12 teaching experience of new hirees, that suggests teacher education faculty members have themselves gone through a teacher preparation program. On-going professional development for IHE teachers is frequently limited to attending and presenting at professional meetings. These meetings often focus on the content of one's discipline, a worthy objective, but only a small part of the effective teaching equation. Given that knowledge about adult learning processes and appropriate and effective teaching strategies for this age of learners is not a requirement to teach at the IHE level, what do universities and colleges do to ensure that their faculty members are effective teachers? If our experiences as teacher educators are anything to go by, not much.

Since few professional development support systems and processes are systematically available to IHE teachers, what do concerned faculty members do to improve their teaching? In our case, we did not wait for institutional support. Instead, we took the initiative, sought out other concerned teacher educators in our region, began to meet on a regular basis to explore issues of mutual interest, and formed a group, Bay Area Teacher Educators (BATE).

History of Bay Area Teacher Educators (BATE)

Much of the literature on effective professional development for teachers stresses the need for supportive communities of learners. This is an element that frequently is absent from our lives as teacher educators and it is a void that we set about filling. In September 1994, a small group of teacher educators in the Greater San Francisco Bay Area met to talk about their practice, something they rarely found time to do. Six months later, in March 1995, we held our first official meeting of a group that we eventually named BATE (Bay Area Teacher Educators).[1] Since that March 1995 meeting, we have continued to meet regularly, about once every two months.

As we live and work in communities that are far apart, we meet at alternate locations throughout the San Francisco Bay Area. Our mailing list, which is updated regularly, contains over thirty names from seven institutions (two large state universities, a small state university, a small state research university, a small private university and two small private colleges). It continues to grow through word-of-mouth. All group members are kept apprised of the content of meetings through email communications. Members who are unable to attend frequently ask that we keep them on the mailing list in hopes that their schedules will free them up and allow them to attend.

A core group of about eight teacher educators from six institutions of higher education attend meetings on a regular basis. All members of BATE teach in graduate teacher education programs, most of us working with K-8 credential program candidates and MA students who are elementary teachers. Although several of us teach language and literacy-related courses, group members' disciplines and areas of content expertise vary considerably.

A basic meeting structure has emerged since the inception of BATE. We devote the morning to a focused discussion on an issue that is of interest to group members regardless of area of expertise (e.g. portfolios and portfolio assessment; facilitating classroom discussions around race, class, gender, and SES; program development; and integrating theory into credential program classrooms). After several meetings, we decided to embark on self-study projects. Since then, we have devoted afternoons to discussions about our action research projects.

Though several of us started action research projects, only four of us continued; in this chapter, we discuss three of them. The method we used in the individual studies was action research, broadly defined (Noffke and Zeichner, 1987). The entire teacher educator group served as our action research team as all participants contributed to the discussions of these three studies. Although action research projects are often conducted

---

[1] We are grateful to the Noyce Foundation for its support of BATE.

collaboratively, they rarely resemble the type of collaboration that we experienced. In the case of BATE, we explored quite different topics in distinct institutions with a group of fellow teacher educators, only some of whom were actively involved in self-study. The three of us became interested in looking at the larger picture, that is, the influence of this form of collaborative self-study on our practices and the broader implications of such work for professional development and school reform.

In order to explore these issues, we kept reflective journals (including email messages) and surveyed BATE members. Using these data, we wrote our individual self-study stories. We then compared these three cases in order to identify common influences of the collaborative structure on self-study and professional development. In the remainder of this chapter, we will share our stories, report on the results of the cross-case comparison, and explore the implications of these findings for professional development and educational reform.

Individual Self-study Stories

Vicki's Story

The question I was trying to address in my individual action research project was, 'How can I improve the ways in which I deal with and prepare new teachers to deal with issues of race, class and gender so that greater social justice for my students and theirs might be achieved?' More specifically, as a Caucasian teacher educator working at Mills College in Oakland, California, one of the most diverse cities in the United States, I was concerned with my abilities to work with student teachers (most of whom are also Caucasian women, but some of whom are not) around issues of race, class and gender. I wanted to be able to do so in ways that would not only enhance our skills and propensities for engaging in critically reflective practice, but would also provide us with some concrete possibilities for making a positive difference in the lives of our students. Fortunately, I work in an institution where all of us who direct and teach in the credential programs have similar goals; we all want to improve in these areas. In fact, over the course of the last two years, we have been in the process of redesigning our programs to fulfill the requirements of a new state certification option called Cross-Cultural Linguistic and Academic Development. Therefore, neither the changes I made, nor the results of those changes, can be understood or evaluated in isolation from the whole.

Many models of action research include in the initial phases a thorough exploration of the nature of the problem. Lewin (1946), for instance, referred to this as the reconnaissance phase. Though my particular study was more of a long-term goal than an immediate problem, I still saw the value in gathering systematic information about how my most recent students were feeling with regard to this goal. Therefore, I began the project by sending a questionnaire to all members of my last two graduating classes. Thirty-five per cent of the graduates replied. I analyzed and summarized the questionnaire responses and shared the results with my action research team and with my colleagues at Mills. Based upon those results, I decided to eliminate an assignment I had given in my spring semester curriculum and instruction course called the multi cultural packet, wherein groups of students researched and reported on selected racial/ ethnic groups. Graduates had seen value in it, but felt that it was too isolated from the rest of our work. I decided instead to aim for a more organic incorporation of the information and issues through such means as ongoing discussion and regularly-occurring mini-assignments.

The action research team was particularly helpful with regard to the latter. They assisted me in designing and evaluating two such activities involving the reading of articles and the studying of children from diverse racial/ethnic groups in my students' student teaching classrooms. With the help of my colleagues, I completed two action research cycles during the course of the formal operation of this project. My own informal observations of the activities, along with spontaneous commentary from students, led me to conclude that these particular assignments were not very successful. But in analyzing the outcomes, my team and I decided that it had more to do with rectifiable details, e.g. the somewhat outdated perspective of one of the articles they read, than with the overall idea of multiple mini-lessons accompanied by ongoing conversation.

Again, since it was an action research project, I wanted to gather more systematic evaluation data. At the end of the year, I gave the students in my credential program a questionnaire designed to elicit information about their reaction to the way that the whole program, including my Elementary Curriculum and Instruction course (C and I), had prepared them to deal with issues of race, class and gender.

Nearly 50 per cent of the students (six out of a possible thirteen) returned the questionnaire. All of the respondents had mixed feelings about how well-prepared they were to deal with issues of race, class and gender in their teaching. The two who seemed most confident said that they had been working on these issues all of their lives. Four of the students did make direct reference to some contribution Mills had made to progress in this area, e.g. 'I don't feel that well-prepared for dealing with these issues, but I do feel I learned how to interrupt the process and talk about the problem. I know that last year (before Mills) I didn't have the ability to do that. So this is a good first step'. In a similar vein, several described the overcoming of racism, sexism, etc. as a lifelong process that meant they did not expect any program to 'do the whole job'. However, all of them felt that Mills could do more. They made two main suggestions for change. The first was to add more content, particularly in the areas of class and, ironically perhaps, gender. The second was to make the conversations we did have about race more 'authentic': 'I thought we spoke about teaching using the words "race, class and gender" but never attacked the deeper, underlying issues'.

All of them named the course Introduction to the Profession of Teaching Diverse Students taught by one of my colleagues as the most helpful in learning to deal with the issues. Five of them mentioned aspects of my course as also being quite helpful. None of them made specific reference to the action research mini-assignments, though they may or may not have been referring to them when they made general comments like the following: 'C and I [second semester] touched on the issues again for reinforcement'. The only two specifically-identified features of the course were readings that were not a part of the mini-assignments. However, the tone of all of the responses supported the general goal of the project — to aim for a more organic incorporation of the information and issues — as the following statements exemplify: 'Your class second semester was also helpful. I felt the two of you [referring to my colleague who teaches the Introduction to the Profession of Teaching Diverse Students course and me] worked together to provide us with exposure to issues of race and class', and 'Vicki, your openness and candor on these issues made these things much easier to talk about'.

Only three other features of the program were referred to at all by anyone: a few course readings from the linguistics class; one of my group's seminar sessions on the topic of homophobia; and the journals. It does appear then that I am having some positive influence in my course since it was cited as the second most helpful aspect of the program, preceded only by the course specifically designed to address the issues of race, class and gender. It is possible, of course, that my students made mention of my course because they were addressing their comments to me. However, our students, including this particular group, are typically quite forthcoming with their comments, concerns and suggestions, both positive and negative.

The results of the questionnaire, combined with the team analysis of the particular actions I took during the year, led me to conclude that though the specific interventions I tried were not very successful, I did make progress with my overall aim of continuous, organic incorporation of the issues. The teacher educator group played a significant role in my ability to carry through with this project in a number of ways, as noted in my response to the group questionnaire:

> I found the group very attentive to my issue and respectful of my concerns and struggles. They raised important questions and offered helpful suggestions. They also helped me to make sense of what happened as a result of my interventions. Very basically, the group provided me with the incentive to carry through. I felt responsible for bringing back some sort of information.

Though I would have worked on this goal anyway, I would not have done it in the same way without the group. Not only were my options increased by their input, but my thinking about and processing of these ideas and experiences was enriched and transformed.

The most significant outcome of this project has been the encouragement to persevere in my efforts to improve the ways that I deal with and prepare new teachers to deal with issues of race, class and gender. I have developed more mini-assignments, but, most importantly, in collaboration with my Mills colleagues, I have continued my own education around these issues in order to better prepare myself to engage authentically in any challenging conversations that may arise. In van Manen's (1990) view, this is the optimal outcome of action research — to be more prepared to act with tact, or 'pedagogical thoughtfulness', in our subsequent educational encounters with our students. One example of a current effort to improve my 'pedagogical thoughtfulness' is my involvement in a Mills credential program faculty seminar led by one of my colleagues with particular expertise in the education of second language learners. In these sessions, we read and discuss current research with regard to diverse learners and reflect critically on our relevant experiences. I agree with my students who said that educating ourselves in these areas is a lifelong process. Thus, I am sure that this particular action research project will go on forever, and hopefully, with much help from BATE.

Katharine's Story

At first, it was difficult for me to select a focus for self-study as I was interested in many aspects of my practice. Eventually, I decided to pursue a topic that has been of great interest and concern to me for several years — the impact of the reading/language arts credential program course that I teach on the classroom practices of former students. Although I get helpful short-term feedback on the course through narrative course assessments, I really don't know how well former students feel that they have been prepared to teach reading/language arts once they have responsibility for their own classes. Consequently, although I am constantly rethinking my practice in order to improve it, any adjustments I make lack the kind of insight that direct feedback from former students can provide.

I mailed a questionnaire to 147 former students in which I asked them to provide some background information (e.g. number of years teaching and grade level), comment on their experiences teaching reading/language arts, reflect upon influences on their development as teachers of reading/language arts (e.g. how well the course prepared them), and offer suggestions for improving the course. I also asked them to rate the impact of particular features of the course on their lives as teachers (e.g. the readings, engaging in our own reading/writing/literacy workshop, setting their own goals, and self-assessment).

Approximately 15 per cent of the teachers responded. Most respondents identified themselves and, when they did, I followed up in writing, usually via email. All of these data helped me better understand the relative effectiveness of my teaching. Most respondents felt that the pre-service course had prepared them to teach reading/language arts. In particular, many commented that they had found the hands-on, in-class experiences in which they had been engaged as literate adults (i.e. events in our own weekly literacy workshop) to be particularly helpful in preparing them for organizing and implementing their own instructional programs. In fact, when describing a successful reading/language arts session that they had taught, all but one of the respondents referred to a learning event that they had been immersed in and learned about in our class (e.g. writers' workshop or literature study circles).

Several years ago, I decided to devote a sizable chunk of time to our own in-class literacy workshop, about one hour a week, almost one-fifth of class time. I made this decision when I realized that the majority of pre-service teachers whom I taught had very negative feelings towards reading and writing. I decided that I needed to address my students' fears and apprehensions by actually engaging them in a regularly-scheduled literacy workshop, a time for them to work on self-selected reading and writing because I believe that the most successful teachers of reading and writing are themselves knowledgeable and enthusiastic readers and writers. I also figured that through this type of hands-on experience (and demonstration) I would be able to introduce them to effective strategies for teaching reading and writing to younger learners.

The structure for the literacy workshop is predictable so that participants can prepare themselves for it prior to coming to class, and involves the following features: a five to ten minute mini-lesson grounded in the needs of participants (e.g. locating poetry, changing point-of-view in one's writing, the use of semi-colons, and writing annotated bibliographies); a five-minute check-in when participants briefly indicate how they will spend their time during literacy workshop (e.g. second draft of an opinion piece, conferring on a final draft of a children's story, reading professional articles); thirty to forty minutes for them to read, write and confer; and a ten-minute whole group sharing time when they share their reading and writing, seek help as readers and writers, and comment on their accomplishments.

Over the years, it has been clear from spontaneous comments and end-of-semester course assessments that students valued and appreciated this opportunity to develop their own literacy (and learn about teaching literacy), but I have often wondered about its impact on their own teaching. I sometimes worried that maybe it was a misuse of classtime, given the enormous range of topics needing to be addressed and the limited amount of time available. This self-study showed me that the decision to continue with a weekly literacy workshop was correct as so many respondents commented that it had been a powerful influence on them as new teachers.

Although the overall content and tone of the questionnaires indicated that the course had a positive impact on these new teachers, several respondents commented that they felt better prepared to teach older students than emergent readers (grades K–3). In particular, they mentioned that they would have liked more attention to teaching (emergent) reading, phonics, spelling and grammar. At first, I was surprised as I knew that we had addressed these issues in class on several occasions. It then occurred to me that two explanations were possible. First, the aspect of the class that had resonated most with them had been their engagement as readers and writers in our literacy workshop. However, as they are literate adults, we did not spend much time on emergent literacy issues such as phonics or grammar. Second, I have always been confronted by a potential dilemma in electing to focus on best practices rather than current practices, even though I know that many former students are much more likely to be hired to teach in schools where, for example, current practices focus on decontextualized skills instruction. As a consequence of the feedback from former students in this area, I have made several changes in my teaching to ensure that pre-service teachers feel much better prepared to teach emergent readers, including the role of and how to teach skills in a learner-centered classroom. They include the following: (a) co-teaching with a primary teacher; (b) requiring that the pre-service teachers work in a primary classroom on a weekly basis; and (c) requiring that the pre-service teachers conduct a series of assessments, observations, and instructional occasions in a primary classroom.

Although I am a former primary grade teacher, most of my recent work in elementary schools has been in upper grade classrooms (grades 3–6). I have kept up with developments in emergent literacy theory, research and practice, but I decided that it would enhance my knowledge of and ability to teach this content if I were to co-teach the course with a primary teacher, Sharon Weight. Sharon is a very experienced primary teacher and has, in recent years, assumed responsibility for emergent literacy staff development in her district. We have just completed co-teaching the course and, as expected, I found it very beneficial in upgrading my skills as a teacher educator.

After my first semester teaching in the credential program, I realized that the pre-service students needed a meaningful classroom experience so that they could connect what they were learning about in class to the real world of elementary teaching. At first, I thought that any classroom would provide them with this kind of practical experience, but I learned very quickly that, unless they were working in carefully-selected classrooms, they were unlikely to see how what they were learning about in class was relevant for elementary classrooms (and was actually implemented by classroom teachers). I then located successful K–8 teachers who are learner-centered and process-oriented. Over the intervening years, this aspect of the course has become increasingly more powerful. This semester, I decided to include only primary teachers to ensure that all students had a K–3 experience with teachers who incorporate best practices. When evaluating the course at mid-semester and at the end of the semester, students repeatedly commented on how much they had learned from the K–3 classroom experience. Their comments, however, were often connected to the third change that I have made in my teaching, requiring that they complete a series of classroom observations (e.g. interactive writing, guided reading, shared reading, writers' workshop), assessments of students (e.g. running records and observation survey tasks), and teaching tasks (e.g. reading and writing conferences and read aloud).

The decision to focus on these elements was arrived at collaboratively with Sharon. We isolated key assessment and teaching strategies and events important for new teachers. We then decided what was reasonable to expect pre-service teachers to complete in a class where they would be relatively infrequent visitors. For example, we decided that it was reasonable to expect them to have conducted one or more running records (a reading assessment) early in the semester, but it wouldn't be reasonable to expect them to be able to make appropriate instructional decisions based on these assessments. Students then wrote up detailed reflections, to which I responded. This K–3 classroom experience was very time-consuming, but I think that it has been extremely worthwhile. In the future, I would limit the number of tasks and spend more time in class working through sample reflections and data as a class so as to enhance the pre-service teachers' abilities to interpret data and make learner-centered instructional decisions.

I was one of the three teacher educators who initially decided to form BATE. I have been a teacher educator for almost twenty years, the last six years at a large state university where there never seems to be time or concerted opportunities to explore our practices with colleagues. I found that I was even more isolated at this university than I had been when working in much smaller programs where colleagues had markedly different responsibilities, backgrounds and interests. My professional development was not on hold as I read, attended conferences, talked from time to time with friends and colleagues, and reflected constantly upon my teaching. However, I did not have opportunities to really engage in sustained conversations or collaborative efforts designed explicitly to address my needs as a teacher educator. I began to feel a terrible sense of discombobulation. On the one hand, as a teacher educator, I stressed the need for school districts to support long-term, focused staff development that K–12 teachers were involved in planning, yet I did not have access to similar opportunities at my own institution.

BATE played a significant role in my self-study. I have lots of questions about my work as a teacher educator and it was hard for me to isolate a topic at first. Having to be prepared for BATE meetings provided me with the incentive to focus on an issue that was very important to me, when there were multiple demands on my time. The group also helped me as I drafted the questionnaire. Although I have often used questionnaires in other research projects and am comfortable constructing them, I found it very helpful to share drafts with group members. Through this focused self-study, I was able to more thoroughly evaluate my effectiveness as a teacher and then take steps to improve.

Because of unusual demands being placed on BATE members, we have not met as regularly this year as in the past and, when we have met, we have often focused on an issue that has become highly politicized in California: the teaching of reading and the role of phonics and phonemic awareness. Consequently, BATE has not focused on self-study this academic year. The impact of the group on my engagement in self-study is reflected in the fact that, although I continue to self-assess and reflect, I am not systematically investigating my own practice. Frankly, I miss the structure for self-study that BATE provided.

Sara's Story

I teach in a small, private, Jesuit university where there has always been an emphasis on teaching for social justice. Most of our candidates are Caucasian and come from economically-privileged backgrounds. Recently, the pre-service credential program in California was changed to include a particular emphasis on the preparation of candidates to teach in linguistically and culturally diverse classrooms. In an effort to respond to these requirements, we restructured the curriculum to coordinate our existing stress on social justice with the new focus on cultural knowledge. We tried to integrate this throughout the program, as well as add some specially-designed experiences, such as visitations to alternative schools and social agencies that serve ethnically diverse communities. I wanted to explore students' thinking about the relationship between social justice and cultural knowledge upon completion of the year-long program (four quarters).

At the end of the academic year, I asked fifty teacher candidates for a closing self-narrative that focused on their feelings about becoming teachers. To capture their reflections, I used a format similar to one I designed for my field practice that is grounded in a series of open-ended questions intended to trigger self-perceptions as they relate to social justice and cultural knowledge. I asked students to tape record their thoughts in a 'story-like' fashion and to think of the faculty as their audience. I asked them to address the following questions: (a) How did you feel about becoming a teacher when you first started the credential program? (b) How do you feel about becoming a teacher now that you are nearly finished? (c) What has changed in your thinking and why? (d) Identify areas for future growth. (e) What is your understanding of social responsibility and/or social justice?

Narrative theory predicts 'disorderly' narration, especially when people are catalyzing experiences through which their political consciousness is fundamentally changed (Kohler-Reissman, 1994). Many of the participants' narratives, especially the lengthy ones, were consistent with Kohler-Reissman's prediction. They were quite disorderly, and the disorderliness seemed to increase over the course of the narrations. The narrative tone also became more intense as students expressed emotive responses to social conditions related to schooling. Through the process of narrating, the students seemed to be trying to make sense of what social responsibility actually meant to them in relation to their teaching. The views expressed by the students were quite similar, though some were more complex than others, and some were presented in a more emotional tone. Most of them went into great detail about various forms of cultural knowledge they felt they had acquired through the process of constant reflection, self-narrative and critical analysis. It is important to note that the questions used to guide these responses did not use the term 'cultural knowledge'.

I asked the students to tape for only fifteen minutes but most recorded both sides of a sixty minute tape. Many students started by narrating how they felt about becoming teachers during their undergraduate experience and, subsequently, covered a multitude of relevant dimensions in constructing their stories. In at least two thirds of the taped narratives, the students reported that there was a clear change in their feelings about becoming teachers. In these comprehensive responses, there were obvious transformations in their thinking. Several of them commented that teaching was a much more complex process than they had originally thought, especially with regard to issues of diversity. Approximately one third of the students only minimally addressed the questions and did not elaborate.

In analyzing the tapes, it appears that the first three guiding questions were just 'warm-up' questions, whereas the last two actually prompted them to reflect on culture. Many students however, did express, even in their responses to the first question, thoughts relevant to working with culturally diverse students in the classroom. Various aspects of their perceptions of cultural knowledge were linked to social justice, as we had hoped. Excerpts that seemed initially incoherent, were the most interesting because in them the students seemed to be struggling to understand how the complex issues surrounding culture, language and ethnicity were linked to their perceptions of themselves as teachers. The reflections of my students seemed to portray a process of striving for inner-balance and for self-understanding of their own development. They articulated how university faculty had helped them shape their perceptions and how often their university experiences attempted to transform their thinking with regard to social justice issues and schooling, but that they felt dissonance when confronted with the 'real' situations in the public school classrooms.

A common theme in the emergent protocols was the notion of 'change.' As the following excerpts illustrate, change in their lives as teachers was evident:

> I want to learn from the parents and use the knowledge that they can bring to me and bring them to my classroom. . . . I am just starting to grow in that area. . . . I hope it will come naturally in my own classroom.

> I feel that my social responsibility as an educator is to affirm each and every student . . . it ranges from affirming students' self identities . . . from the very personal and individual level to the cultural level where we need to affirm the culture that the child comes from. I have really grown already in being able to do that and in having that in front of my mind as I teach. I thank Santa Clara for that because it is not an area that I had realized I needed to work on so much. I appreciate being shown that weakness, I guess, in my thinking.

One thing that is clear from the taped protocols is that the learning with regard to diversity issues and reflective inquiry has only happened at a very fundamental level. It may not be a sufficient foundation for building reflective practice in their growth and development once they get their own classrooms. Theorizing on the academic components of a teacher preparation program may simply not be enough to forge a transformation in thinking, attitude and practice for new teachers. According to Cantor (1997),

> We need to begin to theorize what might be the conditions for changing beginning teachers' beliefs about social justice education, schooling and the teaching profession. Even more important is finding ways to help promote the retention of those values and beliefs, so that when confronted with the cognitive dissonance that occurs when faced with the realities of practice, beginning teachers have both the external and internal support to remain steadfast in their convictions to teach differently from the traditional norms and support changes that lead to social justice education. (p. 21)

As I have noted elsewhere (Garcia, 1997), perhaps new teachers will continue to grow in ways that will make a difference in the quality of schooling for all students, including culturally and linguistically diverse learners, if the process of pre-service teacher development through self-narrative inquiry is continued into the first years of teaching. Clearly articulated in new studies on teacher preparation (Friedlaender, 1997; Darling-Hammond, 1994; Su, 1992) is that the sites where most change occurs is where student teachers, resident teachers and teacher educators are engaging in a constant critical reflection on their practice.

The BATE group for me is the first opportunity I have ever had to reflect with other teacher educators about issues that concern us all. My attitude toward my own practice has changed as a result of working collaboratively with other teacher educators. This is only the beginning of a continual process of growth for me. I now feel that it is very important to provide ongoing staff development to our faculty to facilitate the reflective process in our development as teacher educators in order to lead our group in the exploration of changes that affect our process. Our identities and the validation of one another as teacher educators is important in helping our students become better professionals and better prepared to deal with diversity.

The student reflection tapes I collected at the end of the academic year helped me to gauge how they perceived their own development. As a follow-up, I contacted those students who talked about an intensely transformative experience and have subsequently interviewed them concerning their ongoing growth process. In addition, I have recently formed an action research group of first year teachers from last year's program and am working very closely with them to examine their process. These students are already embracing change and are willing to improve their practice through ongoing reflective inquiry. They are committed to collaboration with colleagues who keep them on task in examining their growth. All of these activities have been a result of my own colla-boration with other teacher educators who have contributed to my own growth and development.

Cross-case Comparison

At the end of the academic year, each of us wrote about how the BATE group interac-tions had influenced our action research projects. In addition, we also responded to the general questionnaire for all BATE members that included a question about the action research discussions. In analyzing these data sources, we discovered three primary ways that the teacher educator group had affected us with regard to our action research projects.

The first and most significant influence was motivational. That is, we all felt that the regular BATE meetings provided us with the incentive to keep going. A group member said, 'The Teacher Educator group was very helpful in keeping me on track. I needed to have done something to share'. A second way that the group seemed to facilitate our studies was by helping each of us to clarify our issues. Another member of the group said, 'The meetings as well as individual feedback on my writing have helped me in legitimizing what I am doing with my research in progress as well as 'tightening up' the focus of what I am doing'. A third way the group helped was by providing specific ideas for change. A third member commented, 'I got some good specific ideas, even though I don't think most of them worked as I had intended, they pointed me in the right direction and as a result of doing them I have a better idea of what to do next year'.

It is clear that in each of our cases it is quite unlikely that the studies would have been done at all had it not been for the group participation. Furthermore, the nature and the form the studies took was influenced by group interactions, and we all seemed to feel that those differences were positive ones. Such teacher educator groups can help to both provide the incentive for self-study and improve the quality of those efforts.

Professional Development and Educational Reform

The work we have done here is significant not only because it has allowed each of us to make improvements in our respective practices, but also because it seems to be exemplary of the kind of professional development efforts being called for in the current school reform literature. Many discussions of school reform suggest that both students and teachers must be actively engaged in establishing and pursuing learning goals. In this vein, Ann Lieberman (1995) suggests that if schools are to be transformed into 'learning organizations', teachers must have opportunities to think about, discuss, try out and hone new practices, and to do so within the context of a professional community.

In arguing for this new model for school reform, one that focuses on the greater capacity of schools and teachers to be responsible for high levels of student learning, Linda Darling-Hammond (1993) points out that for such change to occur, institutions need to invest in the ongoing learning of teachers, what she refers to as 'the human capital of the educational enterprise'. We believe that this is true for teacher educators, also. However, according to Gary Sykes (1996), 'efforts to promote teacher learning that will lead to improved practice on a wide scale have yet to emerge' (p. 465). He suggests that the answer lies in 'approaches [that] often engage teachers in learning about their own learning, in studying their own teaching, and in sustaining relationships with other teachers, both near and far away' (p. 467). Certainly, the action research projects undertaken by us within the context of the BATE group fit this description.

In a similar vein, Judith Warren Little (1993) argues that, because the nature of the educational reforms being proposed is so complex, a transformational approach to professional development is required. She proposes six principles against which such efforts ought to be tested. Our self-study seems to embody most of them, especially the following three:

- Professional development offers meaningful intellectual, social, and emotional engagement with ideas, with materials, and with colleagues both in and out of teaching.
- Professional development takes explicit account of the contexts of teaching and the experiences of teachers. Focused study groups, teacher collaboratives, and long-term partnerships are examples of professional development opportunities that encourage teachers to identify new ideas with respect to their individual and institutional histories, practices and circumstances.
- Professional development prepares teachers to be reflective practitioners, providing possibilities for exploring and questioning one's beliefs and the institutional patterns of practice.

The argument in the current school reform literature is clear: our central aims in education today are to teach our children to be informed, ethical decision-makers, critical problem-posers and solvers, and lifelong learners. To do so, we must have teachers who can do likewise within institutions that encourage and support them in such reflective practice. It follows logically that to prepare teachers to be informed, ethical decision-makers, critical problem-posers and solvers, and lifelong learners, their teachers — teacher educators — must also be encouraged and supported in the acquisition and practice of those attitudes and skills.

The type of collaborative self-study that we engaged in as members of a cross-institutional group of teacher educators seems to hold promise for the improvement of particular aspects of teacher education practice. In addition, it appears to include many of the most salient characteristics of professional development being called for in the current school reform literature, and thus, is very likely to make a valuable contribution to that effort.

References

CANTOR, J. (1997) 'The development of beginning teachers as social justice educators in context of a school–university partnership'. Paper presented at the American Educational Research Association, Chicago, Illinois.

DARLING-HAMMOND, L. (1994) *Professional Development Schools: Schools for Developing a Profession,* New York: Teachers College Press.

DARLING-HAMMOND, L. (1993) 'Reframing the school reform agenda: Developing capacity for school transformation', *Phi Delta Kappan,* **74**, 10, pp. 753–61.

FRIEDLAENDER, D. (1997) 'Giving teachers a voice in the collaboration'. Paper presented at the American Educational Research Association, Chicago, Illinois.

GARCIA, S. (1997) 'Self-narrative inquiry in teacher development: Living and working in just institutions', in KING, J., HOLLINS, E.R. and HAYMAN, W.C. (eds) *Preparing Teachers for Cultural Diversity,* New York: Teachers College Press.

KOHLER-RIESSMAN, C. (1994) *Narrative Analysis,* Newbury Park, CA, Sage.

LEWIN, K. (1946) 'Action research and minority problems', *Journal of Social Issues,* **2**, pp. 34–6.

LIEBERMAN, A. (1995) 'Practices that support teacher development: Transforming conceptions of professional learning', *Phi Delta Kappan,* **76**, 8, pp. 591–6.

LITTLE, J.W. (1993) 'Teachers' professional development in a climate of educational reform', *Educational Evaluation and Policy Analysis,* **15**, 2, pp. 129–52.

NOFFKE, S. and ZEICHNER, K. (1987) 'Action research and teacher thinking: The first phase of the action research on action research at the University of Wisconsin-Madison'. Paper presented at the meeting of the American Education Research Association, Washington, DC.

'THE BUSINESS OF THE BUSINESS' (1989) *Policy Perspectives,* **1**, 3.

SU, J.Z.X. (1992) 'Sources of influence in pre-service teacher socialization', *Journal of Education for Teaching,* **18**, 3, pp. 239–57.

SYKES, G. (1996) 'Reform of and as professional development', *Phi Delta Kappan,* **77**, 7, pp. 465–7.

VAN MANEN, M. (1990) 'Beyond assumptions: Shifting the limits of action research', *Theory into Practice,* **19**, 3, 152–7.

11 For Liberation ... Not Less for Love: A Self-study of Teacher Educators Working with a Group of Teachers Who Teach Pupils with Special Educational Needs

Pam Lomax, Moyra Evans and Zoe Parker

Our particular interests as action researchers involve finding unique ways of representing what we come to know about our practice (Lomax and Parker, 1995; Lomax and Parker, 1996), finding ways of incorporating the affective dimension as part of this knowledge (Belenky, Clinchy, Goldberger and Tarule, 1986; Dadds, 1995), and locating our knowledge within an autobiography of our own learning so that we find authority in our own experience (Lomax, 1994a; Russell, 1995). We aim to help teachers to create theory about their own practice from their action research inquiries (Cochran-Smith and Lytle, 1990; Evans, 1996a; Lomax, 1994b, 1994c, 1995; McNiff, Lomax and Whitehead, 1996). We encourage them to use story as a means of representing their implicit theories about their practice and, subsequently, in a group we help them deconstruct their stories so that their theory becomes more explicit (Carter, 1993; Clandinin, 1992; Convery, 1993; Evans, 1996b; Winter, 1989). We call this living educational theory as it embodies their commitment to live their educational values more fully in their practices (Whitehead, 1993; Lomax, Whitehead and Evans, 1996). For our joint self-study of our practice as teacher educators we have chosen to use this same method because we believe that we should model the learning that we expect in our students and that we should account for ourselves in the same way that they must account for themselves.

This is what we have done in this article. We provide for the reader a demonstration of the process we engaged in during our joint research effort. We invite the reader to be not just an observer but an active participant with us in the process in the same way we are active participants and not simply observers in the action research processes within which our own students engage. Since our own joint self-study emerges from the stories that our students share with us and each other, we begin with a story of one of our students. Then we demonstrate how we use the story with our students to make their values more explicit. Next we represent our method of memory work showing how we build on collective self-reflection. In order to do this we provide one of Moyra's stories followed by our collective engagement with that story examining the issue of vulnerability/liberation. We then move to a deeper examination of the interplay of this dichotomy through our joint presentation and analysis of an experience we had with the group of students that leads us to a deeper understanding of the issue of liberation as we juxtapose it with the idea of colonization of students' minds. Next, we present a poem by Pam and use the poem to capture the aesthetic but almost inexpressible nature of the deepest level of analysis. From there, we interrupt our text with a discussion of a critique of the text by colleagues. This presents the way critique of a text forces a reconsideration of not just the language of the text but sometimes a rethinking of the analysis of the text. The critique in this case causes us to reassert our analysis and our commitment to liberation of our students. At the end, we offer a collective yet individual statement of what we have learned presented in our individual voices.

We invite you, the reader, to experience with us action research as we practice it with our students. We begin with 'Circle Time', a story written by Bernadette Igboaka. The story was read and discussed by the group (tutors and students) and subsequently deconstructed in a written form by Bernadette. Bernadette has given her permission for us to use her work.

Circle Time: Bernadette's Story

Have I escaped Aunt Njideka's question this morning? Would she accept this for an answer? I was too preoccupied with the way it worked. I felt it worked like magic. I did not sleep off but I did not quite listen to the end. Poor Chike. I felt so sorry for him when he arrived. 'Yesterday he scratched me. And me too. He kicked and punched me. There is no room here. We are squashed'. Chike must have been used to hearing this and not the story he came for. Were Obi and Ada really squashed or had Chike squashed out the last drop of patience in them. These were the thoughts that pounded in my mind as I waited for Aunt Njideka to come in with the dreaded question. Dreaded only on days I had not listened or slept off in the moonlight. It was very important that one listens to the moral of the moonlight story as it is in it that one learns about right and wrong and rewards and punishments from the Chi. It was not the moral of Odoziaku's story of last night that appealed most to me. It was her suggestion that we all got up and sat in a circle in order to accommodate Chike and the fact that it worked like magic. Two nights ago Chike had to leave because Okpalanna had said he did not want any trouble. It was not a matter of giving Chike another chance. He had a headache and was not prepared for Chike that night. Last week when Adamma tried to extend her patience it did not work. Chike spoilt it all and had to be sent home. Papa Chike must have punished him. Could either have helped it? Chike's chances had been exhausted. In fact he was already living on borrowed chance.

Making Values More Explicit

Working as a behavior-support teacher in different classrooms in different schools to support teachers who have to deal with children who have educational and behavioral difficulties, Bernadette struggles to live her values in her teaching. In her deconstruction of the story she writes 'I have seen myself living on borrowed chance, clinging to a last ray of hope, the one positive statement that can come as a result of my putting another

Chike in the context of the school and asking specifically how he survived every, say, ten minutes of the school day'. Circle time was written in the early stages of Bernadette's action research. She writes: 'My thoughts have gone back to that morning when I was planning the reply to give to Aunt Njideka and how I felt that I was holding on to something that appeared very important to me for Chike's sake — Odoziaku's magic circle'. The modern day circle is a method of providing a safe and caring context for a particular child whereby the teacher can call on the group to help support the child. Bernadette sees the circle as working against the philosophy of exclusion that seems to be the increasing practice in primary schools. Sharing the story enabled us to empathize with her values and to understand her motivation. More than this, the story encapsulated Bernadette's theories about her practice. In her deconstruction of the story she explores her own position on exclusion and clearly sets out the values that underpin her action research. She states:

> If Chike is possessed by Ajo-mmuo, then such a label for convenience gives the labeler the license to justify wanting to exclude Chike. Okpalanna telling Chike that he did not have the disposition for him on a particular day meant that, much as all the others could join in the moonlight story every night, Chike joining would largely depend on the mood of the person telling the story. If Chike is not present at the moonlight story or sent home, then the storyteller's work will be easier. There will be no interruptions to the story or headaches for the storyteller, nor will there be provocations, in the form of being scratched, kicked, punched, or squashed, for Obi and Ada. But where is equal opportunity for Chike, the eight year old whose behavior is not his making?

Bernadette's story was written for the second session of an eight session course spread over one year. The course involves what we call a staged dissertation, whereby teachers carry out an action inquiry and write it up as they progress. One teaching strategy we use is to encourage teachers to write their concerns into a story at an early stage as we think the act of writing helps them to order their thoughts and the act of offering it to others for discussion enables the author to have a different perspective on the issue. Following on from this, we ask the teachers to provide a written explanation of their story and its link with their developing inquiry. Bernadette's account provides evidence to support our claim that our teaching strategy enables teachers to begin to explore their own implicit theories about their practices. She claims to have made a difference to the inclusion of children with behavioral difficulties within the classrooms where she supports. In fact, she has presented evidence for this assertion at a meeting convened for the specific purpose of validating her research claims with colleagues from work and tutors from the university.

We have chosen Bernadette's story as the flagship of our chapter because it mirrors our own values. We too believe in our own magic circle and its power to create the self confidence for personal liberation. As a student who is part of that circle, Bernadette is well placed to say how important it was for her to have worked within the methodology that we provided. Although we are confident about the testimonial she would provide in answer to such a question, we have chosen instead to answer it through collective self-study. In this, the first of two manuscripts, we explore some aspects of the process of our teaching. The data relates to our work with the students until about the mid point of their program. It includes tape recordings of our classes, our written reflections on the sessions, the students' interim reports, a story and a poem written by Moyra and Pam, respectively, as a stimulus for memory work and the taped memory work. In the second manuscript, completed after the teachers' work is formally assessed, we examine our practice in the light of the evidence of improved practice presented in their dissertations (Lomax, Parker and Evans, 1997).

This is the Use of Memory

Memory work is the name of a technique that involves us using memories of specific events that we have experienced as a basis for group discussion with the intention of deconstructing and reconstructing their meaning. Haug (1987) and Crawford, Kippax, Onyx, Gault and Benton (1992) conceived memory work as active and interventionist, leading to the social reconstruction of meaning rather than to merely personal enlightenment, suggesting that it can contribute to new knowledge. Memory work is a method for a collective investigation of experience, where each person can draw upon her own experience in order to help another understand theirs better. It is a method that rejects the assumption that early experience is a prison of the self in favor of the view that anything a person remembers constitutes a trace in his or her construction of the self (Schratz and Schratz-Hadwich, 1995). We believe that memory work enables us to change that construction of the self so that we can reframe our worlds and become better teachers. The method of memory work often includes the use of story. Individuals write stories about some aspect of their lives and present these to a group to discuss. By drawing upon the others' experiences of similar events, the author can clarify their own active part in the events they have described and place it in a broader social and political setting. It is not just the words of the story, but the gaps and spaces in the account, the things written between the lines, that are explored.

Building on Collective Self-reflection

We wrote two pieces specifically to use as a basis for exploring our work with our students. One is Moyra's fictionalized story, in which she presents her remembered feelings about her first meeting with the students. The other is Pam's poem, intended to express her feelings and her values about working with teachers. Both pieces were written intentionally to focus a memory work session. All the discussions were taped. Subsequently, we listened to the tapes and wrote our further reflections, incorporating quotations from the tapes and other data.

Meanings: Moyra's Story

She was sitting on the steps at the station — a dejected heap, her pale face staring defiantly from the drabness of her clothes and hair. I picked my way round her, pretending not to notice. She reminded me of my childhood — picking my way through the dirty London streets to school. I was alright when I was there, but the journey worried me, then, as now. I remembered that I had skirted around people quickly, got past, walked quicker to avoid them — a different environment. Would I understand them? How would their beliefs and values differ from mine? Could I guess by looking at them? How did their lives touch mine? They taught in inner London. They had stuck it out longer than I had. So it was pretentious that I could advise them. They must struggle with problems I had no idea how to resolve. But my job was not to advise. It was to open out our thinking, to explore meanings, to give them support and confidence to take themselves forward. They started talking, introducing themselves. They didn't mention insurmountable problems. They spoke warmly of the children, of building their self-esteem, of the frustrations of never having enough time, of managing the unmanageable, but they liked each other and extended their warmth to us. We were happy. We could work with these teachers. They told us about the books they had read. We challenged them to criticize what they had read rather than accepting it. They defended themselves. They felt like I often felt. Someone's saying I am wrong. But I need to stand my ground. Keep arguing. Keep saying it is not like that. You have got it wrong. Stop, stop. It is all wrong.

Vulnerability or Liberation?

Pam: Your story . . . focuses very much on you and your fear of the unknown, and that's quite useful. I think it quite useful because it shows us as being vulnerable as teachers, and the teachers' stories are about their fear of the unknown.

Moyra: What about your vulnerable stories?

Pam: Well I haven't got one. I'm not as vulnerable as you are.

Moyra: Why is that?

Pam: I don't know.

Moyra: Well, let's explore it.

Pam: I think it's because I'm quite removed from it.

Moyra: Aren't you vulnerable at all?

Pam: Yes, but I don't consider my work part of my basic me. I don't consider it that way.

I'm incredibly vulnerable about some things, but doing a job of work as best I can, I don't have myself in it in that way.

Does exposing our vulnerabilities to others increase the possibility of empathy between people? Moyra's immediate thought was that her story exposed her own vulnerability. But why should she feel vulnerable? She had been teaching for long enough to feel confident in what she was doing. Were her fears of the unknown or were they fears of people? Might teachers hold views of teaching which she might find difficult to connect with? If so, how would they build the relationships necessary between teacher and learner?

Moyra: Just explore vulnerability. Why don't you think it's a bad thing? What do you mean by that?

Pam: If you can afford to be vulnerable, you can also be strong, I think. If you can afford to let other people see the weakness or the tenderness about things you value strongly, then I think you're being strong. You're more or less saying, I'm showing you this because I'm so strong myself that whatever you do I'll only change if you really persuade me and not because you bully me or do anything else.

Moyra: I like this idea but I need to develop the courage, if it is to be an idea to which I can wholly subscribe. Perhaps the answer hinges on whether one can afford to let the other people see the weakness. Just because you reveal it, does that mean you can afford it? Or might you give it up without affording it, and without realizing it? Why can one person afford it and another cannot? Is the whole situation fraught with political implications? Is that why people cannot afford it? Might they lose credibility in their job if they expose their vulnerability? Can we engage in self-study if we are not willing to expose vulnerability?

Inviting Them Into the House

Pam wanted to explain how much she had learned from the students about their area of expertise, special educational needs. She shared an experience in which she had remarked to some colleagues upon the offensiveness of a poster advertising lager, which depicted a woman in thick lensed glasses with a handsome young man and a slogan that said: 'Her Dad owns the Brewery!' She explained that her colleagues thought she was objecting to the poster as sexist, but she was really offended by the reference to the glasses, and the message this gave about disability. She said to the group that she would not have made the connection before working with them and she thanked Peggy and Nick particularly for her raised awareness of this issue.

Later, in discussion about the day, Zoe reported that Nick was surprised at Pam's lack of awareness about disability. This seemed to suggest a criticism of Pam. Is the prospect of such criticism a reason why people do not expose their vulnerability? Are they afraid that exposing their failures might result in them being criticized for their ignorance, rather than being applauded for sharing their learning?

Moyra: The point was the one that you brought up Pam, about learning from the students.

Pam: Right.

Moyra: Which related back to my story and me feeling worried that these people might be different.

Pam: Yes.

Moyra: But there is a possible problem in that revealing our sudden learning might surprise other people. It might surprise other people that we haven't become aware of this before.

Zoe: Nick had a strong reaction to what you said this morning. He thought about it all morning. Then he said he was shocked that you hadn't thought about disability . . . in that way . . . and he was just shocked at the revelation, really, and surprised.

Pam: That's all right, isn't it? Maybe that will allow him to question his assumptions about how people think about things?

Zoe: No. But it's quite painful for him that it doesn't occur to people. That's what a huge part of his life is about.

Pam: But that's unfortunate for him.

Zoe: Yes

Pam: But it's true.

There is a dilemma here that relates back to Moyra's concerns. How much can a teacher afford to show herself as a learner without the imputed ignorance damaging her relationship with her students or colleagues? Pam's response to Zoe and Moyra in the taped excerpt suggests that she finds no need to pretend to know something of which she is ignorant. This perhaps shows Pam's confidence in her position as an authority that the others do not feel about themselves.

Colonizing Students' Minds?

Zoe: This is to do with how we see things differently and why ... what the reasons might be. To do with our experience ... how we've been differently socialized.

Pam: What you've just said I think makes a really important central point, doesn't it? That the difference of people in a group is as important as their similarity? ... Power relations are key because we do, as teachers, take over the minds of our students and they think our thoughts. How do you get away from that and still help them over hurdles because you know the answers? It's a terrible dilemma.

Zoe: I think that's one of the things that we might find a clue to ... through understanding that we've got different ways of doing things but they are okay in their different ways, and through understanding that our students might have a different way of doing things and it might get them to a better place than we had imagined them getting by the route we had suggested?

Pam: I am delighted today because my three students are doing completely different things. I said to Peggy today, 'Look, if you haven't got much about action research, why don't you just forget it and get on with what you are doing?' And I thought, well, that's an amazing thing for me to say, really. I was quite surprised about myself, but then I was also quite surprised that the other two, Viv and Bernadette, are just leaping forward in their own directions. Somehow I haven't held them back. ...

There is a dilemma between wanting the students to do well within the academy by giving technical guidance and wanting them to develop an independence of 'mind' that is likely to be empowering, but more risky. One of Pam's dilemmas as a teacher educator has to do with what she would call a 'service' or 'vocation' view of her job as a teacher. In relation to her valuing of service, it is important that her students do well within the academy, and generally her experience enables her to guide them with successful outcomes. In fact, she prides herself on the examination success rate of the courses she directs. Yet, she also values an independence of 'mind' for her students. She knows she could help them develop, and is confident that the coursework would lead to them being empowered. But she also knows that this is risky and suspects that her students are not capable of making this choice with full knowledge of possible outcomes. This is not a dialectic that is resolvable; she sees both sides of it being exploitable by critics (and friends) who would reject her right to make either choice.

For Liberation ... Not Less of Love

So beautiful.
The sun sharpening the prismatic glory
Of its hard, brittle surfaces, rusted with a patina like antique bronze.

And despite the prickly pride,
And the beginnings of decomposition on the surface
Which had formed a colorful, rainbow-like iridescence,
Standing for itself.

Its brilliance may have been dulled.
Left uncomprehending.
Blind.
Shattered.

Perhaps mistaken for something inferior
And thrown back from where it had pushed so hesitantly, into the sunlight.
Or worse.
Maliciously defaced
By unscrupulous others
Who would not want its self evident worth to detract from their own superiority.

Look carefully
Beneath the surface of our prejudice and power.
So beautiful.
And standing for itself without any help.

The poem was an experiment in using an aesthetic form of communication and, as such, expresses the dialectic of Pam's life as a teacher educator: the analogy with the beautiful brittle glass that has survived despite the hazards. Perhaps the poem also suggests a tentative answer to the dilemma identified earlier: that it should stand (or fall) for itself without any help. Perhaps this answer is also suggested by Pam's delight in her students, Bernadette and Viv, whose uniqueness is suggested by the different directions they are taking and her joy in being able to learn from Nick and Pam and the others.

And so Liberation from the Future as Well as the Past

Jack Whitehead has taken us to task for not making the word 'love' explicit in our text. His remark has led us to agree that for us the main work is liberation and not love.

> Zoe: I prefer the notion of liberation to empowerment because there seems more scope for me to liberate myself whereas I might have to wait for someone else to empower me.
>
> Moyra: There are things we talk about in school that are acceptable and there are things which we do, ways in which we act towards each other that are good and satisfying, but which we don't go talking about — things like respecting people's rights and being concerned for their welfare, looking out for each other, caring for each other. Is this love? I can cope with trust, but love has so many different connotations to it, that once you start talking about it you really need to define how you're using it. Talking about loving sets you apart and embarrasses people.

Yet, the form in which we have presented our self-studies is not intended to be comfortable but to demonstrate a dialectic between different orders of meaning that are signified by different types of text. We have interspersed personal voices and living theory with more formal or traditional propositional theory. The text moves across the dialectic from one type of text to another in a way that shows a dialogue between these two ways of understanding educational practice. We have punctured our original narrative with insights that we have come to through discussing our texts with different groups of teachers and academics, and this has been a source of enrichment to which the length restriction on the manuscript does not allow us to do full justice. We particularly thank Bernadette Igboaka and our other students whose work has so influenced our thinking. We also thank Mel Lever and Jack Whitehead, who took the trouble to write a detailed response to a draft of our chapter.

We hope that you will take time in judging our work and put up with the discomfort of what we see as a more direct and human approach than has been supported by academic writing in the past. Although the form of representation is different, we are also applying different criteria to the task of selecting meanings we find significant. We have searched our souls and our hearts as well as used our technical expertise to interrogate our data and subject its interpretation to the dialectical critique advocated by Richard Winter (1989). We think we have some uniqueness in terms of starting an inquiry for which we genuinely did not know the answers. Jack Whitehead has challenged us to be clearer about what motivates us in relation to the meanings we might share. He points to Pam's belief in faith, hope and optimism, to Moyra's courage in transcending the anxiety associated with feelings that one is exposing one's vulnerability; and to Zoe's meaning when she speaks of a way that integrated our friendship with our joint inquiry into professional issues. Our response is that our chapter has communicated to him three of the most important criteria that we use to judge our effectiveness as teachers. We have not explicated these in a prepositional form, but they have peeped out between the lines of our chapter and been hinted at when we have been explicit about our fundamental values. Surely allowing for such forms of representation is what we are about?

What have we learned? That we know so little? That we have excluded so much in the past because it did not fit neatly into the dominant paradigm? That we have paid too little attention to individual difference?

Zoe: A turning point in my learning happened during the collective memory work because it felt to me as if we had reached a new way of working together, a way that integrated our friendship with our joint inquiry into professional issues. This went together in my mind with the moment where Pam endorsed an idea I had about working together. This idea was that we all bring different styles to our teaching and we could learn from our differences. I understand now that this turning point was a liberating moment. My own research is about parttime research students' experiences of their work, and my current practice as a teacher educator involves me in facilitating parttime students' action research. I believe that one should not facilitate the actions of others if one has no experience oneself of trying to carry out similar actions. Therefore, my understanding of my own development as an action researcher is a key element that informs my practice.

Being able to explain the process of my own learning can also help others who are carrying out action research. In exposing my process of learning, which includes my points of vulnerability, doubt and difficulty, I believe I can be a better teacher and my students can learn better. I have been developing the idea of an autobiography of learning to help explain this process. This autobiography is an edited version of a life, focusing on the specific concerns that have been chosen to describe and explain the values that underpin a particular practice. The autobiography of my learning is constructed to illuminate specific data about my practice. There are certain special moments which I see as turning points that change my understanding of my learning. The incidents we have individually chosen from our joint discussions are probably such turning points and as such may reflect our uniqueness as teachers.

Moyra: But how can I decide which part of the autobiography of my learning I should share with others? How do I come to understand my own autobiography? Why should I inflict it on other people? Do they want to know or do they need to know in order that they can get on with some learning about improving their teaching? Do they have time to listen?

Pam: These are questions you and I are more able to answer than Zoe because we have already had the temerity to inflict our autobiographies on others (Lomax, 1994a; Evans, 1996a). The feedback about my own account has suggested that many people have been able to empathize with the conclusions I have drawn because they can see where I am coming from. I like the point Mel Lever made in her response to a draft of our manuscript when she said, 'It is important that we do not separate aspects of our learning life . . . any part of our work or our development must have a bearing on our research. If we constructively and openly criticize our own lives, this must be part of the knowledge of ourselves and our development. . . .' (personal communication)

References

BELENKY, M., CLINCHY, B., GOLDBERGER, N. and TARULE, J. (1986) *Women's Ways of Knowing: The Development of Self, Voice, and Mind*, New York: Basic Books.

CARTER, K. (1993) 'The place of story in the study of teaching and teacher education', *Educational Researcher*, **22**, 1, pp. 5–12.

CLANDININ, D.J. (1992) 'Narrative and story in teacher education', in RUSSELL, T. and MUNBY, H. (eds) *Teachers and Teaching: From Classroom To Reflection*, New York: Falmer Press, pp. 124–37.

COCHRAN-SMITH, M. and LYTLE, S. (1990) 'Research on teaching and teacher research: The issues that divide', *Educational Researcher*, **19**, 2, pp. 2–11.

CRAWFORD, J., KIPPAX, S., ONYX, J., GAULT, U. and BENTON, P. (1992) *Emotion and Gender*, London: Sage.

CONVERY, A. (1993) 'Developing fictional writing as a means of stimulating teacher reflection', *Educational Action Research*, **1**, 1, pp. 135–51.

DADDS, M. (1995) *Passionate Enquiry*, London: Falmer Press.

EVANS, M. (1996a) 'An action research enquiry into reflection in action as part of my role as a deputy headteacher'. Unpublished Doctoral Dissertation, Kingston University, Kingston, England.

EVANS, M. (1996b) 'Using story to develop explanations about staff development in a secondary school department', in LOMAX, P. (ed.) *Quality Management to Education: Sustaining the Vision through Action Research*, London: Routledge, pp. 123–35.

HAUG, F. (1987) *Female Sexualisation: A Collective Work on Memory*, London: Verso.

LOMAX, P. (1994a) 'The narrative of an educational journey or crossing the tracks'. Inaugural address at Kingston University.

LOMAX, P. (1994b) 'Standards, criteria and the problematic of action research', *Educational Action Research: An International Journal*, **2**, 1, pp. 113–25.

LOMAX, P. (1994c) 'Action research for managing change', in BENNETT, N., GLATTER, R. and LEVACIC, R. (eds) *Improving Educational Management through Research and Consultancy*, London: Paul Chapman, pp. 156–67.

LOMAX, P. (1995) 'Action research for professional practice', *British Journal of In-Service Education*, **21**, 1, pp. 1–9.

LOMAX, P. and PARKER, Z. (1995) 'Accounting for ourselves: The problematic of representing action research', *Cambridge Journal of Education*, **25**, 3, pp. 301–14.

LOMAX, P. and PARKER, Z. (1996) 'Representing a dialectical form of knowledge within a new epistemology for teaching and teacher education'. Paper presented at the meeting of the American Educational Research Association, New York.

LOMAX, P., PARKER, Z. and EVANS, M. (1997) 'How can we make our practice as teacher educators more effective'? Paper presented at the meeting of the American Educational Research Association, Chicago.

LOMAX, P., WHITEHEAD, J. and EVANS, M. (1996) 'Contributing to an epistemology of quality educational management practice', in LOMAX, P. (ed.) *Bringing Quality Management to Education: Sustaining the Vision through Action Research*, London: Routledge, pp. 1–17.

McNIFF, J., LOMAX, P. and WHITEHEAD, J. (1996) *You and Your Action Research Project*, London: Routledge.

RUSSELL, T. (1995) 'Reconstructing educational theory from the authority of experience', *Studies in Continuing Education*, **17**, 1/2, pp. 6–16.

SCHRATZ, M. and SCHRATZ-HADWICH, B. (1995) 'Collective memory work: The self as a re/source for re/search', in SCHRATZ, M. and WALKER, R. (eds) *Research as Social Change*, London: Routledge, pp. 39–64.

WINTER, R. (1989) *Learning from Experience*, London: Falmer Press.

WHITEHEAD, J. (1993) *The Growth Of Educational Knowledge: Creating Your Own Living Educational Theories*, Bournemouth: Hyde Publications.

12 Tensions and Intentions in Group Inquiry: A Joint Self-study

Carola Conle, William Louden and Denis A. Mildon

Doing Inquiry When the Gods are Silent

Foundations are shaking. Researchers and teachers alike seem to be more hesitant these days in their quests, claims and proofs of truth (Denzin and Lincoln, 1994). Some of us, following Bernstein (1983), are trying to function in a realm beyond the dualism of objectivity and relativism. Here we stumble upon a second, related problem: how to do inquiry when the content and process of knowledge acquisition have lost their singular, essential nature.

In the realm of lived experience, as well as in research, the pull toward one story, toward one right way, is very strong. In the academic tradition, readers and reviewers do not want to be left with ten interpretations at the end of a piece of inquiry. In the teaching tradition, teachers work toward establishing familiarity and routines toward their story of their classroom. Finally, in the human tradition generally, there also is the pull toward a single interpretation: We need firm ground to take our next step and function in what Schutz and Luckman (1973) called the natural attitude to create an atmosphere of predictability for our actions.

Are we then being pulled into two directions at once: toward the need for the one story and toward the need to keep in mind its fragility? In this chapter we came to see this ambivalence as a tension between closure and open-endedness and between determinism and agency. What follows is the story of three inquirers seeking, in a doctoral program, knowledge within this tension. Today each of us is teaching and we feel that this exploration of our collaborative learning will benefit our current work with teachers as well as their work with students in classrooms.

Although the form of the search was collaborative, our work does not fit neatly into descriptions of cooperative work currently prominent in the literature (Slavin, 1990; Johnson and Johnson, 1987). We did not have a method or technique, but the self-study we present here speaks to us today because it seems to shed light on the transition period we and many of our colleagues are experiencing as we move toward new paradigms of research and toward new forms of inquiry (Denzin and Lincoln, 1994). It also gives us food for thought as we currently make curriculum decisions within a non-essentialist paradigm.

The Project

Our group met several times a week over a period of four months. These sessions were of varying length, from one hour to three and a half hours, and yielded over twenty hours of recorded discussion (Tapes A to L). In addition, we participated in a weekly larger group meeting, involving twelve graduate students in a graduate curriculum course.[1] The instructor and the other students in the course were silent partners in our small group meetings to the extent that our concerns were often shared by our inter-actions with the larger group.

Carola, for reasons outlined below, maintained a set of audio-tapes of our meetings as well as a journal of personal reactions to our spontaneous and unscheduled conversa-tions in offices and hallways. The point of our meeting as a group was primarily to help each other to explore topics of mutual interest and we gave only one session to evalua-tion of the process (Tape J). We wished to avoid being self-conscious of our pursuit of understanding and favored being fully 'in the game'[2] during our discussion.

When three learners decide to work together, they create a unit that wants to exist as such, a group that must find a point of balance somewhere between silence and a shouting match. In this chapter we describe the creative tensions and conflicting inten-tions that shaped a sequence of collaborative academic work. We explore the way in which the group's collaboration was built on shared histories, required a mutual com-mitment to inquiry, and sought a common discourse for dealing with topics of mutual interest.[3]

Carola considered the study of collaborative learning as a significant part of her own intellectual journey and took the initiative for listening to the tapes and for produc-ing the first interpretation of the sessions. Her voice carries the narrative in this chapter and the substantive interpretations of the inquiry process. However, our shared views are represented and much of the text was constructed by all three authors.

Carola's description begins with the specific and personal motivations for our coming together, establishes the dialectical themes of our discussions, reveals the emerg-ing interaction of our personal narratives, and with those, the emerging conceptualizations of this inquiry. We conclude with some interpretation of our individual growth and with suggestions about the educational significance of this work.

Similarities and Differences

Denis, Bill and I share backgrounds in language and literature. Denis and Bill have both been classroom teachers of English and have from the first day of their doctoral

---

[1] 'Alternative Theoretical Approaches to the Curriculum' with Professor Michael Connelly.

[2] Gadamer's metaphor for the process of hermeneutic understanding (1960).

[3] Connelly and Clandinin (1988) named this personal reservoir of lived knowledge 'personal practical knowledge'. Personal practical knowledge results from our lived experience, and is continually embod-ied in and expressed through our words, actions and the narratives through which we constitute our lives. 'Knowledge is not only found "in the mind". It is "in the body", and it is seen and found "in our practices"'. In the stories we tell about ourselves it is 'a particular way of reconstructing the past and the intentions for the future to deal with the exigencies of a present situation' (pp. 25–6).

program shared an office. They are surprised to find that in spite of practicing on two different continents, they have discovered similar limitations and possibilities in their teaching. Denis and I fell into a series of hallway conversations fed by a mutual fascination with narration and consciousness. Bill and I have worked together on a project to uncover the personal images and metaphors that inform our interest in academic inquiry. In other words, the group did not begin as a *tabula rasa*: from the first day of our collaborative study, we carried forward relationships developed outside the study group. These relationships helped us to be tolerant of each other's false starts, uncertainties and thought processes, as we stumbled toward understanding.

The three of us also brought common intellectual interests to the group. Some of the questions to which we were eager to find answers included the place of narrative in research, the role of critical reflection in education, and the relationship between theory and practice. We were at approximately the same stage in our work in the first year of a doctoral program and we were all starting to think about our thesis proposals. Denis, in our first session, explained it this way: 'It seems to me what you are interested in is the same thing I'm interested in. I'm using different reference points' (Tape A).

In a sense, it seemed that perhaps we had a common story to tell, and yet, differences in our mutual interests promised each of us rich possibilities of profiting from what we had to offer one another. I hoped to learn from Bill's expertise in curriculum studies and Denis's long years of practical experience and his solid background in literary narrative. Both Bill and Denis have used a collaborative approach with their high school students. I was struggling with this approach in my English as a Second Language (ESL) classrooms. I was also struggling to find a form and style of expression, both orally and in my writing, that would allow me to convey my ideas more successfully. I saw both Bill and Denis handle language well; Denis in a flowing, analytic way, and Bill with a knack for just the right turn of phrase at the right moment. Bill was interested in learning more about Habermas from me, and Denis wanted to look at narrative theory, from the different perspectives Bill and I bring to it. These intellectual similarities and differences among us were to make for a productive learning dynamic.

In addition to these intellectual qualities, there were some emotional qualities that contributed to the cohesion of the group. This affective dimension was important. It lent an intensity to the interaction, a willingness to make ourselves vulnerable, and a passion to our academic efforts.

> *Bill*: Excitement is the key word there . . .
> Some people get excited about ideas, some people simply use them . . .
> A love for the game, for the play of ideas.
> *Denis*: I cannot remember a time when we ever had to negotiate trust.

There was a desire to forge intellectual links between our different ways of thinking:

> *Denis*: I am determined to find the bridge between the world you're working from and the world I come from. I know it's close. I want to see it more clearly.

The excitement was catching and we were turning each other on to one another's special interests, making space for them in our own busy schedules. Here is Denis's report about giving in to my favorite author, Gadamer:

> *Denis:* Bill and I had this chat about Gadamer and both of us, without the other
> knowing about it, bought the first copy of *Philosophical Hermeneutics* (1976)
> we saw. I don't need Gadamer. It's really not on track. But I'm glad I bought
> the book.

And finally there was intense mutual questioning and critique:

> *Denis:* A critical habit of mind is a major component of the process; so that we are
> constantly forcing each other to clarify our ideas, to think things through, yet
> at the same time willing to listen to those ideas empathetically, or with a mix-
> ture of what [the instructor] calls submission and critical commentary.

Two other aspects of the dynamics of the group that I believe contributed to its
effectiveness were centered in tacit dimensions and in personal history. Both, we thought,
are connected. There was a vague but strongly felt notion of something to pursue, as
Denis put it: 'There are certain questions we found interesting — a vague notion that
there is an interesting question and that we should go after it'.

This awareness of something to pursue was not worked out reflectively at this
point. It was rather a tacitly felt urgency that propelled our discussions. I eventually
came to use MacIntyre's (1984) concept of 'telos' to explain this urgency to pursue an
area of interest that was as yet undefined (Conle, 1993). MacIntyre reminded us that
such urgency is quite rightly unspecified, because it is part of a quest that does not have
a predetermined object. In our case, we eventually saw the urgency as arising from
certain lived tensions that had now found an intellectual path. With time and increasing
reflection on the process, we wondered if there was the possibility that the tensions
might have an autobiographical basis. Our common interests, our differences, and our
hopes for answers were all connected to stories in our lives which, however, had not
completely risen to our conscious awareness.

In an attempt to get a conscious grasp of these tacit dynamics, I explored the
personal histories that might be propelling them. I did this by analyzing our taped conversations, looking for biographical details.

Lived Tensions

We usually began our meetings by responding to some issue or phenomenon, but in the
effort to come to terms with it, certain themes continued to arise and be developed
further. These themes themselves did not lead us to inquiry, neither did the abstract
terms that filled our conversations. Rather, themes and terms seemed to first pass through
a filter of personal interest within each of us and it was only then that the inquiry
seemed to take off.

An example from our early discussions that illustrates the way in which issues
passed through a series of personal filters in our sessions was our reaction to Brimfield's
description of a part of her graduate education (Brimfield, Roderick and Yamamoto,
1983). We touched on a continuing tension between citing authorities and writing in our
own individual voices:

> *Bill:* I found this a very irritating piece of work. The argument by authority is very
> irritating to me. . . . It does not strengthen her argument. So, 'Speak in your
> own voice, silly woman!'

> *Carola*: You are actually speaking to me directly here, because I found myself [arguing by citing authorities] in my [MA] thesis a lot and [my advisor] took me to task for it . . . You said, silly woman, and maybe that is typical, because I felt I needed to boost my own voice with these quotes.
>
> *Denis*: This [relates to] the whole point of my description of my present narrative. You'd enjoy reading it because I think, there are other reasons why a person does that. Mine is because I was taught all my life that the higher authority is the Bible and if you can quote a text . . .
>
> *Bill*: My reason for quoting is because someone says it better. (Tape B)

Arguing from authority does not have the same history within each of us, yet the histories could probably be related, since we live in similar cultures and have similar social value systems. There are, among the three of us, similarities and differences connected to that issue, enough similarities to have us recognize the issue, enough difference to make us name various facets of it. One might say, the issue is filled with a dialectical tension for us.

I noted other such dialectical issues and summarize them below rather abstractly, even though I had to first construct the list from lived events as they were told in our conversations:

Reflection vs. the taken-for-granted
Objectification vs. unification
Self-conscious awareness vs. spontaneous interaction
Theory vs. practice
Finding difference vs. finding wholeness
Fragmentation vs. narrative unity
Research vs. fiction
Abstraction vs. concrete expression
Dualism vs. pluralism
Explicit vs. tacit
Citing vs. speaking in our own voice
Free will vs. determinism

Because of the abstract form in which the above dialectical tensions are presented, I emphasize again that the list was constructed from my interpretations of our taped conversations. The tensions are tensions in our lived experience, not abstractions we brought to our discussions. To exemplify their lived quality, I turn to one of these opposing pairs in particular, the one involving freedom and determinism, a theme that is fundamental to our intellectual culture. This choice allows me to identify certain aspects of our interaction and still stay within the scope of a single paper.

Pollyanna Versus Gloom and Doom: 'Tensions with a History' Prompting Personal and Group Learning

The notion of 'Pollyanna' as opposed to 'doom and gloom' is used by Bill to contrast interpretive and critical approaches to ethnography. Through the two expressions, Bill named the dichotomy between an exaggerated view of agency and an over-emphasis of external power. It helped me to reword a central tension that propelled much of our work together: free will and agency versus determinism.

We each had our own personal version of the dialectic embodied in us. As we heard our partners surface their versions, we responded in terms based on our own sedimented histories. I need to become more concrete here, but the process cannot be laid bare through analysis nor can it be represented completely. We can, I think, get a sense of how the tensions shaped our discussion, if we take up a narrative approach, and view each dialectic as existing in story form. The telling, of course, is not a recapturing of original events, but a reconstructing from present perspectives and a negotiation of elements from the present and the past through the present telling. This holds true whether it is a story from my life or from the life of my partners, because in the latter case, the story is negotiated. It is a collaborative narrative about Bill, Denis and me that was first constructed by me, incorporating my own 'prejudices'; then, through the process of review and negotiation, the current text incorporates both Bill's and Denis's 'prejudices'[4] as well.

The stories that stirred in each of us embodied a struggle with gloom and doom, or determinism, that had become significant for each of us in a different way. Denis remembered growing up in a Christian Fundamentalist environment where the authority of the Bible was all powerful. Bill felt that earlier in life his enthusiasm had led him to embrace a series of ideas evangelically. I thought that my own background fostered feelings of a strong authority 'out there', stemming from German political and social conditions, which placed the sense of self 'out there' with an all powerful authority. These three biographical circumstances seemed to be fountainheads of deterministic forces in our lives.

Each, of course, had its own path in our individual experiences. For Denis, determinism took the shape of submission to the authority of text; for me, it meant loss of self in interaction; and for Bill, it existed as the loss of personal agency through the power of social structure and ideologies.

There seemed to be certain resolutions each of us wanted to enact in order to cope with this history. Let us see how the capacity to be an agent was one such resolution, but took a different route in each of our lives. Denis, having felt the need for submission to the authority of the text, had grown to realize that with interpretations of the text came freedom and responsibility. Members of his family were always encouraged to read the Bible and to interpret it themselves. Now Denis often points to the need to create text out of life's fleeting phenomena.

Carola: What do you mean by 'existence as code'?

Denis: Discourse itself, not event, not phenomenon, damn text separate from . . . not event, but representation of the event. . . . Text is a static presentation of utterance.

Carola: How does something become a text?

Denis: The minute you are saying, 'you said . . .' and you begin to address my utterance as a phrase you want to deal with, you begin to deal with it as text (Tape K).

---

[4] The term prejudice is used here in Gadamer's (1960) sense of the inevitable prejudgments (Vorurteile) we all bring to our understandings.

Carola Conle, William Louden and Denis A. Mildon

Denis argues that once we recognize textuality we need not submit to the authority of the text. We become agents who can deconstruct the text.

> *Denis:* Then there is the reader's position; to read by deconstructing, revealing strangeness, its polyphonic voice, revealing the frailty. . . . That's what I was doing [with the document under discussion], deliberately deconstructing its original intention (Tape K).

In Denis's view, our capacity to interpret gives us power to counter the text's authority over us. By extension we can read reality as text and deconstruct it as well. Denis therefore was reluctant whenever anyone suggested that we should submit to the text. He argued vigorously against such a suggestion both in our class and in our small group. Yet in order to understand, one has to submit to a text before making a judgment. Denis struggled with this dialectic between submission and deconstruction. Later, in his dissertation (Mildon, 1992), he used postmodern fiction to investigate the relationship between what he called 'narrative acts' and experience, or at least what we call our knowledge of experience, in order to clarify issues of interpretation in narrative inquiry.

In our discussions, Bill's views on the authority of the text are different, as part of our debate on deconstruction showed.

> *Bill:* [The issue here is] a deconstructive kind of thinking. The 'de' in deconstruction makes you think you can get twelve different interpretations. Carola gave me an article on hermeneutics with twelve different — I found it infuriating, because I'm looking for a whole, for a bloody conclusion. I'm looking for the guy to say: Well, I'm capable of giving you twelve interpretations. The one I like is. . . . (Tape K).

Bill seemed to resent open-endedness, yet it was interesting that in our discussions Bill seemed to be the very person who supported a range of possibilities. More than that, his thesis topic centered on reflection, and the key puzzle for him was to see reflection working in other ways than the highly theoretical and often non-open-ended functions assigned to it by some critical theorists. He also countered his own judgmental tendencies very well. Denis and I both admired his ability to let stand the best aspects of two opposing views; and very often he acted as the peacemaker between the two of us. His voice of reason and concrete examples countered any emotional flights into theory. Often his advice was: 'This cannot be decided theoretically but needs to be looked at in a concrete context'. Yet in order to become aware of the subversive power of social structures over us, Bill saw the need to step out of our taken-for-granted frame of mind and to theoretically reflect on our condition. For him, reflection offered a chance to recover agency. At that point the temptation to come to conclusions and make analytic judgments is very strong. Still, as he functioned in practical everyday situations — as a teacher or researcher of teaching — Bill was not comfortable with theoretically driven approaches, but sought after concrete, practical modes of reflection. This was his dilemma and an ambivalence he lived with.

Bill caught a glimpse of a solution to this tension when he thought about how teachers think on their feet:

Most of us choose to live as if we are the agents of our destiny; or you end up a victim. It is not that there are no social forces, it's that the courageous act is to say: I can act . . .

In parts of my life I have gone on as if I can't act, as if I'm stuck, as if. . . . This is an important thing in reflection. This is what teachers often do, to throw their hands up in the air and say: 'It's the system. I'm stuck. I can't do anything. If only they'd reduce class sizes'. The person next to them who is acting, they like their world better. They are not reforming the world, they are not solving the world's problems, but my practical sense is that there is more pleasure to be had in acting as if. (Tape K)

The tension between theoretical and practical reflection was the dynamic that eventually propelled Bill's thesis that he entitled '*Understanding Teaching: Meaning and Method in Collaborative Research*' (1989). The phrase 'Pollyanna and gloom and doom' reflected Bill's struggle with the structure and agency issues in different modes of reflection.

My own 'gloom and doom' story connected to the lack of agency and free will lived out in a very different setting. The ambivalence for me lay in my need to preserve an outside authority that granted me value. This is probably a female story, one I have in common with many women. I saw two options: giving myself over to that outside authority (usually male), or keeping a safe distance from it, and from experience as well, probably, as I see it now. Experiencing without hesitation might mean losing agency by getting involved in something that, through power, would cause me to lose my ability to act freely. There are private dimensions of this tension I eventually dealt with in my thesis, but shall not narrate here. Intellectually the tension has been lived out by a preference for analysis and theory, which granted distance and therefore control. In other words, I joined a male intellectual tradition.

At the same time, there was a reluctance to take responsibility and speak in my own voice, preferring often to cite the voices of more powerful others. When I asked Bill and Denis for reactions to my work, their advice was: 'Don't cite so much, speak in your own voice; don't weigh down your narrative with those theoretical sections (Tape I); make up your mind whether you are presenting your own views or speaking for your authorities, Gadamer and Habermas' (Tape G). I was struggling with this advice and, at the same time I reacted very strongly against Denis's deconstructionist tendencies (Tape L). I saw them producing distance through language, and objectification of language as well as of real life phenomena, and of people. I saw it as a reification of life and experience and expressed a strong emotional resistance to it. This was my dilemma: to want and not to want agency and the experience and responsibility that went with it.

I became very interested in narrative inquiry because it let me speak in my own voice in a non-distancing way. Yet I had a very strong desire to work theoretically, getting involved with the ideas of philosophers and educational theorists. I eventually wrote a narrative thesis, conceptualizing narrative inquiry as I told my personal stories; and narrativizing academic activities, that is, viewing abstract ideas and processes within their temporal, physical and emotional contexts. This meant I had to act as narrator and accept the agency that this role involves.

Carola Conle, William Louden and Denis A. Mildon

Our stories show how we externalized in our arguments battles we were fighting within; and so often our arguments told us more about where we came from and where we were going, than they did about what we wanted them to do, which was to define clearly and unequivocally our present position. They illustrated the 'tensions with a history' in our personal, practical knowledge, tensions that were embodied within us and were tacitly shaping our inquiry. In order to keep track of these various threads and processes, I shall summarize what has been said so far.

Personal history provided an experiential base for lived tensions in each of our lives: Denis's religious upbringing; Bill's early encounter with, and embracing of, theory; and my life in an authoritarian environment.

The tensions consisted of a dialectical pull between opposites. For Denis it was the submission to text as opposed to the chance to deconstruct it; for Bill it was a lived dialectic between the power of theory and the need for concern with the concrete practicalities of life. I was torn between giving value to outside authorities in order to gain value through them and the need to speak in my own voice.

These were personal 'tensions with a history', yet they had strong connections to cultural practices. Each of the tensions could be characterized as falling into the cultural prototypical tension of the struggle between determinism and agency; the determinism issuing forth from authoritarian practices connected to religion (Denis's case), the authority of theory in our culture (Bill), and the political authority connected to patriarchy and totalitarian regimes (Carola).

In an academic setting where our interchanges took place in a trusting, emotionally permissive and intellectually exciting and refined atmosphere, the lived personal and cultural tensions became learning dynamics. The narrative content of each dynamic was different but, most likely because of the cultural connectedness, there was sufficient similarity among the differences, that the three of us could function as a group in our doctoral studies.

Telos in Collaborative Work

Dichotomies pressed for resolution. Unintentionally, but consistently, the tensions in our histories shaped our agenda. This was not particularly surprising since the 'freedom versus determinism' dichotomy in its various forms was common to all three of us. In different words, or different topics, the same issue offered an ever increasing number of variations on the theme, each slightly different from the other. We each responded to particular variations in our own way, depending on what specific notes within us provided maximum resonance. As we experienced it, of course, it was much less grand than this sounds. It was more a matter of each of us coming every day in search of what we wanted, from the group and from our academic work. What each of us could take away was shaped by our need to maintain the communal life of the group.

We settled into two particular areas of discussion. They seemed to provide the space in which our learning dynamic could evolve. One was 'the game', Gadamer's (1960) metaphor for the hermeneutical process of understanding; the other was an emerging methodology in teacher education, narrative inquiry. Examples from our conversations follow:

Denis: Can one be fully in the game and be aware?

Carola: Intuitively [I would say], no. I want to be in the game spontaneously, the way I want to be in this conversation without constantly thinking and judging it. (Tape K)

Academically, 'the game' requires collaborative work, where answers are not found alone, but in the interplay of mutual interpretations; where authority is diffuse and submission and domination become counterproductive. What is essential is personal involvement without constant distancing analysis of it. In our collaborative work, I tried to refrain from explicit analysis of our interactions at the time they were occurring. I wanted to avoid turning people and interactions into text, until I purposefully decided to do so, as I did in writing this chapter. Being in the game, however, did not prevent us from intellectually grappling with the idea and Gadamer's explanations of it.

Carola: It's a key notion for Gadamer . . . you get drawn into it. You are very — uhh — it's the very opposite of distancing. It's real. It's the image of real dialogue where one draws on the other, one makes demands on the other, draws the other in. The opposite of distancing. . . .

Denis: What is real dialogue?

Carola: Ein Gespräch führen, it's not a chat. That's not serious enough. It's not 'to have a dialogue', that's too much the other way. Intensity, seriousness, being close, being very involved with the partner: to put the minimal distance necessary to communicate. It's not the distance necessary in science, but the distance we keep in language; you distance yourself from your own language only as far as it's necessary in order to bridge the gaps of a dialogue. (Tape E)

Narrative inquiry was also a major focus for us. For me now, working in a narrative framework holds the promise of capturing in text my process of personal inquiry without squeezing the life out of it; it promises to reveal my personal involvement in that inquiry in a rhetorical style that does not pay undue homage to authorities. And importantly, it also carries with it the writer's obligation to be fully responsible for her work. At the time of our work together, these notions were still diffuse and focused on various facets of narrative, e.g. questions of objectivity, of change and of qualities of language.

For example, Bill and I disarmed handling the problem of authorities in his thesis. He was not going to make himself an objective observer.

Carola: So you are continually in there, your story constantly continues. [This is important because in the end] the only way your thesis can be judged is by you being judged, not just the text, because you have put yourself in there.

Bill: You have given them a point where they can take issue with you — not Polanyi (1958), for example — because it's you who have pulled all this from Polanyi. (Tape K)

As our narratives continued to surface, issues were worked through. For example, Gadamer's notion of 'the game' struck a very responsive chord with Bill. He remembered his teaching days, moments where he was thinking on his feet, being fully in the game.

> *Bill*: [The game] strikes me as an excellent description of what it is like to teach . . . the sense of immersion into the game that disconnects you from time and which disconnects you from a conscious sense of yourself; you are just in the game. (Tape K)

What Bill describes is not theoretical reflection as we traditionally know it. It is reflection in action, (Bill connects it to Schön's, 1987, work as well); the reflective process is more or less tacit. Bill was getting in touch here with his desire to free agency from the territory critical theory had claimed to be its true abode: the world of the intellect. The game allowed reflection within practice.

> *Bill*: Classrooms tend to throw you into an existential present . . . and the game is a way of explaining that. . . . You can't reflect without distance and you know the reflection is very poorly articulated to the event because the quality of the event prevents you from getting access to it. (Tape E)

He continued his train of thought after some interjection by Denis and myself, in which I invoked the topic of change within language.

> *Bill*: Speech allows you to think. I like that. And it changes you; so you are working within the system, but the system is sufficiently fluid and has the possibility of creativity and spontaneity.

I think Bill intuitively conceived of the possibility for change through the notion of reflection in practice and, therefore, of agency in practice. The potential of such change was driving his inquiry.

Bill and I were very close in our thinking here, although perhaps for different reasons. Denis's reaction, on the other hand, was not at all the same. He drew attention to the role of discourse in reflection. Being 'in the game' makes it hard to reflect on the moment of action. In discourse outside 'the game' there are more possibilities for reflection.

> *Denis*: Addressing it as game . . . implies nevertheless that there is a taking-part in an agreed upon social activity that has rules and that have a system going in it and purpose. . . . So I put a big question mark by the phrase 'real dialogue'.
> *Bill*: So what is the contradiction?
> *Denis*: [The game] as being drawn in rather than being aloof from — there is a suggestion here that there is this natural condition that we can get to, where we become so totally submitted to the dialogue that we can not escape deception and manipulation. (Tape E)

Denis did not want to leave open any possibilities for submission and domination. What Denis introduced to our work was the theme 'all is fiction'. His challenge to us was to ask whether there is substantive difference between interpretive research and invented reality. Unless a clear distinction can be made, the authority of academic text becomes suspect. Its frailty could then be easily demonstrated. With frailty comes vulnerability which in academic circles needs to be covered up by analytic, judgmental language. Denis knew how to use this language very well but he was no longer comfortable with it. It seemed that there may have been an underlying desire to have that frailty of language recognized as strength, in order to do without the kind of language which at present lends recognition to a speaker and buttresses academic text.

In the collaborative setting, there were again similarities and productive differences in the way we viewed our topics of hermeneutic dialogue and narrative inquiry. As in music, a combination of sameness and difference can produce powerful harmonies. The variations between our tensions, played out in our conversations, seemed to profit from one another, so to speak. For example, Denis's notion of finding voice through the interpretation of text influenced my effort to speak in my own voice as a female inquirer; and Bill's exploration of reflection touched my ambivalence about a distancing kind of analysis. Each of us had struggled with submission: submission to the authority of the Biblical text, submission to powerful ideas, and submission to social and political authority. Each of us was struggling to find agency: through deconstruction of texts, through practical reflection, and through narrative voice.

As we played with the melodies of our personal inquiry those 'tensions with a history' created a powerful impetus for that inquiry. We felt a dynamic propelling our discussions and eventually came to see an 'implicit telos' giving direction to them.

The role of desire and implicit goals driving intellectual activity through an emotional impetus is not new. Garrison (1995), with a view to John Dewey, describes the role of Eros in inquiry; Dewey's (1934) concept of 'interest' is not without emotional dimensions and MacIntyre (1984) points out that intellectual as well as other kinds of quests are propelled by an implicit 'telos'. We eventually saw a process at work in our interactive inquiry that seemed very much driven by shared telos.

In our explorations of hermeneutics and narrative, we each consistently voiced certain wishes or goals that promised an endpoint for our inquiry. They created a certain urgency. We felt that if we just continued our conversations, we would reach an insight that would be a form of resolution to the various issues that concerned us. The resolution was not named at the time. We recognized the nature of our telos only later, with reflection and with analysis of the tapes.

Bill in various ways expressed the wish to explore how 'teachers think on their feet' and the idea of change connected to this. I made comments that could be read as the desire to avoid loss of self in close and spontaneous intellectual interaction and in the use of academic language. Denis's comments suggested a then unrecognized desire to have the frailty of interpretive knowledge recognized as academically valid. These were individual strands of telos that also had their shared dimension, since each strand promised a way to achieve the culturally shared telos of agency in a largely determined universe.

These tacit goals or desires were not thesis questions *per se*, nor even what one could call objectives. They rather resembled emotional needs calling for resolution through intellectual activity. The 'resolution' was not conceptually clear either. However, eventually our dissertations profited from this inquiry dynamic and were shaped by our 'tensions with a history' and our 'tacit telos'.

Denis's dissertation clarified the value of interpretation in narrative inquiry by exploring the nature of 'narrative acts'. The notion of a narrative act, of course, stresses that we shape our experience through the act of narration. It thus provides a resolution of sorts to the agency/determinism dilemma and was therefore consistent with the 'tensions with a history' in our conversations.

Through the narrative act of mediation, we create a text that presumably can change. Denis speaks of an essential indeterminacy inherent in the act of making sense of our experience through narrative. In his view, we construe our experience and should therefore also be able to deconstruct whatever we can know about it. We reaffirm our agency vis-a-vis the determining power of 'what is' through narrative. The indeterminacy of the narrative act, however, not only makes room for this agency, it also points to the frailty of whatever text is created. The text is never permanent but can be acted on.

Bill's dissertation clarified processes of teacher reflection. He pointed out that a teacher's and a researcher's understanding of teaching changes through reflection. He recognized and named four forms of reflection. To do this, he very much relied on theory, namely Schön's work (1987) and the conceptualizations of knowledge and human interests by Habermas (1971). But Bill extended this theoretical work by a fourth interest and form of reflection that he conceptualized through observing and participating in the teaching of grade seven and eight students and by reflecting on teaching with their teacher.

Bill, in one of our conversations remembered having playfully enacted a conversational game with a colleague years ago, where his friend in their discussions was 'Mr Theory' and Bill was 'Mr Practice'. In his dissertation now, the tension between theoretical and practical reflection was no longer a dichotomy for Bill, but became a unified process when teacher and researcher reflected and acted. Through this process of reflection, teachers become their own change agents as they reflect and change their lives through reflection. Bill warns educational theorists not to propose changes in teachers' practice with arrogance and certainty, but consider the agency of teachers. Bill's dissertation seems very much to issue forth from the telos and tensions expressed in our conversations.

I eventually wrote a dissertation that created its own data through personal narrative. I clarified the processes of narrative inquiry by doing one, and by, at the same time, tracking and naming the process theoretically. I used the voices of my theorist/ friends, as I called them, not in a literature search to find an entry point for my work, but in order to help me understand what was happening, practically and theoretically, as I went along. I came to see narrative as creating just enough distance between me and my experiences to keep the door of determinism sufficiently ajar and to let me peek and keep track of what was happening. I took full responsibility for my theoretical work and named everyday communicative processes that were largely ignored by theorists (Conle, 1996). At one point, early in the thesis writing, I saw a telos of narrativization pushing me along, that had me seek to contextualize abstract ideas and processes. This was necessary, I believe, so that my and others' understanding of these processes would be less likely to result in an alienated way of knowing. At other times, the concepts did not emerge except as still embedded in a narrative context. I was in no hurry to disentangle them from that context conceptually because their rich experiential connections helped to move my inquiry along. I had to inquire in order to experience and to experience in order to inquire. Experience was no longer connected to loss of agency. My personal history and cultural background provided the impetus and the resolution for my work.

Joint Inquiry: A Summary

We return to a joint voice to speak from a current vantage point that can look back on our inquiry together. Through the writing of this chapter, our interactions have become text and subject to analysis. Our learning can be viewed as a whole, as a particular process. But its essential quality is the subconscious nature of the methodology. We were on a quest without a consciously known object and without a predetermined path to go after it.

The tacit quality of the essential dynamic seems appropriate if we consider MacIntyre's (1984) characterizations of a quest that, he suggests, 'is not at all that of a search for something already adequately characterized, as miners search for gold or geologists for oil. It is in the course of the quest and only through encountering and coping with the various particular harms, dangers, temptations and distractions which provide any quest its episodes and incidents that the goal of the quest is finally to be understood. A quest is always an education both as to the character of that which is sought and in self-knowledge' (p. 219).

This characterization, we wonder, may very well suit modes of academic inquiry that function outside of technical rationality, in a non-essentialist universe, in a realm that does not require traditional objectivity while avoiding extreme relativism. In this chapter we do not have the scope to work out these conditions, but other conceptions of inquiry also value indeterminacy of goals. For example, Schwab (1970) speaks of a necessary indeterminacy in curriculum inquiry and Dewey (1934) describes dimensions of inquiry in art where the end evolves as the work progresses. In current writing on narrative inquiry, methodology and objectives are seen as emerging and as grounded in personal narrative (Connelly and Clandinin, 1990; Conle, 1996).

All three of us found a path toward a successful, satisfying thesis process. All three of us are now teaching and considering options for inquiry processes for our students. Often collaborative learning is presented in a technical, 'how-to' mode, specifying particular techniques and ways of proceeding. Our learning activity was without a blueprint, without specific objectives and a preordained methodology. Yet the process could be described after the fact as having a particular line of development: lived 'tensions with a history' and 'implicit telos' made for a powerful learning dynamic. The dynamic was an individual as well as a group process. Both personal history and cultural practices were part of it.

Favorable Conditions for Joint Inquiry

Even though we cannot, and do not wish to, prescribe methodological steps, we can point to certain favorable conditions. We seemed to have encouraged the exploitation of personal dynamics for inquiry purposes. Also, the setting was important, since there were opportunities to hear ourselves talk and to hear others offer variations on our themes. A focus on the personal seemed essential. We got to know each other better and this made for more cohesive, trusting and intense interaction, all of which helped develop various expressions of the particular learning dynamic. Since the process touched the whole person, not just the intellect, emotions needed to be touched; and for this to happen, there needed to be a sense of trust, security and mutual respect.

A mix of theory and experiential material was productive. Constant opportunities presented themselves for animating and reworking personal experiences. In all of our sessions, we frequently referred to lived examples. Very often we dwelled on recent incidents or feelings about what happened the other day with so-and-so, etc. At times, some of our more distant past was pulled in. This linking to, and reworking of, experience may very well be the most important educational function of such dynamic-propelled inquiry.

With respect to the educational significance of our rather informal work, it would also seem important that there was not only a movement toward resolution of opposites, but also a movement toward the creation of new productive tensions. Otherwise, there would be eventual stagnation. In our project, we not only worked toward rapprochement, but became aware of differences we had not noticed before, or which had not been part of the way we storied our lives previously. For example, during a final session in which we evaluated our work, Denis wondered, 'For a time I thought Bill and I were similar, but then, as I came to know him, I realized, no, I made this similarity. But in fact we really are quite different. We have found our differences.' This holds out a promise for continued joint learning through the hope that new dynamics are constantly being generated which could propel it further.

Having outlined what seem to be direct lines connecting tensions, telos, desire and possible action, we risk the danger of a deterministic view of ourselves. The storylines Carola traced should not be seen as the only possible ones. The telling is done within a temporal and spatial context and the voice made possible by the present situation does not preclude other interpretations in the future. As situations change, they exert their pull on the images we see and the stories we tell about ourselves. Thus the inquiry stays open-ended in spite of the one story this text provides.

Nor should the need to settle on an interpretation close down the dialogue. There is a polyphony of voices in any given text. Changing situations draw on different voices and storylines. Luckily, in communal situations, as we hear ourselves and others talk, we perceive alternatives. As differences emerge along with sameness, new stories become possible. Yet the alternatives, we believe, are neither arbitrary nor unlimited, because we cannot totally abandon the themes we presently see in our personal narrratives. We can only rework them and perhaps outgrow them. Complete relativism is not an option.

The closure of our story, in our view, is not authoritarian, since the closing interpretations were corporate ones, and came about through the collaborative process. Neither is our story reductionist, since it allowed each of us to bring along our embodied histories. When the gods are silent, perhaps we need to attend more fully to those histories we bring to interpretation, and to our agency in the texts that emerge from interpretive inquiry.

References

BERNSTEIN, R. (1983) *Beyond Objectivism and Relativism: Science, Hermeneutics and Praxis*, Philadelphia: University of Pennsylvania Press.

BRIMFIELD, R., RODERICK, J. and YAMAMOTO, K. (1983) 'Persons as researchers: Observations of participants', *Curriculum Inquiry*, **13**, 1, pp. 5–21.

CONLE, C. (1993) 'Learning culture and embracing contraries: Narrative inquiry through stories of acculturation', Unpublished doctoral dissertation, University of Toronto.

CONLE, C. (1996) 'Resonance in student teacher inquiry', *American Educational Research Journal*, **33**, 2, pp. 297–325.

CONNELLY, F.M. and CLANDININ, D.J. (1988) *Teachers as Curriculum Planners: Narratives of Experience*, New York: Teachers College Press.

CONNELLY, F.M. and CLANDININ, D.J. (1990) 'Stories of experience and narrative inquiry'. *Educational Researcher*, **14**, 5, pp. 2–14.

DENZIN, N. and LINCOLN, Y. (1994) *Handbook of Qualitative Research*, Thousand Oaks, CA: Sage Publications.

DEWEY, J. (1934) *Art as Experience*, New York: Capricorn Books.

GADAMER, H.G. (1960) *Wahrheit und Methode*, Einband, Germany: Offdruk Gutmann and Co. Heilbroon.

GADAMER, H.G. (1976) 'Semantics and hermeneutics', in LINGE, D.E. (ed.) *Philosophical Hermeneutics*, Berkeley: University of California Press.

GARRISON, J. (1995) 'Deweyan prophetic pragmatism, poetry, and the education of Eros', *American Journal of Education*, **103**, 4, pp. 406–31.

HABERMAS, J. (1971) *Knowledge and Human Interest*, Boston, MA: Beacon Press.

JOHNSON, D. and JOHNSON, R. (1987) *Learning Together and Alone*, (2nd ed.) Englewood Cliffs, NJ: Prentice-Hall.

LOUDEN, W. (1989) 'Understanding teaching: Meaning and method in collaborative research', Unpublished doctoral dissertation, University of Toronto.

MacINTYRE, A. (1984) *After Virtue: A Study in Moral Theory*, Notre Dame, IN: University of Notre Dame Press.

MILDON, D. (1992) 'Narrative inquiry in education in the light of contemporary Canadian fiction', Unpublished doctoral dissertation, University of Toronto.

POLANYI, M. (1958) *Personal Knowledge*, Chicago: University of Chicago Press.

SCHÖN, D. (1987) *Educating the Reflective Practitioner*, San Francisco: Jossey-Bass Publishers.

SCHUTZ, A. and LUCKMANN, T. (1973) *The Structure of the Lifeworld*, Evanston, IL: Northwestern University Press.

SCHWAB, J. (1970) 'The practical: A language for curriculum', in WESTBURY, I. and WILKOF, N.J. (eds) *Science, Curriculum, and Liberal Education: Selected Essays*, Chicago, University of Chicago Press.

SLAVIN, R. (1990) *Cooperative Learning: Theory, Research, and Practice*, Englewood Cliffs, NJ, Prentice-Hall.

Part V

Processes and Practices of Self-study

Introduction

John Loughran

This section of the book is designed to document and describe a range of processes and practices that are currently being explored in self-study. This section is in an attempt to illustrate how self-study can, and should be, an integral aspect of the work of teacher educators. The value of self-study in teacher education practice may appear to those working in the field to be self-evident. However, it is important to be able to demonstrate this through the articulation and dissemination of individuals' inquiry and research so that the approaches to learning and understanding through self-study might be open to the scrutiny of others. In so doing, this can help to demonstrate the importance of the relationship between learning about one's practice and the teaching about practice with our students of teaching.

This link between teaching and learning about teaching is at the heart of self-study and should clearly be an essential element of teacher educators' pedagogical intent and practice if teaching about teaching is to be viewed as something more than just the delivery of teaching knowledge and the transmission of theory about practice. The practice itself must demonstrate a high regard for the knowledge base of teaching, hence the need for teacher educators to practice what they preach, and the emergence of self-study as a methodology for encouraging this through teacher educators committed to such a view. If pedagogy is to be better understood and valued within the teaching profession, the same certainly applies to teaching about teaching in the academy. Self-study is seen as one way of attempting to do this.

This section begins with a chapter by Glenda Wilkes in which she outlines how her understanding and practice of self-study emerges through her approach to teacher education. Her chapter is based on the notion of paradox because, as she explains, paradox has an explanatory power that is multi-leveled and can lead to interesting and often illuminating insights, and, in many ways, this is indeed an important impetus for pursuing self-study. Perhaps one of the most salient features of Wilkes' chapter is that it is the recognition of a paradox that must first be grasped by a teacher educator. It is reasonable to suggest that a teacher educator juggling the array of tasks, roles and their practice may not recognize the paradox that might be readily apparent to others. Yet it is the recognition itself that is the starting point for self-study and should not be too easily overlooked or ignored.

John Johnston, Rebecca Anderson and Lisa DeMeulle's chapter illustrates one practical and exciting approach to addressing concerns within their practice as they explain how they conducted a collaborative self-study on the Internet through a MOO. One aspect of this chapter that is indicative of many self-studies is the importance of the relationship between the collaborators whereby the inquiry into practice and the concurrent learning through inquiry is the important issue. This is well illustrated through John, Rebecca and Lisa's work as they push, probe and examine each other's practice through dialogue that is not inhibited by perceived positions of authority or hierarchy. In fact, the impetus for the study was a result of the collaboration in teaching whereby the need for appropriate practice was seen to be essential for anticipated learning outcomes. Again, the importance of the links between teaching and learning needing to be both explicit and recognizable is a key to this work. John recognized an inconsistency between his teaching philosophy and his practice. He chose to learn new methods and approaches to teaching that would help him to address this disjunction between philosophy and practice. The extension of Wilkes' notion is therefore evident in this work.

Yet there is another important issue raised in this study. There is an affective component to self-study which is easily overlooked. John found it increasingly dissatisfying to teach pre-service and in-service early childhood teachers in a traditional style whilst advocating teaching students for understanding and encouraging teaching practice that enhanced learner's responsibility for learning. Although John had questions and reservations about other approaches, he wanted to know more about them. Through this recognition of a need for action, his approach to Becky was as an invitation of collaboration and learning through team-teaching an early childhood literacy class, an invitation that fitted snugly with Becky's understanding of teaching, learning and self-study. The processes they developed for self-study through this opportunity to better understand practice was enhanced through the involvement of Lisa and became a powerful tool for the development of a very interesting self-study. This self-study clearly demonstrates the importance of the need for teacher educators to practice what they preach and to examine their attempts to better learn to do so.

This section appropriately concludes with a chapter by Ardra Cole and Gary Knowles. Ardra and Gary extend the work described in the previous two chapters by outlining how the self-study of teacher education practices can be a powerful mechanism for the reform of teacher education. As they articulate and build on their understanding of the general nature and purposes of self-study research, they build a persuasive argument for the self-study of teacher education practices to be seen as a vehicle for teacher education reform. They build their argument in such a way as to demonstrate that there are some important (and natural) consequences of self-study that offer teacher educators opportunities to advance the reform agenda in teacher education both individually and collectively.

Through a series of important and timely questions about self-study, the chapter unfolds. As Wilkes so eloquently explains, through paradox, the surface level contradiction gives way, upon closer examination, to a deeper level of insight that is not contradictory, and can be informative and even illuminating. The value of paradox to self-study is then that the search for illumination is something that needs to be valued by the individual.

It is all well and good to recognize apparent contradictions in practice, but it is something very different to decide to address the issue and search for a greater understanding. This point is implicit in Johnston, Anderson and DeMuelle's chapter. They demonstrate how their views of self-study enhance our understanding of the processes and practices of self-study in teacher education.

Cole and Knowles build on the ideas proposed through the previous two chapters in such a way as to make clear the collective responsibility that teacher educators have to address concerns of practice, and in so doing, to pursue reform in teacher education, which is in many instances long overdue. Moreover, Cole and Knowles' argument is thoughtful and powerful as it highlights the need for beliefs and practice in teacher education to be in harmony if the outcomes of learning about teaching are to be in accord with the intent of the educators and education faculties which are responsible for the development of, not only our teachers, but our teacher educators.

13   Seams of Paradoxes in Teaching

Glenda Wilkes

Background: Three Strands

As is usually the case with important events in life, several parallel strands intersect at a point in time, and that intersection then becomes a starting point for something new. Such is the case with how I came to see the importance of self-study in my own teaching practice. For me, three separate strands slowly began to converge.

The first was a theme that emerged from my work with my university students studying to become elementary teachers. The second theme was an interest in the nature of paradox. The third theme was my introduction to and pursuit of the idea of studying one's own teaching practice, which was fostered by a special interest group within a large international organization of teacher educators.

There are many possible frameworks for engaging in a self-study. This is true, perhaps, because there are many ways to teach well. One possible framework is to follow a theme that appears repeatedly in the literature in one's field or in one's teaching practice, and to turn that theme inward and use it as a vehicle for exploration.

A theme that has arisen frequently from the literature on teaching is that many elements of good teaching practice are counterintuitive. For example, it seems to follow logically that if praising students is a good thing to do, and we all like to be praised, then it does not seem unreasonable to suggest that being conscious of attempting to praise students and, as a result therefore, giving more praise would be beneficial. This may not necessarily be a conscious push to praise students, rather it is a response to teachers wanting students to feel empowered in learning environments, hence praise may be a way of doing so. Once it becomes a part of a teacher's script (White, 1988), it may happen more and more in their practice. However, the literature suggests that this response may not be helpful. Praise is more effective if it is used sparingly and for specific performance (Good and Brophy, 1995). Therefore, a natural response to attempting to praise students can develop in such a way as to hinder the development initially intended.

Another example that highlights this point is demonstrated by our response as teachers when a student is having difficulty understanding elements of the curriculum. Our intuition tells us to pay more attention to the pace of our teaching, to increase the examples we offer to help clarify an issue, and to allow students more time to 'get the point'. But for the at-risk student, for whom understanding is often problematic, slowing down the curriculum may have the opposite effect of burying the student in minutia and making the development of understanding even more difficult. Therefore, as strange as it may seem, implementing the opposite strategy may actually work better, that is, to speed up the curriculum, move through the material more quickly and thereby give the student a broader picture from which to see the patterns and connections (Richardson, Casanova, Placier and Guilfoyle, 1989). Although this does not feel like the right thing to do, it may be the effective thing to do and it may well produce the desired result, even though it is counterintuitive.

So, in the process of preparing university students to be elementary teachers, I engage in conversations with them about situations in which the novice teacher might follow her intuition in a given situation whereas the expert teacher, because of both experience and a knowledge of the literature on teaching, might employ a counterintuitive practice. In my own teaching practice, I find the same principle applies. Often when a student comes to me for help, and they are truly struggling, my intuition tells me to help them by either giving them the answer or telling them where to find it. It is painful for me to listen to them struggle and not give them the information they need. I often have to resist mightily what I want to do, what my gut tells me, and fix the momentary crisis. But I have learned that if I become the source of answers, then I often enable students to stop searching for themselves. So I now employ what, for me, is a counter-intuitive practice. I just ask them questions instead, such as, 'Why do you think it is important to know this?, What does this issue have to do with children and classrooms?, What type of research might be relevant here?' and so on. Later they often come back and thank me for not telling them the answer. But at the time, they often leave angry with me for withholding information from them. This ongoing conversation provided the first strand of my self-study.

The second strand of what was to eventually become my framework for self-study was a long time interest in paradox as a literary technique. One day, while reading an article on paradoxes in literature, I realized that some of the counterintuitive teaching practices I had been discussing with my students, could be thought of as paradoxes. Although not all counterintuitive ideas are paradoxes, some are, and I began to think about the use of paradox in teaching.

The third strand of this story was my participation in the formation of a Special Interest Group (SIG) within the American Educational Research Association. This SIG was eventually named the Self-study of Teacher Education Practice (S-STEP), and has provided a gathering place for teacher educators from around the world to talk about and develop ways of thinking, writing, and doing self-study. As I continued to discuss with my students those counterintuitive teaching practices, I also continued to think about the nature of paradox, and I continued to read and interact with my colleagues around our shared interest in self-study. These three strands eventually intersected and my own framework for the study of my own teaching practice was born.

The Nature of Paradox

What is a paradox, and why is it a useful vehicle for thinking about teaching? A paradox is a seemingly contradictory assertion which is nonetheless true. It is a statement that seems contradictory, but when the seams of the paradox are unraveled a little, it is possible to see that the contradiction is not a contradiction at all. Two things separate paradox from other literary techniques such as a dilemma, enigma, absurdity, ambiguity, or mystery, to name a few. One is that a paradox has multiple levels of meaning, more like a French seam, to continue to seam metaphor. A French seam has two levels of stitches in it — one level sews the two pieces of fabric together initially, and then one side of this seam is trimmed and the other side folded over the trimmed side and stitched again. A French seam is sturdier because of the double stitching, and garments sewn with French seams are considered to be higher quality. A paradox is somewhat like a French seam. Once you unravel the initial incongruity, which is the visible seam on the top, you find underneath another seam, in the case of paradox, another level of meaning. So the paradox is operating on at least two levels, the surface level and then the secondary level, but without some investigation and thought the secondary level remains hidden. So it seems, or seams, that paradox has an explanatory power that is multi-leveled and can lead to interesting and often illuminating insights.

The second aspect of the paradox which sets it apart is that it is not in need of being resolved. A dilemma, two equally unfavorable or disagreeable choices, must be solved before one can move forward. One is paralyzed until a decision is made. For example, consider the dilemma created when considering two equally unfavorable positions such as, do I have surgery, or take medication and hope it will suffice? Or do I have the car repaired, or is it time to buy a new one? We all face dilemmas and we address them because (using the examples above) until a decision is made, I have no transportation, or I will continue to be ill. But a paradox does not need to be resolved, because the surface contradiction, which makes us think it is a dilemma, is in fact not a contradiction at all. So, once we uncover the nature of the compatibility that is underneath that French seam, we can chuckle to ourselves and feel relieved that we do not have to make a decision.

Examples of paradox are many, but I will choose one from Shakespeare as the quintessential example because it offers both form and explanation. In Shakespeare's *Twelfth Night*, Act V, Scene I, the Duke of Orsino greets Feste, the Clown or Fool, saying, 'How dost thou, my good fellow?' The Clown replies, 'Truly, sir, the better for my foes and the worse for my friends'. This statement seems illogical; it seems absurd. How can someone be better for one's enemies and worse for one's friends? The Duke, focusing on the apparent contradiction, challenges Feste's claim, to which Feste replies, 'No, sir, the worse . . . Marry sir, they [my friends] praise me and make an ass of me; now my foes tell me plainly I am an ass; so that by my foes I profit in the knowledge of myself, and by my friends I am abused'.

Feste is certainly no fool. As one ponders what Feste has said, one begins to see the explanatory power of paradox. Friends often tell us what we want to hear in order to protect us from being hurt and to keep our friendship intact. Foes, on the other hand, feel no such obligation, and so we might want to carefully cultivate a few stalwart foes who will tell us the truth so that we might 'profit in the knowledge' of ourselves.

The paradox of a best enemy is well known to academics — that trusted colleague who will critically review our ideas and give us honest feedback — and certainly we profit from the knowledge of our thinking that comes from such criticism. Paradox, it seems, has much to teach us. The surface level contradiction gives way, upon closer examination, to a deeper level of insight that is not contradictory, and can be informative and even illuminating; just as the seam analogy earlier illustrated.

Paradox in my Own Teaching

I will discuss three aspects of a single paradox that comes up for me over and over in my own teaching and what I have learned from attempting to unravel these seams. One of the paradoxes I think about a great deal is the paradox of teaching content and manner (Fenstermacher, 1986).

In one sense, our role as a professor is to teach content — some body of knowledge that we have acquired through study and experience that may be, or should be, relevant to the future careers of our students. We prepare ourselves to teach this content by reading, studying, and pulling together information from a variety of sources, and also by assigning to our students things to read which we can then discuss, talk and write about. Perhaps we even test the learning from such processes on this thing called content. But, content alone is quite sterile and uninteresting — by itself it may well be easily conveyed through a computer or a television. But when the content is lived, so to speak, through us, it becomes dynamic, and we become the medium through which our students learn and remember the concepts or content we are trying to teach them.

For example, in talking about classroom management with pre-service teachers, I frequently tell two stories from my own teaching experience. In one story I handle a crisis poorly, getting angry at the students involved and, in general, not responding in a manner I was proud of then or now. In the second story, I responded to the crisis in a much different way — one that was helpful to students and one in which, upon reflection, I felt I had acted professionally and respectfully of my students. Often when my former teacher education students come back and visit me, they remind me of those stories I told them years before. They cannot recall the names of the theories of classroom management, but they can clearly recall my manner of responding to these two disparate examples of my own classroom management. By sharing these stories with them I am inviting them into my own private world — of successes and failures, of embarrassing moments and triumphant moments.

So, why is this a paradox? It seems to me to be a paradox for several reasons. First, it is common to think that we have never been taught how to teach ourselves. Yet, others perceive college professors to be highly trained in the academic world. However, the one thing we all teach may be the one thing for which we have not been trained. We are trained to teach content — we read, we study, we know things — and we justify our paychecks by assuming that we bring about in our students the process of learning, or at least that we provide an opportunity for them to bring about the process of learning in themselves. Why would we be paid to teach ourselves? On the surface, the paradox of content and manner seems to be contradictory and irreconcilable. To use Shakespeare's form, the paradox might look like this: That for which I am paid much, I teach little, and that for which I am paid nothing, I teach much.

There is another level of meaning beneath the surface that will begin to unravel this seam. When students enroll in our courses, they assume that they will be learning the content. They have no idea that when they learn, they are learning the content in the context of the teaching situation. Students could reasonably assume that the content is basically the same from year to year, allowing for perhaps slow but continuous upgrading of the knowledge. They might reasonably assume that in each course there is a core body of content that is the same from teacher to teacher, allowing for differences in preference and style. But this is more a stereotype than reality. In reality, the same course, taught by two different people may differ dramatically. So, students come to us to learn some body of knowledge called content. When they leave our course, they think they have learned this thing called content. But what has really happened is that they have been molded by our own thinking, and perhaps even changed. They have seen the content through our eyes and through our experience — our story has become woven into the content. And then, of course, as our students begin their own teaching careers, that content again becomes woven into their own stories. Howard Gardner (1982) said it well when he said that a scholar is his [or her] teacher, his [or her] own master, poorly or artfully reconstructed and recombined. It is not only content that figures into that recombination and reconstruction, but manner as well. Manner is a combination of things — it is the way we conduct ourselves every time we are in a teaching occasion, both in the classroom and in our offices with individual students. It is also our recollection of the experiences and moments that have prodded us and allowed us to grow as teachers ourselves. It is the bringing to life for our students, both by our example and our stories, the human aspect of teaching.

As one begins to unravel the seams of a paradox, one finds that the seams connect to other seams, often beautifully as in a well-constructed and elegant garment. And so, as one undertakes the following of a paradox wherever it leads, some of the seams may surprise us. It is difficult for me to think about the paradox of content and manner in teaching without thinking of other parts of my life in which the same paradox occurs. One of those seams, for me, is in parenting. Gardner's notion of reconstruction is powerfully illustrated in patterns of parenting. No doubt that parenting and teaching have much in common, and one of those intersections is this idea of reconstruction. For most of us, the models that we have for parenting are our own parents. When we become parents ourselves, we draw upon the models of our own parents, and poorly or artfully reconstruct them. We have all said, at one time or another, 'I will never do this or that or whatever to my own children. I will be different. I will be better'. And in a moment of stress, when we are tired or angry, what model do we fall back on? We have all caught ourselves saying or doing the very thing we promised ourselves we would never say or do. So, then we reconstruct that reality, by reflecting on that particular inadequacy and consciously mapping for ourselves a different course of action. But as we all know, that is very hard work. I predict that most of us are thoughtful, reflective, concerned parents. I also predict that most of us make a genuine effort to interact with our children in a positive, uplifting, growth-producing manner. There is ample evidence from social psychology and other related fields, to suggest that the models we create as parents live on for generations, poorly or artfully reconstructed.

The cycle of abuse is a powerful example of this model recurring in a negative, destructive way. The model of the abuser is so powerfully inscripted on the mind and psyche of the abused child that it is nearly impossible for the child, grown to adulthood, to artfully reconstruct it. It is not totally impossible, but nearly so. I often wonder, what models am I giving my own children to work with in their own reconstruction. As they take the content of my 'lectures', they combine what I have said with what I am — the manner of my behavior. Whatever I am saying is cast in the mold of my manner, and if the two are inconsistent, the manner will win. It is the old adage of 'Do as I say, not as I do' and then the child promptly does exactly the thing we are doing, and ignores what we are saying. The lessons our children and our students learn from our manner are the most potent and long lasting messages we teach them.

I have often wondered about what messages I am really teaching my soon-to-be teachers. I assume that I am teaching them about a framework such as locus of control — being in charge of their own learning so they can in turn teach their own students the same thing. But am I a perfect model of this concept? Do I, on occasion, undermine my own students by giving them messages by my manner that are incompatible with what I am trying to teach? Is my own model more powerful than the framework itself when the two are at odds with each other? Am I even aware when this is happening? How can I know when my model is inconsistent? Or can I even know?

For example, I talk with my pre-service teachers a great deal about authoritative management techniques — clear communication of expectations, mistakes as an opportunity for instruction not punishment, responsiveness to students' point of view, firm but flexible rules that are enforced with reason and negotiation. Then I continually bump up against situations in which I am required to actually live these concepts in my own teaching practice. So, when a student comes in to talk to me about an exam, and perhaps to complain about a question they thought was unfair, I am at the same time responding on two levels. I am responding to the content of the question, ascertaining the student's understanding of the concept contained in the question, but more importantly I am modeling, by my manner, the authoritative management style I have been teaching in class. I am living the concept through my own manner. And later in the day, when I review in my own mind my interaction with that student, and evaluate my own behavior for the purposes of studying my own teaching practice, I must evaluate whether or not the content and manner were compatible.

These seams lead me to think about another piece of this paradox — that of perspective. I must, to some degree, teach the content of my courses from my perspective — from the perspective, or hopefully multiple perspectives, that I have developed over the years of reading, study and teaching. And yet, every time I engage in a conversation with a student, stand in front of a class, or interact with one of my children, I have the opportunity to understand the world from another person's point of view. I have the privilege of seeing into someone else's patterns of thought. When I stop and think about what an enormous privilege that is, and the opportunity that these interactions provide for me to grow and mature far beyond what I could even achieve on my own, I realize that I am continually reconstructing my own self as a learner through the perspective of my students and my children. I never leave the classroom the exact same person that I was when I entered. My students continually change my thinking. As I try and see the world from their perspective, I become different. They teach me things I have never thought of before.

Thinking about perspective then leads me to think about the unequal nature of the teacher/student and parent/child relationships. In each of these, the adult of teacher/parent has the great power and the child/student has less. That is an inherent piece of teaching and parenting. As teachers and parents, we make decisions every day about what we think is best for our students and children to know, do, understand, learn, participate in, and talk about. If we are not very careful, we can become astonishingly arrogant in the process. Continually trying to put ourselves in the place of our students helps us to guard against this arrogance — validating their perspective when possible, and always the right to have and voice that perspective, is critical to unbinding the unequal nature of these relationships. Because of this inequality, I struggle with the ethical considerations in my relationships with my students and my children. At what point does imposing my own thinking upon them become unethical? Where do my rights as a teacher/parent and their rights as a student/child begin and end, overlap, mutually enhance, or begin to be at odds? I can not even begin to answer these questions. Indeed, I am just beginning to be able to ask the questions themselves.

I teach a graduate course that I have developed entitled *Gender issues in Education*. One of my purposes in this course is to get the students to develop multiple perspectives, or at least to see that multiple valid perspectives are possible and probable for almost all gender-related topics. In this process, I have to be very careful to keep my own perspective silent until the very end, lest the students adopt my perspective as their own. Often, I never tell them my opinion at all because I do not want to interfere with their own evolving awareness of what gender means in their own lives. Sometimes they will say, 'Will you tell us what you think when the semester is over?' and I always say, 'Yes' because I know that by then, my opinion will not matter so much any more. They will have formed their own views by then.

And so this one paradox — content and manner — continues to evolve in my own mind, as I begin to ask these questions and think about my own teaching in these terms. Paradoxes become generative. As I think about and struggle with the various seams of paradox inherent in my own teaching and parenting, I realize how fortunate I am to have chosen a profession that allows my professional life to inform my private life. I have conceptualized parenting as the process of getting my children to know themselves as well as I know them. When they can anticipate what lies ahead as well or better than I can, then my job is over. When they know what thought patterns lead to troublesome behavior and can anticipate the latter by recognizing the former, then they no longer need me to ask questions such as, 'Let's think about why this happened. What were you thinking when you did this? Can we talk about what the pattern is here? Does this pattern occur in other things? What are the warning signals? and How can we be sensitive to them in the future?' When my children can ask themselves those questions, then I am no longer needed. My methodology for self-study, then, becomes a series of questions that arise from my interactions with my students and my children in which I question my motivations, my consistency, and my actions. It is the continual enactment of the paradox between content and manner that provides the platform for my questioning, and the continual striving to make my actions consistent with my belief system.

In parallel, it seems to me that one of the purposes of teaching is to help our students come to know themselves as learners. If we can help them see the patterns of their own thinking and how their own lives are relevant to everything they learn, then our job is finished. They no longer need us. And that, I think, is what we want to happen. Part of that process, I have come to learn, is helping them to see the paradoxes in their own lives, and the multiple seams in which those paradoxes have meaning and influence. Then our students, and children, can move forward into territory we have been too limited to explore. This is one of the great privileges we have as teachers and parents — that is of condensing our own experience, the things it has taken us years to understand and learn, into lessons our students and children can grasp and then move forward — in some cases far beyond our own thinking, which in many ways is limited by the very experiences that produced the learning. We can only go so far, but they can go much farther.

My friend, Jody, a divorced mother of a 24-year-old daughter, related to me a conversation she had with her daughter Ashley. Ashley called from New York to tell her mother she was planning to get married the following summer. As they talked about the wedding, Jody told her daughter how much money she could contribute to the financing of the wedding, and then after they hung up she worried that what she had offered wasn't enough. Shortly, the phone rang again, and it was Ashley, calling back to talk about possible dates for the wedding. The mother confided to me that when she heard the phone ring, and heard Ashley's voice, she thought she was calling back because she was upset about the amount of money. After the conversation about dates was finished, and Jody shared with Ashley what her fear had been, Ashley's reply was, 'That's your issue, mother, not mine'. The mother, in relating this to me, said, 'My own daughter, at 24 is more evolved than I am at 50'. My response was, 'Isn't that what we want?'

I remember a colleague of mine being very upset that one of her students had taken ideas presented in class and done some very good, interesting and insightful work on those ideas. My colleague felt chagrined that her student had been able to take her own work farther than she, a professor, had been able to do. My response was again, 'Isn't that what we want?' Just follow my thinking with me for a minute. It is a bit like a relay race, with the baton being the idea or set of ideas, and every time we pass it on to someone else, in a burst of renewed energy and speed, they carry it on faster and further than we who are tired from getting it to that point are able to do.

I find that I am continually learning from my students. One of my students just completed an extraordinary set of comprehensive exams in which she built on reading done in the Gender Class and wrote about adolescent girls and self image, a topic we hear a lot about in the popular media. She pulled together sources I have not read, and drawing heavily from her own experience in a dysfunctional family, she provided insight to me that will change the way I teach this course in the future.

Another student, who plans to go to Law School after completing an advanced Degree in Education, is interested in children's courtroom testimony. He wrote an exam in which he proposed a set of guidelines for questioning children on the witness stand based on gender, development, and moral reasoning. Once again, I will teach these topics forever differently because of insight and understanding of the literature.

There may be no end to this race, no finish line to cross. The ideas keep expanding and travelling from learner to learner, passed from one generation of thinkers to another, each one more vibrant, more exuberant than the one who went before. We have received the baton from our own teachers, mentors, models. We carry it for a time, but we run with it slightly differently than they did. Our arm movement, head movement, leg movement, and breathing patterns are our own. But we run as fast and as well as we are able. Ahead, we can see our team mate — ready and poised to take over the race. As we hand over the baton to them and watch them explode forward, we stand contentedly and cheer them on. When my students go into elementary school classrooms to become teachers themselves and, when they come back and tell me the stories of their own experience, often they have taken the ideas I have taught them in class and acted upon those ideas in much more thoughtful and consistent ways than I have. They have moved way beyond me not only in their thinking but in their practice. I am always moved by the experience of having a former student relate to me an experience from their own teaching in which the content and manner of their own teaching practice was completely in harmony.

Other Paradoxes

Although this is where my thinking has taken me as I have considered the paradox of content and manner, several additional paradoxes often come to mind. There is a paradox between autonomy and collaboration in the academy — the ability to work autonomously is an aspect of teaching at this level that appeals to many of us — and yet we also know that our professional lives are so much richer if we collaborate and work together as colleagues and students. Where would this paradox take us if we began to explore the multiple seams in it. There is a paradox of silence in the classroom — silence is the most productive and the least productive use of classroom time. Issues of power and control enter into the use of silence in the classroom, and a host of other seams. What about the paradox between structure and freedom. We all want our students to have and make choices regarding their own learning, but complete freedom is often chaos. How must structure and what kind of structure allows freedom to be maximized?

Some paradoxes are gendered in nature. In other words, some paradoxes may be different for men and women. Classroom silence is one of those. The disempowerment of silence is real for most women, especially in classrooms. How hard do I push my female students? Can I, as a female myself, understand the paradoxes of my male students? The list goes on and on. In studying my own teaching practice, in questioning the content and manner of my day-to-day interactions with my own students, I am continually pushing at these questions, observing how my students act and react and interact and those observations inform my practice in observable ways.

Conclusion

Brookfield (1995) suggests that reflection becomes critical when it has two distinctive purposes: the first is to understand how considerations of power undergird, frame, and distort educational processes and interactions. The second is to question assumptions and practices that seem to make our teaching lives easier but actually work against our own best long-term interests, and I would add those of our students. It seems to me that using paradox as a vehicle for self-reflection accomplishes both of these purposes.

So, what have I learned so far? I have learned that Ruskin was right when he said that 'The highest reward for a person's work is not what he [she] gets for it, but what he [she] becomes by it'. I have learned that the key to reflection is not what we know about ourselves, but the continual quest for what we do not know about ourselves. I've learned about the importance of tranquillity. Insights rarely come in the midst of it all — they usually come for me in those precious tranquil moments I carve out for myself when I can be alone and think. They are too few and much too short. And I have learned that I can not really know and understand my teaching without attempting to know and understand the other parts of my life as well.

References

BROOKFIELD, S.D. (1995) *Becoming a Critically Reflective Teacher*, San Francisco: Jossey-Bass.
FENSTERMACHER, G.D. (1986) 'Philosophy of research on teaching: Three aspects', in WITTROCK, M.C. (ed.) *Handbook of Research on Teaching, 3rd Edition*, New York: McMillan.

GARDNER, H. (1982) *Art, Mind, & Brain*, New York: Basic Books.

GOOD, T.L. and BROPHY, J. (1995) *Contemporary Educational Psychology, Fifth Edition*, New York: Longman.

RICHARDSON, V., CASANOVA, U., PLACIER, P. and GUILFOYLE, K. (1989) *School Children At-Risk*, New York: Falmer Press.

WHITE, R.T. (1988) *Learning Science*, London: Blackwell Press.

14   Prospects for Collaborative Self-study on the Internet[1]

John M. Johnston, Rebecca S. Anderson and Lisa DeMeulle

Introduction

Our story is about three colleagues who, for very different reasons, engaged in a collaborative self-study in a particular Internet environment known as a MOO. A MOO, mercifully short for Multiple user dimension Object Oriented, is an on-line computer environment that supports real time (synchronous) written conversations within a text based computer environment. Unlike email, its asynchronous cousin, when communicating using a MOO environment two or more individuals at different physical locations can meet on-line and conduct real time written conversations in which all participants can read and respond to what every other participant writes as soon as it is written.

This project began when John, a full professor of early childhood education, became aware that he was using instructional methods that were inconsistent with his teaching philosophy and wanted to learn new methods and approaches to teaching that were grounded in constructivist philosophy. Given his work in developing and assessing state and national teacher education standards, he found it increasingly unsatisfying to teach pre-service and in-service early childhood teachers using a traditional lecture, test, term paper approach. Though he had questions and reservations about new approaches, John wanted to know more about teaching and learning, using, for instance, new approaches to writing to learn, literature study groups, group projects, peer feedback, peer assessment, developing and using rubrics, portfolios and portfolio assessment. He approached Becky, a new member of the elementary/middle school reading faculty, who was using these practices and proposed that they co-teach an early childhood literacy class. Becky was excited with the prospect because she had found value in previous team-teaching (Anderson and Speck, 1997). In her mind, team-teaching and self-study went together (Anderson and Reid, 1994) so she suggested conducting a collaborative self-study as part of their team-teaching experience.

Over pizza one night after class, we discussed our plans with Lisa, another new faculty colleague. Lisa, an elementary teacher educator, was hired at the same time as

---

[1] The authors gratefully acknowledge the editors of *Teaching Education* for permission to publish here a revised edition of the article that appeared first in the Spring/Summer 1997 issue.

Becky and shared a similar constructivist orientation that had already prompted professional collaboration and a growing personal friendship between the two. Lisa also shared an office suite with John and they often lunched together and shared ideas about their respective teacher education programs. During our three way brainstorm about using emerging on-line technology to conduct our self-study, John proposed using the MOO since he had recently become acquainted with its attributes. During our conversation, Lisa agreed to participate in our self-study by moderating our weekly on-line conversations.

Among other reasons for engaging in a collaborative self-study, clearly the most powerful motivation for each of us was the idea of using on-line technology. Lisa was in the process of developing a new course on Internet integration and wanted to learn more about MOO environments. Because Becky previously used email in a self-study (Anderson and Speck, 1997), she was intrigued with experiencing a different form of technology. John was just beginning to investigate using MOOs for social interaction and was curious about the potential they held to facilitate self-study.

The intent of this chapter is to tell the story of how we reflected on our practice using a collaborative method that includes two forms of technology. First, we exchanged dialogue journals via email, and then met once a week on-line to converse about our teaching. This chapter explores our on-line conversations by addressing the following questions: (1) What was the purpose of engaging in on-line collaborative self-study? (2) How did we do it? (3) What were the attributes of this method?

Purpose of Engaging in On-line Collaborative Self-study

We, like many other teacher educators (Hamilton, 1996; Loughran, 1996; Munby, 1995; Olson, 1996; Russell, 1995), value self-study as a form of reflective practice. As with parallel forms of inquiry such as teacher research and action research, self-study places an emphasis on the intentional and systematic study of one's practice: in this case, teacher educators. We engaged in self-study to become aware of our beliefs and practices, and to develop our professional knowledge as teacher educators (Munby and Russell, 1995) and to contribute to the knowledge base in teacher education (Zeichner, 1995).

Even though many teacher educators value self-study, there are a variety of issues that must be confronted. Cole and Knowles (1995) offer a useful framework for self-study that addresses technical, interpersonal, procedural, ethical, political, and educational issues. We were particularly concerned with the technical, interpersonal, and procedural issues, because these seemed salient to a method based on technology and collaboration. For instance, teacher educators often lack the time and money to carry out systematic studies of their teaching. Perhaps more importantly, teacher educators generally work in isolation and the collegial support needed is often missing.

In response to these issues, there is growing evidence of efforts by teacher educators to foster communities for supporting self-study. For instance, the American Educational Research Association now includes Self-study of Teacher Education Practices (S-STEP): a large, active special interest group with an international membership which sponsored an international conference on self-study in teacher education at Herstmonceaux Castle in England in August 1996, with a second conference scheduled for 1998. Can a particular method of self-study encourage collaboration between novice and experienced teacher educators in a way that overcomes the paradigm of teacher educators learning by themselves, through trial and error (Korthagen and Russell, 1995)? Our study sought to address these issues.

There were three additional reasons we engaged in on-line collaborative self-study. First and foremost, we wanted to improve our own teaching. Second, we wanted to experience and model what we advocate to our students. We expect our students to engage in teacher research (Cochran-Smith and Lytle, 1993), because as our students learn to become producers and disseminators of knowledge, they gain power to influence educational decisions (Hollingsworth and Sockett, 1994). Finally, as the Internet becomes more common in schools, we feel it is our professional responsibility to explore ways in which this technology can enhance our teaching and learning, as well as our students' learning. Indeed, new teacher education standards in our state (Tennessee State Board of Education, 1996) require students to be able to integrate a variety of Internet tools into their practice.

How we did it

For one semester John and Becky team-taught a graduate early childhood literacy course. Becky and John reflected on their teaching and sent journal entries to each other via email after each class meeting. The purpose of these weekly journal entries was to exchange ideas, thoughts, and perceptions about teaching the class. They addressed three areas in each journal entry. First, in these weekly journals they reacted to the class in general with specific attention to the topic of peer assessment. Second, they focused on new knowledge and understandings they had gained about their class, again focusing on peer assessment. Third, they considered how these new understandings might guide their future teaching. Lisa also received a copy of these journal entries via email. The three of us met on-line each week to engage in a written conversation about our teaching before the next class meeting. Lisa's role was to serve as a facilitator for these conversations. Although there are multiple environments on the Internet in which to engage in on-line dialogue, our conversations occurred in a MOO environment.

Conversing in a MOO Environment

A MOO is a computer program, accessed via Telnet, in which multiple users located anywhere in the world can simultaneously interact with each other. Communication on a MOO occurs as users write and transmit text (talk). The generated text is visible on each user's monitor and can be read by all others logged on to the same virtual location. Participants can respond by typing and sending their response that is immediately visible to all others at that location. As participants enter new text, it appears at the bottom of each participants' monitor, with text scrolling upward as the conversation continues. Similar to the now popular Internet chat rooms, MOOs are purposeful virtual communities that are social in nature and where community members gather, chat, meet friends, make jokes, and discuss things. There are a number of loosely themed social MOOs (e.g. Lambda, River, CowsGoMOO), role playing or strongly themed MOOs (e.g. ChibaMoo, ZenMOO, StMOO), and educational or academic MOOs (e.g. Media-

MOO, Diversity U, LinguaMoo). MOOsaico (Universidade do Minho, Portugal) was the MOO we chose for our conversations since it was not as crowded as some other MOOs and thus we would experience fewer technical delays.

In contrast to email which is asynchronous, and thus similar to mailing a letter, this form of communication is synchronous, and is analogous to a telephone conference call. The MOO conversational medium is usable by anyone who understands the basic operation of word processing. It is simply a matter of typing what one wants to say, and then entering a RETURN command to send the communication.

Obtaining a MOO Character and Password

Each participant needed access to Telnet as well as a character name and password for MOOsaico. To obtain a character and a password, we each connected to MOOsaico using its Telnet network address and port number:

```
moo.di.uminho.pt/port=77.77
Once we connected, Figure 14.1 shows what we saw on our screens:
$    Telnet moo.di.uminho.pt/port=7777
Trying . . .
Connected to ALFA.DI.UMINHO.PT, a SPARCSERVER 1000 running SUNOS 5.3.

        \\V/                    M u l t i l i n g u a l
        (. .)                   Using LambdaMOO 1.7.8p4
     ooO(_)Ooo
   #*#*#*#*#*#*#*#*#*#*#*#*#*#*      lOcAtEd At UnIvErSiDaDe Do MiNhO
   # Welcome to MOOsaico #           InFoRmAtIc DePaRtMenT
   #*#*#*#*#*#*#*#*#*#*#*#*#*#*
                        Wed Sep 20 17:27:00 1995 MET DST
Please type the following commands,
to connect to your character                'connect <user-name> <password>',
to see how to get a character of your own   'create',
to connect to a guest character             'connect Guest',
just to see who's logged in right now            '@who',
or, to disconnect, either now or later      '@quit'.

Para ver este ecran em portugueˆs, digite 'ajuda'.

After you've connected, type 'help' for      Please email bug/crash reports to
documentation and 'help manners' to see
the behavior we're expecting from you.       pmoo@di.uminho.pt
```

Figure 14.1: MOOsaico start up screen.

By following these directions in our first visit to MOOsaico, we connected as guests by typing:
connect Guest
Then following the MOOsaico program instructions we typed:
create
and received the following response:
create

To get a character, connect as a guest and use the command '@request <character-name> for <email-address>'. The character will be created and the password mailed to the email address. Only one character per person. If, for some reason, the system does not allow you to automatically register, send regular email to pmoo@moo.di.unimho.pt. Please do try @request first. If @request doesn't work, please mention the reason it gave in your email message.

We then sent email requests for our character names and our passwords. Confirmation of character names and assignment of passwords was returned immediately by the MOO host program via email. After logging on to MOOsaico with our new names and passwords, we each created descriptions for our characters:

> *John*: Ernestine
> The priceless patina of middle-age warms the tall and slender gray haired figure who greets your inquiring gaze with twinkling brown eyes and a gentle smile.
>
> *Lisa*: Lisa
> A young intellectual genius type, eager for fame and fortune. Needless to say, she has neither, but she is hopeful. She is friendly, fun, and easy going.
>
> *Becky*: Andy
> A grand lady who has tired eyes. Too much to do. Would love to smell the roses more often.

Finally, John created and then described a room location for our meetings: Project CD [Collegial Dialogue] Office (#3701) is owned by Ernestine (#2309). This sunny office contains three desks with comfortable chairs, a conference table, a project board, and a chalk board. On each desk is a MacIntosh computer. The three Project CD team members are hard at work. It was in this sunny room each Thursday from 1:00 to 2:00 p.m. that our conversations occurred.

Our Weekly Procedure

Every Thursday from 1:00–2:00, each of us would close ourselves up in our university offices, sit down at our computers, and Telnet to MOOsaico. Once connected, a password gave us access to a reserved space that allowed us to converse privately. Acting in her capacity as facilitator, Lisa would begin the conversation with observations taken from her reading of the dialogue journals that Becky and John had written. At the completion of each session, we saved an electronic version and printed a hard copy transcript of our written conversations.

Data Analysis

Our approach to analyzing the data was threefold. First, prior to beginning each weekly on-line dialogue we individually made notes on printed copies of John and Becky's email journal entries. John and Becky's notes consisted of ideas for future classes, questions for each other and insights about their teaching. Lisa's notes were open-codings (Strauss and Corbin, 1990) of topics and/or themes she saw in each of the entries. These notes then helped launch and frame our weekly dialogues. For instance, in the fourth week of the study, John and Becky made notations such as, 'This goes back to the purpose for this journal — are they clear about the purpose?' and, 'Have you ever established criteria with your students or is this something you have always done?' Lisa had open-codings such as 'criteria for journals', 'revisit criteria issues', and 'criteria for grading'. This emphasis on criteria then launched the following conversation:

ON-LINE Conversation #4

L: You both made comments about the journal criteria and your struggles with it. Any comments?

J: My impression was that the students were not clear about creating criteria . . . several possible reasons . . . one, they were not sure what a criterion for a journal was, or they didn't want to deal with this assignment, or they didn't have a context for establishing criteria . . .

B: I liked your suggestion of identifying the purpose of the task for them.

Second, in seven of the twelve dialogues, a portion of our weekly conversation was devoted to reflection (Kaplan, 1990) on the use of on-line collaborative self-study. We made explicit what each of us was learning, explored ideas for dealing with technologically-related problems, and shared thoughts about our various research procedures used. For instance:

ON-LINE CONVERSATION #10

B: At AERA we learned that one of the dangers in self-study is that the researchers don't look at what the students are learning. Are we doing this?

L: I thought a lot about this because it is important, then I wondered if it was part of OUR research questions. Is it?

J: We are, I think to some extent, but are you implying that it should be in a cause and effect mode?

L: Not cause and effect, but why study yourself if you don't know what impact it is having on your students?

In the above conversation, we spent time reflecting on the need to examine student learning as a part of our study. These conversations were important because they provided us with a mechanism to clarify assumptions of the study, rethink the framing of our research questions, and develop ideas.

Finally, we analyzed the data at the completion of the study. Our data set consisted of twelve transcripts of one hour on-line conversations, thirteen sets of weekly email journal entries, and researcher notes taken during these on-line conversations. We began by independently reading the E-mail journals and transcripts in their entirety to get a feel for the nature of our conversations. We then did a second reading as a group. Using open-coding, we noted issues and topics of conversation for each transcript (Strauss and Corbin, 1990). It was at this point that two salient features emerged.

John M. Johnston, Rebecca S. Anderson and Lisa DeMeulle

The Attributes of On-line Collaborative Self-study

We identified two features of using the MOO for on-line collaborative self-study: (a) negotiating the mechanics of written conversation, and (b) the impact of the medium on the nature of our conversations.

The Mechanics of Conversing on the MOO

The mechanical attributes of conversing in a MOO environment can be discussed in terms of (a) access, (b) interruptions, (c) time and timing, and (d) conventions of writing.

Access

The procedure of gaining access to the MOO involved connecting to our university VAX mainframe that provided access to Telnet, and then connecting to the host computer acting as the MOO server. Occasionally, we experienced problems logging on to the VAX, and at times we were disconnected:

ON-LINE CONVERSATION #6
BECKY HAS DISCONNECTED
J: I'd like to hear about Wendee . . .
L: Where's Becky?
BECKY HAS CONNECTED
B: I'm here!
J: She is here!
L: Where were we?

These interruptions naturally interfered with the flow of conversation. MOO servers and network linkages can also crash often and are thus unavailable for use, although we never experienced this problem during our study. Both of these types of mechanical failures are problematic when one or more participants are not able to log on, requiring conversations to be rescheduled.

Interruptions

Since interacting with others is the *raison d'être* for logging on to a MOO, our conversations were often interrupted by others who wished to socialize. These interruptions occurred in two ways. First, we were 'paged' by others. Paging is a function that allows a person to send messages to others logged on anywhere in the MOO. Even though we were dialoguing in a private space that we had secured so others could not enter, we could still be paged. We found these interruptions to be associated with gender and the descriptions we provided about ourselves. For instance, given Lisa's initial character description she received the following message:

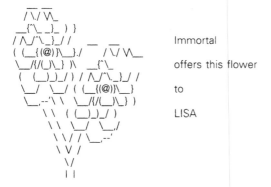

Immortal

offers this flower

to

LISA

Figure 14.2: The message sent to Lisa here

Lisa says 'John, I had a guy sending me flowers on the screen. I really need to change my name to something like Goofus'. Lisa did indeed later change her name to 'Buster', using the following description: 'A large, hairy, gruff dude, very unsociable'. It made a difference; she was never paged again.

The second form of interruption occurred when we forgot to secure our private space, and as a result, other people 'joined' us. This allowed them to see and participate in our dialogue, and forced us to stop our conversation, explain to them that we were having a private meeting, and ask them to leave. Interruptions are a way of life on the MOO, but can be reduced greatly if participants remember to secure their private spaces and use personal descriptions that are not appealing to others or do not use a description at all.

Time and timing

We experienced two forms of lag in our on-line conversations. First, delay was caused by the time it took to type, as opposed to speak, a response. Although the delay was only seconds, others in the conversation were required to wait to make sure the speaker was finished before replying.

A second type of delay was associated with the technology itself, and is referred to as net lag. Net lag is a time lag between a user's input and the Moo's reception of that input. A function of how many users are logged onto the MOO, net lag delays can be a minute or more. These forms of lag time had both positive and negative influences on our conversations that are discussed in the next section.

Conventions of writing

During our first conversation we immediately became aware that we needed a convention to follow so that all three of us were not talking at the same time. John told us to use a MOO convention by breaking our sentences into fragments followed by three ellipsis points to indicate that we were in the middle of a thought, and a period when we were finished. It took only a couple of sessions to master the necessary skills to communicate. As the semester proceeded, we also learned other writing conventions such as using acronyms to abbreviate words. For instance peer assessment, a topic we frequently discussed, became 'pa'. Thus, the conventions of communicating in this environment were relatively easy to learn and developed naturally over time.

In summary, we now understand that on-line collaborative self-study is affected by mechanical attributes. Mechanical attributes related to accessing a MOO, and interruptions to conversation, are always problematic and negative. Access problems are random and beyond the users control; however, interruptions are preventable for the most part. We encountered an important truth when engaging in collaborative self-study online — it takes a longer time to type a thought than to speak it. We had to accommodate a new style of conversing. We found it easy to use and learn this new style, and found it was less problematic as we became more fluent. Finally, we discovered that conversations in the MOO medium are sometimes affected by technical delays that retard or sometimes interrupt the flow of conversation. In the next section, we discuss the impact of a MOO environment on our conversations.

Impact of a MOO Environment on our Conversations

While we found that our conversations tended to center around several themes related to democratic classrooms: peer assessment, developing criteria and standards with students, feedback versus grading, and student-centered assignments, we discovered several ways that the MOO environment influenced these conversations. First, the nature of our dialogues changed over time. Second, our conversations tended to remain on one topic for an extended period of time. Third, we found we were able to merge practical and theoretical knowledge. Finally, we found that scheduling a specific time to meet each week was not always conducive to reflective thinking.

Our changing conversations

Our first two conversations were awkward. We jumped from topic to topic, talked over one another, and explored our roles as co-researchers in this study. During metacognitive processing in the second conversation, Lisa was trying to make meaning of her role in our collaborative effort:

ON-LINE CONVERSATION #2
J: Do you have expectations about what you will get from it [self-study]?
L: That the three of us can join together and talk about ourselves as teachers, something I don't get to do very often. No expectations other than self-insight.
B: Do you think it can influence your teaching?
L: Sure, I'm already thinking about the issues you two have and how they are prevalent in my own classes.

By the third session, we were more comfortable with the conventions and procedures of MOO conversations, more focused on one topic of conversation, and our roles were less of a concern. Toward the completion of the study, we had moved to a point in our dialogues where we were able to reflect back over the semester and articulate what we had learned as a result of engaging in our collaborative self-study. For instance:

ON-LINE CONVERSATION #12

L: What if we discuss what we've learned about peer eval, and what questions we still have now? What have you learned that you didn't know before?

J: I've learned new strategies that I hadn't used before, and had an opportunity to try them out in a class to see how they worked.

L: I've learned that peer assessment is one way to evaluate student learning, and that its main purpose is to help promote self-understanding. This was new for me.

B: I guess I'm still struggling with the grades vs. learning issue. Should peer assessment be just for facilitating learning? I get concerned/confused about students giving each other grades.

In summary, even though our conversations began somewhat awkwardly, we were having focused professional dialogue about things we had learned, as well as posing new questions for future inquiry after fourteen weeks.

Time on topic

We found that on-line dialogue was conducive to in-depth discussion and reflection for two reasons related to lag time. Both net lag and the lag time involved in typing responses forced us to wait longer to respond than if we were speaking directly to each other. We discussed this aspect in our fifth conversation:

ON-LINE CONVERSATION #5

L: I have a hypothesis. I think we stay more on one topic than we would in a conversation. In a conversation, you drift with the dialogue, but here, you stay more focused on one point because it takes longer to respond. Do you agree?

B: Yes.

J: Yes.

We became reluctant to start a new topic until we were sure that no one had further comments to make. This wait time encouraged us to keep reflecting on the topic at hand. For instance, in the beginning of our ninth dialogue we engaged in an in-depth discussion about the difference between criteria and standards:

ON-LINE CONVERSATION #9

J: Could we pause a moment and reflect on what we mean by criteria?

L: I found a great article on the difference between standards and criteria... Criteria specify general requirements while standards represent the degree to which these requirements need to be satisfied in particular instances.

> J: I have been confusing criteria and standards. I wonder if the students have been confusing them too?
>
> As this dialogue continued, we were able to move from defining terms to implications for our practice:
>
> J: It now makes sense to me to discuss standards after students are well into writing their paper, but criteria need to come closer to the front end. I am learning!

Lag time offered the opportunity to spend more time on a topic, thereby creating sustained reflection that resulted in gaining new understandings about our theory and practice.

The merging of theory and practice

For us, a major strength of our approach was that our discussions became a time for reflecting not only on our practice, but also for examining the personal theories we held in connection with those practices. This is illustrated in our seventh conversation:

> **ON-LINE CONVERSATION #7**
> B: Last semester when the student teachers developed the categories/criteria, they felt that it was worth it. This semester, I don't think that . . . it would create less tension for the students if we told them the categories, but they will also end up having less ownership . . .
> J: . . . but the way people respond to categories is what is looked at, that tells the tale, so the issue becomes how to preserve ownership with 'laid on' categories.
> B: I see it connected to the power/democratic issues. Who has the power to decide what the categories should be — who knows?

In this excerpt, we discussed a practical concern of creating criteria with students, which led us to explore more theoretical issues of democracy and power in the classroom. However, we discovered that we were unable to reflect on more global or theoretical issues if one of us had a specific classroom concern.

> **ON-LINE CONVERSATION #9**
> L: Your journal entries appear to indicate that there is a 'flow' to your class now. Things seem to be running smoothly.
> B: I would like . . .
> J: You are right, things are running fairly smoothly.
> B: . . . for us to discuss when to develop criteria with students.

Here we see that Lisa attempted to begin a more global conversation, but Becky had a specific need to discuss, and thus changed the direction of the conversation to meet her needs. This phenomenon occurred in many of our discussions. Once a specific need was met through discussion, we would often return to a more social, political, or theoretical issue related to education.

Scheduled reflection

In most of our on-line conversations, we were fully engaged in the discussion; however, our eighth conversation proved to be an exception. During this conversation, we had problems staying focused:

ON-LINE CONVERSATION #8

B: I still feel the need for a lit review!
L: On peer eval?
B: Yes.
L: I'm feeling very distracted, hard to focus today, sorry.
J: Regarding the feedback during the writers celebration . . .
B: Maybe then we could talk about the dialogue . . .
J: I was just thinking the same thing!
L: What dialogue?
B: Thinking what John?

The problems we experienced staying focused during this conversation made us question the effectiveness of a scheduled time for reflection. Although maintaining focus occurs in verbal conversations, participants can use non-verbal cues to re-engage others in the conversation or to direct its flow. However, these affect-laden cues are missing from MOO conversations. We had fewer ways of helping one another to become focused on the topic again or understand the intensity of another's need for a different conversational focus if we found ourselves distracted.

In summary, we now understand that a MOO environment influenced our conversations in at least four ways. First, our conversations moved from being awkward and unfocused to being more specific, reflective and fluent as we recognized and mastered the conventions of written conversation in a MOO environment. We found conversing on-line in a MOO environment to be user-friendly. Second, these on-line conversations were conducive to in-depth discussion because the pacing of written conversation is slower than spoken conversation. We learned that a conversation will cover less ground but in greater depth. Less is more is a characteristic of this approach. Third, this medium supported the merging of theory and practice, a primary goal of self-study. For us, this occurred naturally and unconsciously. Finally, we learned that scheduling a specific time to meet each week was not always conducive to reflective thinking. In addition, we found that the lack of non-verbal cues required us to work harder to make sure everyone maintained focus and was engaged in the conversation.

Discussion and Implications

We entered into this study not knowing what to expect when using the Internet for collaborative self-study. We found MOOs to be very engaging and highly conducive to collaborative self-study. Indeed, this method demands collaboration. Below we make meaning of our findings using Cole and Knowles' (1995) categories of technical, interpersonal and procedural issues of self-study, and discuss implications for teacher educators.

Technical Issues

Technical issues 'revolve around the initial facilitation and ongoing continuance of the inquiry process' (Cole and Knowles, 1995, p. 143). Many forms of collaborative self-study are time intensive due to methods of data collection such as interviewing, participant observation, and recorded meetings and discussions among collaborators, all of which can be impeded or influenced by technology.

We found that using a MOO environment is very advantageous in dealing with technical issues. As a form of data collection, it was convenient to stay in our own offices and easy to participate on the MOO. There is no cost in this form of self-study for those who have access to Telnet. This process provides a free electronic and hard copy transcript without the time usually involved in transcription — a task made more complex when collaborative meetings and discussions are a source of data. These written records leave a trail that would not normally exist in verbal conversations and in a form that is virtually ready to code and analyze on a computer. We did, however, experience some access and interruption problems with the technology, but these were insignificant in terms of time. Although it took longer to type our responses than it would to speak them, this turned out to be to our benefit by helping us reflect more thoughtfully. On-line conversation appears to strongly support collaborative self-study and so may alleviate isolation, a significant barrier often associated with self-study. Educators who do not have local colleagues with whom to study their teaching can collaborate with colleagues at other locations.

Interpersonal Issues

When examining interpersonal issues, attention is given to the relationships, roles, and responsibilities involved in collaborative self-study. We found that using a MOO for a collaborative self-study had interpersonal advantages and drawbacks. This method is grounded in social interaction, and cannot occur unless there are two people who are willing to do it. It requires collaboration based on mutual interest. Responsibilities are naturally shared during data collection. Because commitment is made to dialogue on a regular basis, this can help sustain participants during those weeks when schedules are overly demanding. If studying one's practice alone, documentation might not be kept as faithfully. This method helps support commitment, an essential element in sustaining collaborative effort.

Procedural Issues

On-line collaborative self-study can also overcome problems associated with the time and cost of data analysis and collection. If educators want to analyze their conversations systematically, this process provides a hard copy at no cost and without the time usually involved in transcription. These written records leave a trail that would not normally exist in verbal conversations and in a form that is ready to code and analyze on a computer.

In addition to the specific findings of our own collaborative effort, we also identified some larger implications related to using a MOO environment for self-study. For educators who are intimidated by emerging technologies, collaborative self-study in a MOO environment is user-friendly. Lisa and Becky entered this experience only with knowledge of email and word processing. With John's help they found this Internet environment to be easy to learn, and available to them at no extra cost since they already had access to Telnet.

Final Reflections

Finally, we learned that this method of self-study made a difference in our professional lives. We feel that we are better teachers. For instance, in his tripartite role as a student, teacher and researcher, John learned from Becky how to plan and implement constructivist teacher education classroom practices. He applied his learning as he explored and mastered these new approaches while team teaching each weekly class. He was able to reflect on his efforts, discuss difficulties he was having, and clarify issues surrounding constructivist teacher education practices during the weekly on-line conversations with Lisa and Becky. The team teaching and collaborative self-study brought about major changes in John's teaching. Lecture and term papers have been replaced by approaches including among others, literature study groups, journals, collaborative group projects, and authentic assessment strategies.

We have more confidence in our ability to use new technologies. For instance, Lisa has moved to integrate technology into all of her courses and feels comfortable in meeting any new technology standard in teacher education. Becky is currently developing a new course integrating technology into the literacy curriculum. John is teaching a new course about technology and teaching and learning in the early childhood curriculum. Because of our first-hand experience in a MOO environment and our continued integration of technology into our teaching, we know that MOOs and other Internet technology can lend powerful support for collaborative self-study.

As a result of our collaborative experience, we have stronger collegial relationships with one another. In fact, our self-study resulted in us developing jointly a new required departmental core course in teacher research. We also have new questions to explore. It was personally exciting to us to make linkages between our theory and practice. This method gave us the basis for understanding and challenging our beliefs, and in turn, influencing our actions.

Looking forward, we recognize the need for our future research to focus on the impact of this method on student learning. The purpose of this study was exploratory. We wanted to gain a greater understanding of MOO environments as a venue for collaborative self-study. Next, we would like to see if it makes a difference in students' lives. We need to explore the linkages between our changing understandings, the impact of this knowledge on our practice, and most importantly, the influence on student learning. Finally, given our increased knowledge and skill in using the MOO environment for self-study, we are interested in exploring how the barriers we encountered can be overcome. The continuing evolution of Internet technology, computer hardware and software will certainly ensure even easier use of on-line environments for collaborative self-study of one's teaching practice. Given that the evolutionary history of technology predicts easier and wider access to an increasingly user friendly Internet, it is important to continue exploring MOOs and other interactive environments as a venue and method for collaborative self-study.

References

ANDERSON, R.S. and REID, S.S. (1994) 'A collaborative conversation about learning: Using dialogue journals for professional development', in KINDER, C. and LEU, D.J. (eds) *Multi-dimensional Aspects of Literacy Research, Theory, and Practice*, Forty-third Yearbook of The National Reading Conference, pp. 361–9.

ANDERSON, R.S. and SPECK, B.W. (April, 1997) 'Working together: Studying our team teaching', in J. Richards (Chair), 'Expanding the knowledge base about self-inquiry: Merging academic perspectives with practitioner voices'. Symposium conducted at the annual meeting of the American Educational Research Association, Chicago.

COCHRAN-SMITH and LYTLE, S. (1990) 'Research on teaching and teacher research: The issues that divide', *Educational Researcher*, **19**, 2, pp. 2–11.

COCHRAN-SMITH, M. and LYTLE, S. (1993) *Inside/outside: Teacher Research and Knowledge*, New York: Teachers College Press.

COLE, A.L. and KNOWLES, J.G. (1995) 'Methods and issues in a life history approach to self-study', in RUSSELL, T. and KORTHAGEN, F. (eds) *Teachers Who Teach Teachers*, London: Falmer Press, pp. 130–51.

HAMILTON, M.L. (1996) 'Mapping a landscape: Identifying and exploring self-study'. Paper presented at the annual meeting of the American Educational Research Association.

HOLLINGSWORTH, S. and SOCKETT, H. (1994) 'Teacher research and educational reform'. Chicago: National Society for the Study of Education, University of Chicago Press.

KAPLAN, S.N. (1990) 'Building better thinkers: The start-up stage', *Learning*, **90**, February.

KORTHAGEN, F. and RUSSELL, T. (1995) 'Teachers who teach teachers: Some final considerations', in RUSSELL, T. and KORTHAGEN, F. (eds) *Teachers Who Teach Teachers*, London: Falmer Press, pp. 187–92.

LOUGHRAN, J. (1996) 'Self-study in teaching and research'. Paper presented at the annual meeting of the American Educational Research Association, New York.

MISHLER, E.G. (1986) *Research Interviewing: Context and Narrative*, Cambridge: Harvard University Press.

MUNBY, H. (1995) 'Gazing in the mirror: Asking basic questions about self-study'. Paper presented at the annual meeting of the American Educational Research Association, San Francisco.

MUNBY, H. and RUSSELL, T. (1995) 'Towards rigor with relevance: How can teachers and teacher educators claim to know?' in RUSSELL, T. and KORTHAGEN, F. (eds) *Teachers Who Teach Teachers*, London: Falmer Press, pp. 172–84.

OLSON, M.R. (1996) 'Collaborative reflections: Letter writing as a form of collaborative self-study'. Paper presented at the annual meeting of the American Educational Research Association, New York.

RUSSELL, T. (1995) 'Giving authority to personal experience: Studying myself as student teachers study themselves'. Paper presented at the annual meeting of the American Educational Research Association, San Francisco.

STRAUSS, A. and CORBIN, J. (1990) *Basics of Qualitative Research: Grounded Theory Procedures and Techniques*, Newbury Park, CA: Sage Publications.

TENNESSEE STATE BOARD OF EDUCATION AND TENNESSEE DEPARTMENT OF EDUCATION (1996) *Teacher Education Policy Implementation: Licensure Standards and Induction Guidelines*, Nashville: Author.

ZEICHNER, K.M. (1995) 'Reflections of a teacher educator working for social change', in RUSSELL, T. and KORTHAGEN, F. (eds) *Teachers Who Teach Teachers*, London: Falmer Press, pp. 11–24.

15 The Self-study of Teacher Education Practices and the Reform of Teacher Education[1]

Ardra L. Cole and J. Gary Knowles

Introduction

We begin with an assumption: self-study of teacher education practices is a powerful mechanism for the reform of teacher education. In this chapter, we provide an overview of the general nature and purposes of self-study research and work, its current role and status in the academy, and its emerging role and status in the teacher education community. In so doing, we hope to characterize the self-study of teacher education practices as a vehicle for teacher education reform, and offer some ideas on how those involved in self-study work might advance the reform agenda through a course of individual and collective action. We organize the chapter with a series of questions:

- What is self-study of teacher education practice?
- What is the broad intention of those who engage in self-study of teacher education practices?
- What concerns do self-study researcher-practitioners have about engaging in such work?
- What are the reasons for and bases of these concerns?
- How is the status quo challenged by self-study?
- How and why is self-study research?

We conclude with a discussion of the role of self-study in teacher education reform and a call for community action to promote self-study as a powerful reform mechanism.

The Nature and Intention of Self-study of Teacher Education Practice

What is self-study of teacher education practice? What is the broad intention of those who engage in self-study of teacher education practices? Although self-study of teacher

[1] We acknowledge the generous support of the Social Sciences and Humanities Research Council, Canada. Ideas in this paper exploring the relationship between self-study and teacher education reform were facilitated by a research project on beginning teacher educators and teacher education reform.

education practices takes many forms, it has two main purposes. Teacher educators, many of whom were classroom teachers prior to entering the academy as university-based educators, engage in self-study both for purposes of their own personal-professional development and for broader purposes of enhanced understanding of teacher education practices, processes, programs, and contexts. Sometimes both are made explicit in self-study work; sometimes one is implicit in the other. The purposes are not mutually exclusive. The former purpose typically has a largely practical (often pedagogical) focus and is usually self-oriented in that the general aim relates to the ongoing improvement of one's own (pedagogical) practice. The latter purpose has a broader aim more generally related to the production and advancement of knowledge about teacher education practices and the programs and contexts within which they are situated. Both purposes have to do with refining, reforming, and rearticulating teacher education.

Self-study for purposes of self-understanding and professional development is essentially being thoughtful (in a Deweyan sense) about one's work. It is reflective inquiry, similar to that widely advocated for teachers. As a form of professional development self-study is inherently valid and defensible as sound pedagogical, professional practice. Its practice has obvious inherent benefits for learners as well as for teachers, and within academic contexts where progressive teaching is valued, so too are those who engage in self-study.

Concerns About Self-study

What concerns might self-study researcher-practitioners have about engaging in such work? What are the reasons for and bases of teacher educators' concerns about engaging in self-study? Concerns about institutional responses to self-study mainly are rooted in issues associated with tenure and promotion since most of those engaged in self-study research do not have full rank and status security. For others, concerns may relate to marginalization or isolation. The reward structure of the academy is straightforward and, for the most part, universal. Publications are seen as most meritorious: the more the better especially those of a particular perspective, style, or genre, published in prestigious refereed journals. Getting self-study work published in most education journals is a challenge. Those who have had self-study work (or other reflexive accounts) reviewed for publication by unsympathetic contemporaries can attest to the conserving nature of the review and publication process. Characterizations such as 'narcissistic', 'self-indulgent', 'egocentric', 'solipsistic' are often used to describe self-study work.

In many presented and published accounts and, even moreso, in informal conversations, self-study researchers themselves voice concerns about the perceived legitimacy or validity of their work within the context of the academy. For example, in a reflection on a self-study of his teaching Munby (1996) wonders, 'While I welcome the impact the self-study had on me, I have to question its value for others: 'Why would anyone be interested in what I experienced?' Furthermore, he questions whether his self-study and, by extension, others can be considered valid research (p. 65).

In an earlier publication we commented on the professional development merits for us of our self-study work but raised questions about how that work might be perceived by our respective institutions:

> From a pedagogical standpoint, and based on our beliefs about the importance of understanding ourselves as persons and professionals in the contexts within which we live and work, there is no question that we need to continue to commit ourselves and our time to self-study work. . . . What we do not yet know, however, is whether our [research] currency of self-study has a sufficiently high exchange value. In other words, in the eyes of institutional evaluations and assessments: Are the publications viewed by those who work with us as contributing to the institution and field? Is 'this work published in "the best" journals? Do funding agencies have sufficient interest in the kind of work we do? How does it contribute to work within the local institutional context? Will it contribute to "institutional recognition"-elevated status for the employing body?' (Cole and Knowles, 1995, p. 148)

As it turned out, our respective institutions (at that time) did indeed attach very different value to self-study work.

In the epilogue of *Teachers Who Teach Teachers*, Russell and Korthagen (1995) comment on the historical tensions and dilemmas — which we would say still exist — associated with attempts to challenge the traditions of the academy. They assert that survival, for those who engage in alternative forms of research and practice including self-study, depends on individuals' abilities to keep hidden their non-traditional beliefs and practices and show a traditional face to the academic public.

A failure to live with this split-personality syndrome was, and still is, punished by expulsion from academia — tenure positions generally open only to staff members with a sufficiently long list of publications in the field's traditional journals. Such journals generally support the old research paradigm. Furthermore, the academic world has other means to safeguard dominant paradigms: publications regarded out of the mainstream are often just not cited [or reviewed favourably] by the veterans in teacher education (Russell and Korthagen, 1995, pp. 188–9).

The punishment of 'expulsion from academia-tenure positions' is a practice with a long history, and the espoused grounds for such action generally relate to the individual's demonstrated competence in carrying out professorial responsibilities or the individual's 'fit' with the institution's values, mission or mandate. The real grounds for denial of tenure are seldom made public and are likely known only to the one or more individuals responsible for the decision. Despite the meticulously defined procedures and requirements articulated by some institutions, two points about the tenure system are well known: First, if an individual is not wanted in the institution, a way will be found to deny tenure regardless of the strength of their tenure case; and second, the tenure review process is one of the academy's great mysteries. The tenure system, instituted to protect academic freedom, also works counter to that intention for pretenure faculty. As Tierney and Bensimon (1996) observe,

> If one of the reasons for the creation of tenure was to protect faculty so that they could engage in intellectual battle without fear of reprisal, then that purpose has been lost . . . If a faculty member does not walk the ideological line, he or she will be at risk of not attaining promotion and tenure. (p. 8)

When the topic of tenure denials is raised in informal conversations among academics, it is only a matter of minutes before collective remembering produces a lengthy list of names of prominent and not so prominent scholars, who Tierney and Bensimon might call 'radical riff-raffs purged by their universities'. Given the profile and reputation of many of these scholars and the perspectives they reflect, there is little doubt about the real, though not necessarily stated, grounds for their dismissals. In some way — ideological, personal or political — they represented a threat and challenge to the status quo of the institution and were not content to play the split-personality game.

Many academics have openly engaged in research and professional practices counter to the dominant discourse of the institution and have successfully achieved tenure and the protection of academic freedom, among them are those who engage in self-study. We suggest, however, that because the self-study of teacher education practices represents a challenge to the status quo, those who engage in self-study work might also be considered radical riff-raff. The following two examples are cases in point.

Gary Knowles, who described himself in a recent interview as 'someone who challenged the status quo and came off second best' (Cole and Knowles, 1996, p. 118), was recently denied tenure at a high profile research university in the United States of America. We cite a passage from that interview.

> [Gary]: . . . For the most part it seems, the [negative tenure] decision rested on an assessment of my scholarship . . . Also, given that a good part of my scholarship was directly related to my responsibilities as a teacher [educator] [brackets in original], and some of it was 'self study', it's my guess that those of the committee who were very traditional researchers had difficulty with the practical orientation of much of my work. (p. 112)

Although the 'real' reasons for the tenure decision will never be known to anyone but the committee members who made it, we surmise without a great deal of risk, that the decision rested in Gary's blatant insistence to 'be true to himself', 'to look in the mirror each day and say that I haven't sold out in order to obtain some level of professional security and intellectual freedom' (p. 116). He was unwilling to play the split-personality game, and he was punished by expulsion.

Another example, which is perhaps more obvious and straightforward in its explanation, is that provided by Jack Whitehead who is at the University of Bath in the United Kingdom. Jack is well known within the self-study of teacher education practices community for his notion of 'living educational theory' which presents a challenge to teacher educators to understand the educational theories and values they practice and to make themselves accountable to themselves and their students. To many teacher educators, and especially those committed to self-study, this is not an outrageous viewpoint by any means; interestingly, but not surprisingly, it is also very close in spirit and intent to Gary's position. To the status quo of the academy, however, Jack's ideas were seen as 'disturb[ing] of the good order and morale of the School of Education' (Whitehead, 1994, p. 5). Beginning in the 1970s, his attempts to challenge the traditions of the university by freely expressing the values that constitute his educational relationships were met with abject rejection: failures of his two PhD dissertation submissions and a threat to terminate his employment. As is indicated in a letter from the University Council from which Jack quotes, several years later he was punished once again for his writing and education activities: 'Your activities and writings are a challenge to the present and proper organization of the University and are not consistent with the duties the University wish you to pursue in teaching and research' (p. 6). Hence, while engaging in self-study research may seem like an innocent and well meaning endeavour, it is not necessarily perceived as such by the governing forces of the academy. There are, at present, many snares for the unwary.

Self-study and the Status Quo Perspective of the Academy

How is the status quo challenged by self-study research? In conservative-minded in-stitutions value is attached to those individuals who uphold through their work the dominant ideology of the institution. Usually, this means that research should follow the scientific doctrines of positivism and meet criteria of objectivity, measurement and quantification, predictability, and generalizability, and be presented in relatively de-tached, impersonal ways. Self-study research is based in an epistemology of science which is antithetical to these principles. Although multiple means of representation are possible and are used, in general self-study research is personal, subjective, practically-oriented, qualitative in nature, and often creatively communicated in narrative form.

In addition, universities tend to base their status and reputations on the construc-tion of academic knowledge which is judged by standards of abstraction and obscurity. According to Myers (1995), abstraction and obscurity are built-in safety features that help to conserve, insulate, and protect academic reputations. Self-study research, by its 'up-close and personal' nature, renders both individuals who conduct it and their affili-ated institutions vulnerable and accountable. Self-study researchers lay bare for public scrutiny aspects of themselves, their practices, and their institutions. This effectively disarms the safety features that render academic institutions, and those within them, untouchable. It razes the ivory tower since it enables commoners to peek inside.

It has been only in the last decade that the teacher education professoriate has been the subject of any significant amount of research reported in the teacher education literature. And until recently most of these reports were traditionally-oriented examina-tions of the professoriate, its responsibilities and roles, and its problems. Reports on self-study of teacher education practices are an even more recent occurrence and litera-ture on the topic is, relatively speaking, scant. But over the past few years the self-study of teacher education practices has begun to acquire a scholarly and organizational presence in the teacher education community. Publications such as *Teachers Who Teach Teachers* (Russell and Korthagen, 1995), two special issues of *Teacher Education Quar-terly*: 'Self-study and Living Educational Theory' (Pinnegar and Russell, 1995) and 'Beginning Professors and Teacher Education Reform' (Knowles and Cole, 1996), and the recently published, though with limited distribution, *Empowering Our Future: Con-ference Proceedings of the First International Conference on Self-study of Teacher Education Practices* (Richards and Russell, 1996) are substantial volumes on the topic. They are preceded and followed by numerous other journal articles by a variety of authors in the area. Thus, self-study has achieved a presence as a bona fide research methodology and topic of interest and focus in the teacher education community. Within the context of the academy, however, self-study is still very much an alternative form of research and practice. It represents a challenge to the status quo and, as such, it is as yet a marginalized activity.

We do not mean to suggest that teacher education institutions are not interested in the improvement of teacher education; they just do not want to see themselves as part of the problem. After all, historically, the academy's role is to be seen as offering solutions to social and practical problems not as the source of such problems. Veblen (1918/ 1962) as cited by Schon (1983) describes the situation this way:

> Quite simply, the professions are to give their practical problems to the university, and the university, the unique source of research, is to give back to the profession the new scientific knowledge which it will be their business to apply and test. Under no conditions are the technical men [sic] of the lower schools to be allowed into the university. (p. 36)

And, we would add, under no conditions are those in 'higher schools' to be allowed to behave or to be seen as the technical men and women of the lower schools.

Publicized research that is both personal and practical in its orientation not only endangers the reputation of the academy but also is, by virtue of its very nature, part of a political agenda to challenge traditional conceptions of what counts as knowledge and research. It is not in the best interests of the academy (and those who align themselves with the academy) to support such an agenda. (Self-study work that is true to its nature and spirit leaves no holds barred, no processes sanctioned, and no topic sacred.) Self-study researchers' vulnerability might be further explained by their status within the academy. Typically, those engaged in self-study are teacher educators committed to teaching, the teaching profession, and teacher education reform. As such, they already are self-identified marginals and typically do not hold positions of power within the academy. Ducharme (1993) indicates that many faculty in education and other disciplines who are involved in the preparation of teachers choose not to identify themselves as teacher educators, most likely because of the low status of teacher education in the academy. It is no secret that schools of education are the least powerful members of the academic community. Hence, self-study researchers remain a marginalized group challenged to demonstrate how their scholarly work counts as research.

Self-study as Research for Teachers and Teacher Educators

How and why is self-study research? In many ways self-study researchers vying for legitimacy in the academy face challenges similar to those met by qualitative educational researchers over the past couple decades. In essence, self-study research is qualitative research focused inward. Utilizing the characteristic qualitative research tools of observation, interview, and artifact collection, although clearly with different kinds of goals and emphases, it adheres to the same standards of rigour as qualitative research. Given how qualitative research has gained in status, there is hope for a similar outcome for self-study research. But, of course, unless self-study processes are applied more widely, such as in the disciplines of sociology, anthropology, chances are that this progression of acceptance will not happen with the same potency nor at the same pace.

A similar parallel might be drawn between self-study of teacher education practices research and the teacher research movement. In effect, self-study of teacher education practices is a form of action research, the hallmark of the teacher research movement. As such, and by extension, we might think it would be granted the same kind of acceptability (although it must be noted that action research also has a long history of contentious struggle in the academy). The action research and teacher research movement have very successfully fought for the legitimacy of teacher research. In the struggle, the political stance of the movement as an epistemological challenge to the traditional and modernist conception of both knowledge and research have been made explicit. Kincheloe (1991) notes:

> The critically-grounded teacher-as-researcher movement is designed to provide teachers with the analytical tools to overcome ... conservative and liberal blindness. Researching teachers would possess the ability to challenge the culture of positivism, exposing the origins of many of the constraints which obstruct their ability to implement educational strategies that respond to the experiences and lived worlds of students from all backgrounds. (pp. 65–6)

But while there are obvious similarities between teacher research and teacher educator research, which in theory suggest a similar kind of acceptance, in practice acceptance is curtailed by a major contextual distinction. The successful acceptance of teacher research as bone fide research is conditional. The condition relates to the traditional hierarchical relationship between schools (as sites of practice) and universities (as sites of theory). Even though the teacher research movement was successful in removing total control over educational research and theory development (especially as it pertains to the improvement of classroom practice) from those socially and traditionally granted primacy as academic experts, the hierarchy of status still applies. Kincheloe observes,

> Even after their involvement in educational action research teachers are reluctant to say that they really did research; even if they admit to having done research they maintain that it was unscholarly or of low quality. (p. 18)

'Real' research is carried out by 'real' researchers — experts from the academy: Examine any teacher action research periodical and it is clear that members of the academy still dominate those of the classroom. And, as John Elliott (1989) reminds us, action research already has been coopted by educational managers and policy makers (and we would add academics) who have and apply a technocratic agenda. Thus, in a very real sense, while action research is accepted as a research methodology for classroom teachers, it has yet to meet with wide acceptance as a strategy for knowledge production in the academy. Especially questionable is that work which obviously incorporates socio-political agenda.

What would happen, then, if researchers in the academy were sanctioned by their institutions and the broader academic community to throw off their 'expert' mantles and act like ordinary, curious people with practically-oriented questions, including questions that might challenge 'the system'? How then could universities hold onto their status as elite societal institutions? Even if self-study research 'measures up' according to criteria used to judge qualitative research in general or action research in particular, it is not likely to be readily sanctioned by the academy — not because it is methodologically flawed but because it is epistemologically and politically challenging. Thus, the more important question is not how or whether self-study is research but rather how can it be openly practiced by teacher educators without fear of reprisal from the academic community.

Self-study of Teacher Education Practices and Teacher Education Reform

Self-study researchers are individually and collectively committed to teacher education reform. As Guilfoyle, Hamilton, Pinnegar and Placier (1995) observe:

> We study our own practices . . . Whatever we want our students to do in their own practices — study and reflect, use innovative pedagogy, be a change agent — we ask of ourselves . . . Our practices as teacher educators re-create and redefine teacher education . . . They have the most potential to help us understand what it means to teach, to teach teachers, and to gradually re-create education practices. (p. 53)

Action research or teacher research is noted for its reformative purpose and power. Yet we know reform is a slow, uphill struggle. The self-study of teacher education practices movement has the same kind of potential for substantive, systemic reform of teacher education.

Whitehead (1995) suggests that through self-study teacher educators can help to transform what counts as educational knowledge and educational theory in the academy. While we agree that individual and local change efforts often have greater impact than systemic top-down measures, it seems to us that in order for the power of self-study as a reform mechanism to be realized, collective will and action are required. The struggle for legitimacy in the academy is a political struggle. And, as in other political struggles, organization and solidarity are key.

To conclude we offer several practical ideas for moving forward with self-study research. In so doing we do not intend to define or map out the scope of self-study work, but, rather, to frame and propel individual and collective action. The ideas are listed in four clusters: research and publishing, community building, political action, and critical guiding principles.

Research and Publishing

To promote self-study research, researchers could endeavour to:

- take care to explicate goals, intentions, and processes of individual and collective self-study work so that appropriate appraisals can be made about the value of such work;
- work toward maintaining the integrity of self-study research through explicit adherence to methodological standards (broadly defined);
- make clear the epistemological and methodological issues associated with self-study work by focusing on its unique strengths rather than on its dichotomous relationship with more traditional research approaches;
- focus self-study work on issues/matters/processes/problems that also have value to others and make explicit how self-study work contributes to the broader understanding (and reform) of teacher education.

Ardra L. Cole and J. Gary Knowles

Community Building

To further develop and extend our organizational presence self-study researchers could strive to:

- continue community building activities such as meetings, conference, newsletters, electronic mail networking;
- maintain and build on the various networking efforts already established by self-study researchers so that those who are at the boundaries of self-study and more traditional research practices can enter the conversations;
- facilitate the work of colleagues and graduate students who wish to initiate their own self-study research and, if appropriate, join with them in collaborative self-study work;
- work towards establishing 'centres' of self-study in local institutional contexts.

Political Action

To effect more thoughtful and sustained responses to self-study; self-study researchers could commit to:

- engage other faculty and administrators in conversations about the integral value and place of self-study in ongoing professional, program, and institutional health and development;
- make self-study processes (and work) a central component of ongoing course, teaching, and program evaluation;
- increase the scope of activities of self-study work by writing for 'popular' audiences as well as scholarly and professional ones;
- become part of publishing, tenure and promotion, and grant agency decision-making groups wherever and whenever possible;
- become politically savvy, active, and expressive with regard to focused energies on academy and school reform through self-study.

Critical Guiding Principle

To sustain focus and overall purpose it is important for each of us engaged in self-study work to:

- acknowledge that individual self-study activities are part of a larger teacher education reform movement.

A Closing Note

Systematic inquiry into elements of our practice (teaching, supervision, research, writing); the contexts within which we work (our institutional, academic, and teacher education programs more specifically) is an integral part of who we are and what we do as teacher educators and educational researchers. We believe that professional self-study, which leads to self-knowledge and informed practice, is part of our moral responsibility as teachers of teachers. When we engage in ongoing reflection on, and analysis of what we do, we better understand the reasons, influences, and principles which underpin our actions; we can then make appropriately informed decisions regarding future action. This form of self-study is a vital part of our professional development. It keeps us honest with ourselves and for the students and others with whom we work.

Honesty is also part of our self-study agenda which is situated in the broader educational context — the kind of self-study we named earlier as that concerned with the production and advancement of knowledge about teacher education. As part of a formal research agenda, we study teacher education programs and the contexts within which they are situated, the teacher education professoriate, and the various agendas to reform teacher education. For the most part, it is not 'pretty' work; yet, we sense that for too long the academy, as purveyor and controller of research, has escaped scrutiny. It is time to turn the research lens inward, to lay bare for examination programs, policies, and practices that govern the preparation and development of teachers.

Such self-study also permits us to better understand and learn from successful efforts to change and improve teacher education. The reform of teacher education is on the agenda of most schools and faculties of education. Contextual differences notwith-standing, the similarities of issues with which teacher educators around the globe are grappling are remarkable. And yet, for the most part, it seems like we are all engaged in singular efforts. It has been said that innovation typically does not spread; it is also well known that we, in the academy, do not talk much with each other about our programs. Focused attention, analysis, and description of teacher education programs, processes, and contexts through self-study may be a vehicle to help improve communication and the spread of innovation. We have much to learn from one another.

References

COLE, A.L. and KNOWLES, J.G. (1995) 'Methods and issues in a life history approach to self-study', in RUSSELL, T. and KORTHAGEN, F. (eds) *Teachers Who Teach Teachers: Reflections on Teacher Education*, London: Falmer Press, pp. 130–51.

COLE, A.L. and KNOWLES, J.G. (1996) 'Reform and "being true to oneself": Pedagogy, professional practice, and the promotional process', *Teacher Education Quarterly*, **23**, 3, pp. 109–26.

DUCHARME, E.R. (1993) *The Lives of Teacher Educators*, New York: Teachers College Press.

ELLIOTT, J. (1989) 'Studying the school curriculum through insider research'. Paper presented at the International Conference on School-based Innovations: Looking Forward to the 1990s, Hong Kong.

GUILFOYLE, K., HAMILTON, M.L., PINNEGAR, S. and PLACIER, M. (1995) 'Becoming teachers of teachers: The paths of four beginners', in RUSSELL, T. and KORTHAGEN, F. (eds) *Teachers Who Teach Teachers: Reflections on Teacher Education*, London: Falmer Press, pp. 35–55.

KINCHELOE, J.L. (1991) *Teachers as Researchers: Qualitative Inquiry as a Path to Empowerment*, London: Falmer Press.

KNOWLES, J.G. and COLE, A.L. (eds) (1996) 'Beginning professors and teacher education reform', [theme issue], *Teacher Education Quarterly*, **23**, 3.

MUNBY, H. (1996) 'Being taught by my teaching: Self-study in the realm of educational computing', in RICHARDS, J. and RUSSELL, T. (eds) *Empowering our Future in Teacher Education: Proceedings of the First International Conference on Self-study of Teacher Education Practices*, Kingston, Ontario: Self-study of Teacher Education Practices Special Interest Group of the American Educational Research Association, pp. 62–6.

MYERS, C.B. (1995) 'The importance of self-study in teacher education reform and reaccreditation efforts'. Paper presented at the Annual Meeting of the American Educational Research Association, San Francisco, CA.

PINNEGAR, S. and RUSSELL, T. (eds) (1995) 'Self study and living educational theory', [theme issue], *Teacher Education Quarterly*, **22**, 3.

RICHARDS, J. and RUSSELL, T. (eds) (1996) *Empowering our Future in Teacher Education: Proceedings of the First International Conference on Self-study of Teacher Education Practices*, Kingston, Ontario: Self-study of Teacher Education Practices Special Interest Group of the American Educational Research Association.

RUSSELL, T. and KORTHAGEN, F. (eds) (1995) *Teachers Who Teach Teachers: Reflections on Teacher Education*, London: Falmer Press.

SCHON, D.A. (1983) *The Reflective Practitioner: How Professionals Think in Action*, New York: Basic Books.

TIERNEY, W.G. and BENSIMON, E.M. (1996) *Promotion and tenure: Community and Socialization in Academe*, Albany, NY: State University of New York Press.

WHITEHEAD, J. (1994) 'Creating a living educational theory from an analysis of my own educational practices: How do you create and test the validity of your living educational theory?' Paper presented at the Annual Meeting of the American Educational Research Association, New Orleans, LA.

WHITEHEAD, J. (1995) 'Educative relationships with the writings of others', in RUSSELL, T. and KORTHAGEN, F. (eds) *Teachers Who Teach Teachers: Reflections on Teacher Education*, London: Falmer Press, pp. 113–29.

Conclusion: The Value and the Promise of Self-study

Mary Lynn Hamilton and Stefinee Pinnegar

At the heart of the work found within this text lies the impassioned desires not only to be the best teachers possible and empower others toward that goal, but to reconceptualize the ways in which academics generally and teacher educators specifically view teaching practice. From our vantage many educators in higher education still pursue *THE* right way to teach or *THE* one best way to deliver information. As sentinels of change, the authors within this text and others committed to the work of self-study stand as provocateurs of traditional teaching strategies. Instead, we offer possibilities and examples of classrooms where students and teachers consciously examine their actions so as to align them with their beliefs. Furthermore, we suggest that the work of self-study represents legitimate, albeit non-traditional, scholarship.

In our role of messenger, we should expect that those with more traditional approaches to teacher education might resist our innovative inroads. Further, we might even predict a more vehement resistance to change within the academic community in response to our work. As Kuhn (1970) points out, resistance to shifts in ways of knowing is not only expected but can also be extensive. The more inevitable the change becomes, the greater the resistance. In the face of such resistance, innovators strengthen their vision. For the work of self-study scholars, this has proved to be the case.

Within our cadre, younger scholars have fought hard to be heard and more experienced scholars have endured challenges — each with varied degrees of success, each with a strong sense of vision. Because self-study is post-modern in its perspective, resistance has combined with uncertainty. The work of self-study acknowledges that and rejoices in the uncertainty of the current world. More than a qualitative approach to a situation, self-study scholars attempt to embrace that uncertainty and reject calls for validity and reliability as they are traditionally known. The multilayered, critically-imbued, reality-ladened world is the text of the self-study scholars and the chapters within this text begin to provide evidence of that.

The Self-study of Teacher Education Practices Special Interest Group began in 1993 with a rush of excitement and enthusiasm. Teacher educators studying their own practice seemed quite unique, yet timely, as they generated practical inquiry to substantiate their formal theorizing. Too often our work has been discounted with allegations of shallowness or accusations of claiming theory where there is none. We think this text meets these indictments directly with our selection from the aspects of self-study and articulation of the theoretical perspectives with which we claim affiliation. In this concluding chapter we revisit themes addressed in this text, including philosophy, methodology, and processes and practice with the hope that you will revisit the chapters as you locate your self within our work and begin to reconsider your own practice. After a brief discussion of self-study definitions, we turn to text themes to provide a larger context for the chapters. Next, we address a critical aspect of the self-study group — community. Finally, we examine the value of self-study and its promise for developing new knowledge and understandings of teaching and learning.

Definitions of Self-study

Considerable research has been done on the process of teacher development, but most of it has centered on beginning classroom teachers and has been conducted by researchers outside the classroom. The research on the development of teacher educators has been much more limited and, until recently, that too has been investigated by researchers who were not necessarily teacher educators. Consequently, most of our knowledge about developing as teachers and teaching teachers has not been grounded in practice or personal experience. The emergence of self-study and teacher research has shifted this trend.

Recently, in teacher education, studies have attempted to capture the process of teaching in academia from the 'inside' — from the students' and the teacher educators' perspectives. Some of these attempts have developed from Schön's (1983) notions about reflection-on-practice (Russell and Munby, 1992, for example), while others (Guilfoyle, 1994; Hamilton, 1994; Pinnegar, 1994; Placier, 1994; Russell, 1994, for example) seem to center on the power of personal theorizing in the development of knowledge about teaching and learning.

What is self-study? Self-study is the study of one's self, one's actions, one's ideas, as well as the 'not self'. It is autobiographical, historical, cultural, and political and it draws on one's life, but it is more than that. Self-study also involves a thoughtful look at texts read, experiences had, people known, and ideas considered. These are investigated for their connections with and relationships to practice as a teacher educator.

Self has been defined in many ways. Some anthropological studies reveal that beliefs are a division of self from non-self (Wallace, 1970, for example). From a more psychological view, Bohm (1994) suggests that the Self is the quintessence of everything. Rather than a static form, beings are always revealing themselves. Philosophically, Heidegger (1993) suggests that to locate self, we must return to a more primeval place, a place 'before influence'; Foucault (1973) addresses the imagined self; Gadamer (1976) encourages a constructive way of understanding self; and Derrida (1987) calls for deconstruction of that which we call self to analyze the invisible. Self can also have many aspects specific to a given situation (Bullough, Knowles and Crow, 1991).

Without the ground-breaking work of scholars in teacher thinking who were concerned with capturing the tacit knowledge of teachers, with studying the development of reflective practice (Zeichner, 1981, 1989) and who embraced concerns with difference in formal and informal knowledge and began work in practical knowledge (Fenstermacher, 1986), we would have taken longer, perhaps, to develop our current understandings of the teaching experience. These scholars influenced our interest in self-study, although we did not all arrive at our involvement in quite the same way. Connelly and Clandinin

(1990) find that knowing is experiential rather than conceptual and they use narrative to reveal teachers knowing. In addition, they find that knowing to be multifaceted, embodied, biographical, historical experience. The Arizona Group began studying their own movement from the role of graduate student to the role of teacher educator. Fairly quickly they became aware of how central an understanding of their teaching practice and its improvement was to their development as faculty members. A symposium they presented at AERA was the actual organizational site of the special interest group. The Queen's interest naturally developed from their seminal work in the development of Schön's (1983, 1987) work. It has continued to develop through their individual and collective study of the evolution of their teacher education program. Many of the English advocates, have come to their interests in self-study through their work in action research. McNiff (1991), Whitehead (1993), and Lomax (1994) have worked strongly to develop not only published guidance for such work but institutional support as well. Cole and Knowles began their work by reflecting through their letters on the impact of their autobiographies on their development as teacher educators. Subsequently their students have continued and pushed forward their research in autobiographical self-study methods. Their work emerged from Knowles' early tutelage by Bullough (Bullough et al., 1991). The Australians' interest grew from reflection as defined and discussed in Dewey and their long-term relationships with PEEL (Baird and Northfield, 1992).

Philosophical Discussions of the Practical and the Formal

We live in a chaotic universe. Our attempts to claim one right answer for ways of doing things, is our effort to control the situation. As researchers we wonder: What is the relevance of propositional, law-like statements discussed by those researchers who are looking at practical inquiry as a less-than methodology? Will we find TRUTH outside? Is it important to pursue THE TRUTH? Is the world so disordered, because researchers are looking for non-existent things or through clouded and archaic lenses?

Many of the critics use the terms formal and practical knowledge to make distinctions between the work of real educational researchers and the work of researchers involved in practical inquiry. While technically we do not mind the distinctions, we rankle at the implied dismissal and reduction in status of the term *practical*. Practical knowledge and research has been viewed as work that contributes to formal research, but does not stand alone. According to Fenstermacher (1994), for example, practical knowledge is not epistemologically plausible because teachers or teacher educators doing practical inquiry do not have evidence for what they know. Instead, these authors suggest they have beliefs about what they think they see. Fenstermacher asserts the need for propositional knowledge, arguing that knowing and believing are not the same (Ironically, he then bases his argument on a personal statement of his belief about the requirements for surety in knowing). He claims that for practical inquiry to attain the level of validity that formal knowledge has, teachers must show that they know something and that they consciously recognize that. Other researchers (Wong, 1995 for example) also support this notion.

In support of practical inquiry, Wilson (1995) believes that the self is an integral part of research. Carter (1993) suggests that teachers and teacher educators need to attend to the meaning involved in learning-to-teach instead of the simple technical aspects involved in particular settings. This would help develop an understanding of practical inquiry.

Previously, when we thought of educational research, we thought of formal research that would add to the general educational knowledge base. While this approach to research contributes to our understanding of classrooms and helps us learn about the ways that teachers generate the knowledge they use in classrooms, 'we [still] know little about how to work with teachers' (Richardson, 1994, p. 9). This formal research does not provide teachers with the kinds of immediate answers they need for their classroom problems, nor teacher educators with the tools to best support their students.

Often not undertaken to contribute beyond a particular classroom, practical inquiry helps teachers and teacher educators explore their situations, experiences, and stories. And do we have evidence for our work? Yes — usually. While Richardson (1994) points out that some of us in self-study do not use formal research methodology when we are considering our practice, all serious scholars do, use formal, though perhaps not traditional, research methods in systematic studies of practice that are undertaken as scholarly academic work. Most use qualitative data collection methods even in informal studies of their practice, since evidence of student learning and the context under examination are needed for the most fruitful kinds of reflection-on-practice. Consequently, this allows them to go over their notes or other documentation to provide evidence of how they know what they know.

Many times, teachers engage in practical inquiry because they experience a problem or have a concern within the classroom that causes a moral dilemma. This can also be called a 'living contradiction' (Whitehead, 1993). When experiencing these contradictions, questions arise about practice and belief. An examination of responses to these questions provides arenas of fruitful inquiry about education. These inferences are only now being well-studied and it would help to know how teachers and teacher educators carefully think through these processes. This conscious examination for evidence helps develop personal theories about education, teaching and practice. Bullough and Baughman (1997) suggest that teachers' knowledge is tacit instead of propositional in form. They suggest that we need to create strategies to support teachers to link their beliefs and actions as a way to improve their practice. Further, Clandinin and Connelly (1995) assert that teacher knowledge comes from the context, the particular experience, and the specific situation. Is that true? Teachers are producers and generators of knowledge; do teachers view themselves in that way? Lomax and Parker (1996) provide evidence that teacher knowledge is dialectical and they demonstrate that teachers have knowledge and produce knowledge (using the living theory work of Whitehead).

Teaching and Practice

Why do critics of self-study persist? We speak with not just passion but a purpose of continuous improvement in teacher education research and teaching. This is found in the voice of LaBoskey (1997) when she says,

> All students deserve teachers who are primarily guided by student needs and interests and who are both willing and able to construct and examine their practice in conscientious, principled and judicious ways. I design my portfolio assignment and the rest of

my curriculum and instruction as I do because I owe it to the children to try . . . and try again. (p. 162)

LaBoskey holds not only her students accountable for being conscientious, principled, and judicious, but she holds that expectation for herself. It is evident in her 'try . . . and try again' phrase that she is not always successful but continues to try.

A popular phrase in this community, as in other research communities, is the phrase 'walking our talk'. The Arizona Group (1996) provides a complex analysis of this idea in an article in a whole issue of *Teacher Education Quarterly* edited by Cole and Knowles (1996) which looks at the lives of beginning professors, provides several examples of this struggle of teacher educators to walk their talk. Elijah (1996) explores this theme in her examination of the conflict that a commitment of 'teaching' causes for teacher educators in most university contexts and articulates the triumvirate commitment to service, teaching, research of the professoriate generally as pedagogy and the implications of this for the new professor. Allender's (1996) address is a multilayered analysis of this. Framed as the narrative of a teacher educator's narrative of a student's understanding of what teacher education is about, Allender's provocative paper is a clear articulation of most of what is known about a student's development as a teacher and provides evidence of his own response to that in her teacher education curriculum.

Walking our talk actually represents another necessary characteristic of strong work in self-study. This is integrity or the bringing together of belief and action. Strong work in self-study requires integrity. One way this integrity is captured is in multi-layered collaborative analysis and data sources. Loughran and Northfield (1996) provide a carefully worked through example of this in their multilayered analysis and collaboration in their study of Northfield's return to public school teaching. Personal integrity led Northfield to return to public schools. Reading of Russell's (1995) attempt to teach high school physics, Northfield decided that he owed it to his own teacher education students to return to the classroom not just to provide evidence that he could 'do it', but also to develop a better personal and public understanding of how teaching actually occurred and the struggles of competent professionals to be good at teaching. His own account of his learning process is coupled with accounts of his students' views of his teaching, his response to their views, and Loughran's analysis of both of these accounts. Featherstone, Chin, and Russell (1996) provide a powerful examination of their own integrity in their work with each other (Russell and Chin were Featherstone's teachers in his process of becoming a teacher) as Featherstone enters his first year of teaching and attempts to learn what he has been taught in teacher education in his own classroom and the impact of his email reflections on Russell and Chin's teaching.

Methodology

According to critics, self-study research lacks methodology. From the critic's perspective, those engaged in self-study and action research just common-sensically look at a problem and reason it out. While there are those researchers that do not follow a traditional research paradigm, all self-study scholars use extant research methods drawn from a number of traditions and chosen for their ability to provide insight into the question of practice under consideration. As we argue earlier in this text (see Pinnegar's introduction to her section) self-study research is a new methodology for research even if the researcher employs common and established methods from other research traditions. Following natural research strategies many involved with action research ask questions, think about solutions, and proceed through trial-and-error until we determine a suitable answer. Yet, as self-study research demonstrates convincingly formalizing an examination of practice leads to important insights about process, contexts, and development in educational practice. Self-study research is a research methodology in which researchers and practitioners use whatever methods will provide the needed evidence and context for understanding their practice.

As we prepare to do a self-study we imagine, if you will, that each of us is a text to be reviewed for present and absent ideas and intimately distance our selves from our selves as if we were a text. As with text, we bring to our reading of self, all the other textual understandings we have developed over time. No two readings are the same. It is as if we are undertaking a hermeneutic study of self. What are we reading? What ideas informed the text? Who informed the text? Why are these ideas and people important to the text? In what ways do these ideas and people miss the point? As we read our 'self-text', we are looking for the events that influenced my thinking. Why do we have these perspectives? How were we influenced by our ethnicity, gender, and social status? Certainly not everyone engaged in self-study follows our example — some do not employ such deep-mining strategies. The common element is the reflective, critical examination of the self's involvement both in aspects of the study and in the phenomenon under study.

According to Britzman (1991) our voices bring meaning from our stories and our lives, while the use of our voices helps us participate within our communities. Self-study, a tool for developing voice, uses field records, journals, unstructured interviews, lived stories, letter writing, and auto/biographical writing as strategies. Yet these are not the only strategies. For the teacher educator involved in self-study, there are no quick answers. Instead, the information develops over time. What may not appear obvious initially may emerge by the end of the project.

One of the research by-products of self-study is the way in which it pushes the boundaries of what counts as research. Finley's artistic renderings of collaborative autobiography work she did with beginning professors is just one stunning example. Another is Hamilton's (1995) use of the story of the Wizard of Oz to account for her journey to becoming a teacher educator. Smith's multilayered spider stories (1994, 1995, 1996) are another. The self-study researcher struggles to find ways to capture insight for the reader. In the process of both coming to understand their own practices and instantiate that understanding for the reader (or audience), the self-study researcher begins to push boundaries of what counts as data, how to collect data, how to report data, and what counts as research. Representing living educational theory is more problematic than communicating statements about practice that work and about which the researcher only feels compelled to state that it works.

Examples

The need to honestly hold up practice to critique by colleagues, by oneself, and by ones' students is an important hallmark of self-study work. Both Hoban (1997) and Loughran

(1996) provide accounts of how this might occur. Hoban develops tapes of student accounts of teacher practice which teachers can then use to support their current practice (where student reports are congruent), come to understand their practices better, and change practices where needed. He demonstrates the way in which this occurs in the practice of teachers he worked with as a curriculum specialist. Loughran's work provides a clear account and analysis of how a teacher educator can, through public reflection, make teaching practice more clearly available for understanding by students. In teacher education, this work is represented further by a recent book by Featherstone, Munby and Russell (1997). This book provides reflective accounts of teacher education students about their own experience as students. It makes an interesting companion piece with the Bullough and Gitlin (1995) book. The Bullough and Gitlin book provides a guide for having students create such accounts. The Featherstone et al. work provides accounts written by students engaged in such enterprise. This shows the ways in which authentic work, played out against each other, move understanding forward in research in teacher education. The accounts in the Featherstone book lead to support for practices articulated by Bullough and Gitlin, questions about particular teacher education practices, which if pursued can lead to improvement and new ways of conceptualizing teacher education, and understanding for why certain practices are productive. Unlike the assertions about what works, which were the hallmark of earlier teacher education research (Wittrock, 1986, for example), this research leads teacher educators to understand their work, question what might be possible in their practice, and then move to create such practice that more might be learned both by the future teachers thus educated and by teacher educators studying what they are doing.

Processes and Practice — The Overlooked Political Nature of Self-study

Concomitant with the support of personal theorizing is the recognition that knowing and understanding the self is an essential aspect for generating change and developing new knowledge. Potentially unfortunate political labeling has developed, formal research and practical inquiry for example, which could undermine the shift in understanding the research process. Certainly there are practical, experientially-based aspects to the research done by teachers/teacher educators/teacher researchers, but that research is not necessarily without formal research methodology as suggested by some (Richardson, 1994, for example), nor without a desire to offer generalizable rules, if generalizable rules are appropriate within this new understanding of the research process. In fact, the formal research/practical inquiry dichotomy offers a binary description of a world that is, instead, far more dynamic and complex. Cochran-Smith and Lytle (1990, 1993) ask who constructs the knowledge base? They find that the technical model of the profession encourages teachers to use others' knowledge and others' strategies. For us, this is a very political issue.

Importantly, though, we believe that when we discuss the formal research–practical inquiry continuum, the political nature of the relationship is not addressed. In fact, I have found few articles that deal with that aspect of the issue. Here, as Cochran-Smith and Lytle (1990, 1993) suggest, we must ask ourselves — who owns the knowledge? Whose knowledge is of most worth? And who stands to lose if we value private theory more than public theory? Instead, who stands to lose if we empower teachers at all levels to account for themselves in ways that support rather than hinder inquiry?

Self-study research, in an ironic counter to its name, often requires collaboration. Critical friends represent a central concept of such work. Lomax, Evans and Parker in this text and in other work they have produced provide the most authentic accounts of what critical friendship might look like. Their absolute honesty with each other while sometimes difficult in the hearing leads to improvement. At the Castle Conference, the Alaskan Teachers Research Network (1996) provided a play that clearly revealed the way that such collaboration and critical friendship worked. In keeping with this collaborative, critical friend group that is much the way this community has emerged. There are small clusters of critical friend groups which link and intertwine in the group as a whole. The chapters in the collaboration section provide some examples of these groups. Others that form the core of this enterprise include the Allender–Lighthall group who have been doing work like this privately and independently for years as well as the Queen's faculty group and other authors like Tidwell and Heston and Knowles and Cole.

Finding a Community

As the examples articulated suggest, this kind of work brings insight. Munby and Russell (1994) have captured this idea quite clearly in their assertion of the authority of experience as one of the strong qualifying foundations of this work. Northfield (1996) presented a controversial overhead that suggested that good work in self-study work always leads researchers to reframe practices. Reframing practice leads to reconceptualizing what it means to be a teacher educator and what it means to engage in research in teacher education. It also leads to new understandings of what is worth knowing about teacher education. While many accuse self-study research as solipsism, those who do it well provide clear evidence to the contrary. That clear evidence is visible in their own practice as teachers, educators, and researchers. It should also be evident in their research accounts as well as through multilayered sets of data and analysis, through accounts of their practice collected from various perspectives of their practice, by a willingness to admit failure and fiasco and learn from it, by evidence that productive change and steady growth characterize their practice and by the reported and usually obvious influence of critical friends. Teacher education is a moral endeavor. The evidence of our understanding about teaching should appear not just in our own practice but, also in the practice of our students and, therefore, in the lives and actions of their students.

What is unique about the chapters in this book, is made most apparent by a phrase from the Wilcox chapter where she speaks of teaching as a 'witness' to the need to learn. What is implied by this statement and by other segments of this book is the commitment of this group not just to understand or to discover 'new knowledge' though there is plenty of commitment to do that, what is unique here is the commitment to provide insight for others of how the understandings of the authors become part of their actual day-to-day practice. Whitehead, in his 1994 AERA address, raised the need for living educational theory. We have thought through this phrase often and assert that this book generally and self-study specifically is indeed an example of living educational theory in two ways. It is living because, as people engage in understanding it, they learn more and their theory changes as they understand more. Further, because they are living what they learn, new knowledge emerges. The work in a special issue of *Teacher Educational Quarterly* (Russell and Pinnegar, 1995) provides one example of that, while McNiff's *Teaching as Learning* (1993) is another good example. McNiff explains action research techniques that might be used to not just create better classroom practice and thus learn as one teaches, but also to conduct systematic study of the practice using action research principles so that educational theory continues to grow. As one's educational practice improves, accounts of it and therefore knowledge about it is added to the knowledge base of the teaching and research community.

The belief in this process is always apparent in Guilfoyle's work. This is especially evident in her 1995 piece where she explores the entanglement of teaching/learning/researching in her own struggle to create particular kinds of complex learning environments with her own students. In addition, Pinnegar's (1995) piece captures this in her study of the way she uses storytelling with her own students. In studying the ways she tells stories in her classroom, she comes to understand herself what is strategic and helpful and what is not in her storytelling. She sees the ways in which her storytelling helps her understand how her storytelling patterns are an attempt to help students create particular patterns of thinking about themselves in their future practice.

What makes such a process rich and the community that accompanies it an important one is the moral ethos of the community. Barnes alludes to this in his *Foreword* and *Afterword* of this book. Humility, which we have never heard spoken of much in the larger research community, speaks from the pages of almost every chapter in this book. It is eloquently apparent in Hutchinson's work, radiating from her willingness to alter practice in response to her students. It is there in Wilkes' concept of the dilemma of practice, as the recognition that learning comes when two strongly-held ideas conflict in ways that may not allow for resolution, we may not always be able to uphold both aspects of our practice. Hamilton alludes to this in a chapter in the Loughran and Russell (1997) book, *Teaching About Teaching*, where she talks about promoting equity and democracy for teachers until it relates to her own son and how she always wants the best for him. It is also evident in Placier's work (1995) in her headings 'Fiasco #1' and 'Fiasco #2'. This willingness to admit that we stumble in our teaching practice is a central part of work in self-study. From this stumbling and our efforts to both understand and act differently that the knowledge we produce about teaching emerges. Being vulnerable in this authentic way and not in some Uriah Heap hand-wringing act is what makes this work ring with genuineness for most readers.

Conclusion

As teacher educators, we recognize that we are teachers. We believe that research on teaching practice by teachers holds invaluable promise for developing new understandings and producing new knowledge about teaching and learning. Formalizing such study of practice through self-study is imperative. The formalization of self-study then provides both kinds of living educational theory: the practice of the researchers and the accounts of their new understanding of and knowledge about their practice. The value of self-study depends on the researcher/teacher providing convincing evidence that they know what they claim to know. This book provides evidence that self-study undertaken with rigor produces living educational theory that will lead to both reconstruction and

Mary Lynn Hamilton and Stefinee Pinnegar

reconceptualization of teacher education. Our work can be judged on the credibility and integrity of the self-study voices found in this book and on the evidence these accounts provide.

References

ALASKAN TRN. (AUSTIN, T., GABORIK, B., KEEP-BARNES, A., McCRACKEN, J. and SMITH, B.) (1996) 'Gretel and Hansel research in the woods: A modern fairy tale', in RICHARDS, J. and RUSSELL, T. (eds) *Empowering our Future in Teacher Education, Proceedings*, Canada: Queens University.

ALLENDER, J. (1996) 'From student self to teacher self: A reflective mirror'. Paper presented at the annual AERA conference, New York.

ARIZONA GROUP (GUILFOYLE, K., HAMILTON, M., PINNEGAR, S. and PLACIER, P.) (1996) 'Becoming teachers of teachers: The paths of four beginners', *Teacher Education Quarterly*, **23**, 3, pp. 35–55.

BAIRD, J. and NORTHFIELD, J. (eds) (1992) *Learning from the PEEL experience*, Melbourne: Monash University.

BOHM, D. (1994) *Thought as a System*, London: Routledge.

BRITZMAN, D.P. (1991) *Practice Makes Practice: A Critical Study of Learning to Teach*, Albany: State University of New York Press.

BULLOUGH, R. and BAUGHMAN, K. (1997) *First Year Teacher Eight Years Later*, New York: Teachers College Press.

BULLOUGH, R.V. and GITLIN, A. (1995) *Becoming a Student of Teaching: Methodologies for Exploring Self and School Context*, New York: Garland.

BULLOUGH, R.V., KNOWLES, J.G. and CROW, N.A. (1991) *Emerging as a Teacher*, London: Routledge and Kegan Paul.

CARTER, K. (1990) 'Teachers' knowledge and learning to teach', in HOUSTON, W.R. (ed.) *Handbook of Research on Teacher Education*, New York: Macmillan Publishing Company, pp. 291–310.

CARTER, K. (1993) 'The place of story in the study of teaching and teacher education', *Educational Researcher*, **22**, 1, pp. 5–12.

CLANDININ, D.J. and CONNELLY, F.M. (1995) *Teachers' Professional Knowledge Landscapes*, New York: Teachers College Press.

CONNELLY, F.M. and CLANDININ, D.J. (1990) 'Stories of experience and narrative inquiry', *Educational Researcher*, **19**, 5, pp. 2–11.

COCHRAN-SMITH, M. and LYTLE, S. (1990) 'Research on teaching and teacher research: The issues that divide', *Educational Researcher*, **19**, 2, pp. 2–11.

COCHRAN-SMITH, M. and LYTLE, S. (1993) *Inside Outside*, NY: Teachers College Press.

DERRIDA, J. (1987) *The Post Card: From Socrates to Freud and Beyond*, (Alan Bass, trans.). Chicago: University of Chicago Press.

ELIJAH, R. (1996) 'Professional lives: Institutional contexts: Coherence and Contradictions', *Teacher Education Quarterly*, **23**, 3, pp. 69–90.

FEATHERSTONE, D., MUNBY, H. and RUSSELL, T. (1997) *Finding a Voice While Learning to Teach*, London: Falmer Press.

FEATHERSTONE, D., CHIN, P. and RUSSELL, T. (1996) 'Extending professional trialogue: Self-study across the teaching spectrum', in RICHARDS, J. and RUSSELL, T. (eds) *Empowering our Future in Teacher Education*, proceedings from the Castle Conference, pp. 16–20.

FENSTERMACHER, G.D. (1986) 'Philosophy of research on teaching: Three aspects', in WITTROCK, M.C. (ed.) *Handbook of Research on Teaching*, 3rd Edition, New York: Macmillan, pp. 37–49.

FENSTERMACHER, G.D. (1994) 'The knower and the known: The nature of knowledge in research on teaching', in DARLING-HAMMOND, L. (ed.) *Review of Research in Education 20*, Washington, D.C.: American Educational Research Association, pp. 3–56.

FOUCAULT, M. (1973) *The Order of Things*, New York: Vintage.

GADAMER, H.G. (1976) 'Semantics and hermeneutics', in LINGE, D.E. (ed.) *Philosophical Hermeneutics*, Berkeley: University of California Press.

GUILFOYLE, K. (1994) 'Finding out more than I want to know: Using teacher research and critical pedagogy in teacher education'. Paper presented at the annual meeting of the American Educational Research Association, New Orleans.

GUILFOYLE, K. (1995) 'Constructing the meaning of teacher educator: The struggle to learn the roles', *Teaching Education Quarterly*, **22**, 3, pp. 11–27.

HAMILTON, M.L. (1994) 'A teaching odyssey: Sailing through the straits of teaching through the gales of academia'. Paper presented at the annual meeting of the American Educational Research Association, New Orleans.

HAMILTON, M.L. (1995) 'Confronting Self: Passion and promise in the act of teaching', *Teaching Education Quarterly*, **22**, 3, pp. 29–43.

HEIDEGGER, M. (1993) *Being and Time* (J. MacQuaurie and E. Robinson, trans.). New York: Harper and Row.

HOBAN, G. (1996) 'A professional development model based on interrelated principles of teacher learning'. Unpublished doctoral dissertation, University of British Columbia, Vancouver, Canada.

KUHN, T. (1970) *The Structure of Scientific Revolutions*, (2nd edition). Chicago: University of Chicago Press.

LABOSKEY, V. (1997) in LOUGHRAN, J. and RUSSELL, T. (eds) *Teaching about Teaching*, London: Falmer Press, pp. 150–63.

LOMAX, P. (1994) 'Standards, criteria and the problematic of action research within an award bearing course', *Educational Action Research*, **2**, 1, pp. 113–26.

LOMAX, P. and PARKER, Z. (1996) 'Representing a dialectical form of knowledge within a new epistemology for teaching and teacher education'. Paper presented at the annual AERA conference, New York.

LOUGHRAN, J.J. (1996) *Developing Reflective Practice: Learning about Teaching and Learning through Modelling*, London: Falmer Press.

LOUGHRAN, J.J. and NORTHFIELD, J.R. (1996) *Opening the Classroom Door: Teacher Researcher Learner*, London: Falmer Press.

LOUGHRAN, J. and RUSSELL, T. (1997) *Teaching about Teaching*, London: Falmer Press.

McNIFF, J. (1991) *Action Research: Principles and Practice*, London: Routledge.

McNIFF, J. (1993) *Teaching as Learning: An Action Research Approach*, London: Routledge.

MUNBY, H. and RUSSELL, T. (1994) 'The authority of experience in learning to teach: Messages from a physics methods class', *Journal of Teacher Education*, **45**, pp. 86–95.

NORTHFIELD, J.R. (1996) 'Quality and the Self-study Perspective on Research'. Paper presented at the Annual Meeting of the American Educational Research Association, New York. (ERIC Document Reproduction Service No. ED 397 034).

PINNEGAR, S. (1994) 'Negotiating balance between context, colleagues, students, families, and institutions: Responding to lived experience in the second year'. Paper presented at the annual meeting of the American Educational Research Association, New Orleans.

PINNEGAR, S. (1995) (Re-) Experiencing Beginning, *Teaching Education Quarterly*, **22**, 3, pp. 65–83.

PLACIER, P. (1994) 'A action research approach to a contradiction in teaching: Recounciling grades with democratic education'. Paper presented at the annual meeting of the American Educational Research Association, New Orleans.

PLACIER, P. (1995) 'But I have to have an A: Probing the cultural meanings and ethical dilemmas of grades in teacher education', *Teaching Education Quarterly*, **22**, 3, pp. 45–63.

RICHARDSON, V. (1994) 'Conducting research on practice', *Educational Researcher*, **23**, 5, pp. 5–10.

RUSSELL, T. (1994) 'Returning from the field: Did recent relevant and successful teaching experience make a difference?' Paper presented at the annual meeting of the American Educational Research Association, New Orleans.

RUSSELL, T. (1995) 'Returning to the physics classroom to re-think how one learns physics', in RUSSELL, T. and KORTHAGEN, F. (eds) *Teachers Who Teach Teachers: Reflections on Teacher Education*, London: Falmer Press, pp. 95–109.

RUSSELL, T. and MUNBY, H. (1992) 'Transforming chemistry research into teaching: The complexities of adopting new frames for experience', in RUSSELL, T. and MUNBY, H. (eds) *Teachers and Teaching: From Classroom to Reflection*, London: Falmer Press.

RUSSELL, T. and PINNEGAR, S. (1995) (Whole Issue Editor). *Teaching Education Quarterly*, **22**, 3.

SCHÖN, D. (1983) *The Reflective Practitioner*. New York: Basic Books.

SCHÖN, D. (1987) *Educating the Reflective Practitioner: Toward a New Design for Teaching and Learning in the Professions*, San Francisco, CA: Jossey Bass.

SMITH, B. (1994) 'Learning how to awaken the moral imaginations of pre-service teachers'. Paper presented at the annual AERA conference, New Orleans.

SMITH, B. (1995) 'Self-reflection of the whole me: A soulful helper of other'. Paper presented at the annual AERA conference, San Francisco.

SMITH, B. (1996) 'Creating the spirit of community in my teacher education courses by awakening and nourishing individual and collective soul'. Paper presented at the annual AERA conference, New York.

WALLACE, A. (1970) *Culture and Personality*, New York: Random House.

WHITEHEAD, J. (1993) *The Growth of Educational Knowledge*, Bournemouth, Dorset: Hyde Publications.

WILSON, S. (1995) 'Teaching and studenting: Implementing teaching reforms in teacher education'. Interactive symposium presentation at the annual AERA conference, San Francisco.

WITTROCK, M. (ed.) (1986) *Handbook of Research on Teaching*, 2nd edition, New York: Macmillan.

WONG, E.D. (1995) 'Challenges confronting the research/teacher', *Educational Researcher*, **24**, 3, pp. 22–8.

ZEICHNER, K.M. (1981) 'Reflective teaching and field based experience in teacher education', *Interchange*, **12**, 4, pp. 1–22.

ZEICHNER, K. (1989) 'Kenneth Zeichner reflecting on reflection', *NCRTE Colloquy*, **3**, 2, pp. 15–21.

Afterword[1]

Douglas Barnes

I will end with a suggestion for a later conference. It may well be that at this stage, while the group is still developing a consensus about what kinds of activity are to be included in *self-study*, a conference should be like this one, wide-ranging rather than focused. This conference has clearly been of great value to many participants for whom it has been timely and appropriate to share values, engage in mutually supportive discussion and to find from others what their experience of taking part in action research of this kind has been. For many the culmination of the conference was the decision to make new commitments to self-study in spite of the risks. However, I predict that one day a sharpening of focus will be felt to be necessary, and then a policy-forming conference will be needed. I suggest that it should take this form. There should be invited speakers on the central topics, and the majority of the time — perhaps not more than two days — spent in working parties whose task would be to formulate and agree statements of policy. The outcome would be a written document that could be voted upon section by section. On the basis of the present conference I would suggest as topics the following:

1 The preconditions of successful self-study
2 The meaning of *validity* in self-study
3 The processes of self-study

Of course, the future may bring other important concerns. The purpose would be to produce an explicit framework for future conferences, based on the 'case law' assembled in the course of other open conferences like this one.

So, LONG LIVE SELF-STUDY!

---

[1] The beginning of Douglas Barnes' afterword on the Conference forms the foreword of this text, see page ix.

Notes on Contributors

Rebecca S. Anderson is an Assistant Professor at the University of Memphis and Co-Director of the Memphis Urban Writing Institute. She is a literacy teacher educator whose research interests focus on alternative assessment practices and technology integration.

Douglas Barnes was Reader in Education at the University of Leeds, England until 1989, where his main research interest was the role of spoken language in classroom learning and teaching. His publications include: *From Communication to Curriculum*, *Practical Curriculum Study*, and (with co-authors) *Language, the Learner and the School*, and *Communication and Learning Revisited*.

Ardra Cole is Associate Professor in the Department of Adult Education and Counselling Psychology at the Ontario Institute for Studies in Education of the University of Toronto. Her main areas of research and teaching are teacher development, teacher education reform, and qualitative research methodologies, particularly (auto)biography and life history approaches. The role of self-study in teacher education reform is a topic in a forthcoming book, *The Heart of the Matter: Teacher Education Reform Perspectives and Possibilities* co-edited with Rosebud Elijah and J. Gary Knowles.

Carola Conle teaches Cross-cultural Education, Foundations of Curriculum, and Narrative Inquiry at OISE/University of Toronto. She has published in *AERJ*, *Educational Theory*, *Curriculum Inquiry* and other journals and received AACTE's 'Outstanding Writing Award' in 1996 for her article, 'Resonance in Pre-service Teacher Inquiry'. Her current research is in ethics and the imagination.

Katherine Davies-Samway is a Professor in the Division of Teacher Education at San Jose State University in San Jose, California. She teaches language and literacy courses in the teacher preparation program and engages in collaborative, classroom-based research with K–8 teachers. These experiences have a profound impact on her own teaching, and she is constantly rethinking and revising her role as a university-based teacher.

Lisa DeMuelle is an Assistant Professor in the Dept. of Instruction and Curriculum Leadership at the University of Memphis. Her professional interests revolve around Curriculum and Pedagogical Inquiry for teachers and teacher educators, Integration of Internet into Curriculum, and Elementary Teacher Education. Personally, she is engaged in family life with her husband and two young boys, Benjy and Nicholas.

Moyra Evans is a deputy head teacher in a United Kingdom mixed comprehensive school of 1200 pupils, age range 12–18+. She has been working, in partnership with Kingston University, to create learning communities of teachers within her school, so that they can address effectively the issues detailed in the School Development Plan, and so that teachers have the support they need in order to further develop their practice. Her current research interests include action research, the concept of leadership in schools, including the gender dimension, the use of story as an aid to reflection, and self-study within teacher education.

Sara Garcia is an Assistant Professor and Director of teacher education at Santa Clara University. She is an educational psychologist with specialization in cognition, language development and learning theory. She has written a chapter on teachers' cultural knowledge in the recently published book, *Meeting the Challenge of Cultural Diversity in Teacher Education* (Teachers College Press). She also has a special interest in Mexican ballads, or corridos, which represent the oral tradition in Mexican culture.

Joan Gipe is Research Professor and Seraphia D. Leyda Teaching Fellow at the University of New Orleans, Department of Curriculum and Instruction. She teaches undergraduate courses for teacher preparation in elementary and literacy education. At the graduate level she works with masters and doctoral students in a variety of professional development areas including the integration of technology in teaching and assessment alternatives in literacy. She is currently involved in a project to assist teachers and faculty in developing their own professional portfolios. Dr. Gipe is the author of *Multiple Paths to Literacy: Corrective Reading Techniques for Classroom Teachers*, available in its fourth edition from Merrill/Prentice Hall.

Mary Lynn Hamilton is an Associate Professor at the University of Kansas. She was a high school social studies teacher and a program coordinator for gender-related and multicultural programs before returning to university to work in teacher education. Her research interests include self-study of teacher education practices, teacher beliefs, multicultural issues, and the professional development of teachers. Some of her most recent publications include: Confronting the self: Passion and practice in the act of teaching or My Oz-dacious journey to Kansas! in *Teacher Education Quarterly* and Cultural knowledge, school culture, and teaching in the Zambelli and Cherubini edited text *Teachers and Teaching*.

Melissa Heston received her PhD in Educational Psychology from Indiana University in 1989. She is currently an Associate Professor in Educational Psychology at the University of Northern Iowa. Dr. Heston's professional interests include self-study of teaching practices, constructivist approaches to teacher education, risk and resiliency among children and adolescents, and early childhood education.

Nancy Hutchinson is an Associate Professor in the Faculty of Education at Queen's University. She is a member of the four-person committee that has led the development and implementation of a field-based program of teacher education at Queen's. Earlier versions of this chapter were presented at the First International Conference on Self-study of Teacher Education Practices (Herstmonceux Castle, England, 1996) and the Canadian Society for the Study of Education (St. Catharine's, Canada, 1996).

John M. Johnston is a Professor at the University of Memphis, in the Department of Instruction and Curriculum Leadership where he directs and teaches in the Early Childhood Teacher Education Program. He has participated in developing guidelines for preparation of early childhood professionals adopted by the National Association for the Education of Young Children, the Division of Early Childhood of the Council for Exceptional Children, and the National Board for Professional Teaching Standards. He currently serves on the National Council for Accreditation of Teacher Education Board of Examiners. His current research interests include using Internet technologies to support community within teacher education programs.

J. Gary Knowles is an Associate Professor within the Department of Adult Education at the Ontario Institute for Studies in Education of The University of Toronto, Toronto, Canada. As a one-time classroom teacher and principal Gary taught a variety of school subjects although specialized in teaching geography and history from an experiential learning perspective — a framework which included accessing principles of outdoor education. As a university teacher and teacher educator Gary has developed innovative graduate teacher preparation programs grounded in a reflexive inquiry perspective and has researched issues of teacher development, also using a reflexive inquiry approach, alongside new and experienced teachers. He is also particularly interested in developing arts-based (or inter-modal) educational research approaches which honour, among other things, alternative representations of research data. Gary is an exhibiting artist who works in water media on paper and canvas.

Vicki Kubler LaBoskey is an Associate Professor of Education at Mills College in Oakland CA and Director of the elementary portion of their Teachers for Tomorrow's Schools Credential Program. Her current areas of interest are in elementary pre-service education with a focus on reflective teaching and teaching as a moral and political act. She is also interested in action research, portfolios, teacher educator self-study, narrative knowing, and new teacher support (teacher development as a vehicle for educational reform).

Pam Lomax is Professor of Educational Research at Kingston University, UK. She has a BSc in Sociology and a BA in Fine Art. Her masters degree and PhD were in the Sociology of Education. She has taught in secondary schools in the UK and for a short time lectured at Kenya Polytechnic in Nairobi. Her current research interest is action research and her most recent books are *You and Your Action Research Project*, co-authored with Jean McNiff and Jack Whitehead and *Quality Management in Education*, both published by Routledge in London and New York.

John Loughran is the Director of Pre-service Education and Professional Development, School of Graduate Studies, Faculty of Education, Monash University. John was a high school science teacher for ten years before returning to University to work in Teacher Education. His research interests include teaching and learning, science education and the professional development of teachers. Recent books include *Developing Reflective Practice* (Falmer Press, 1996) and *Teaching About Teaching* a co-edited book with Tom Russell (Falmer Press, 1997).

Jeff Northfield was the Head of the Peninsula School of Education, Monash University until recently when he moved to work more closely with schools as a researcher and professional development leader pursuing his long held views about the need to better link academics of education with practising classroom teachers in an attempt to better align theory and practice in teaching. This move is an extension of his recent book *Opening the Classroom Door* (Falmer Press, 1996) co-authored with John Loughran which documents his learning and the research knowledge developed through a return to classroom teaching with a Year 7 class of High School Students.

Linda Oda is an Associate Professor in the College of Education, Weber State University, Ogden, Utah. She was formerly a public school teacher, teacher supervisor, principal and administrator. She teaches the language arts and reading methods and multicultural courses.

Zoe Parker is a lecturer in the School of Education at Kingston University in the UK. Her principal interest is in the ways we construct ourselves as learners, teachers and researchers through the stories we tell about our auto/biographies of learning. She is an action researcher, primarily fascinated by the notion of the self as text and how we relate our professionalism to our personal lives. Her current research is about providing support for beleaguered professional educators who are undertaking doctoral studies against the backdrop of continuous reform in the politics of education in the UK.

Stefinee Pinnegar is a teacher educator at Brigham Young University. Through research with the Arizona Group and her own students she continues to study the development of teacher knowledge, narrative, and self-study research methodology.

Janet Richards is an Associate Professor in the Division of Education and Psychology where she supervises a literature-based literacy partnership between USM and a multicultural elementary school. The pre-service teachers whose self-portraits appear in this chapter have graciously given permission for their drawings to be shared.

Tom Russell is a Professor of Education at Queen's University, Kingston, Ontario, where he continues to pursue longstanding interests in the nature and development of teachers' knowledge. He teaches secondary science methods courses and an experience-based course on research, theory and professional practice in the pre-service program at Queen's, as well as a course on action research in the MEd program. He is co-editor of four titles published by Falmer Press, including *Finding a Voice While Learning to Teach* (with Derek Featherstone and Hugh Munby).

Howard A. Smith (PhD Toronto) is Associate Professor of Education (Educational Psychology) at Queen's University in Kingston, Ontario. He has also been a visiting or research scholar at Stanford and Indiana Universities and at the University of Bologna. During the past 20 years, his major research interests and publications have been in the areas of nonverbal communication in teaching, classroom learning, adolescent development, and semiotics of education.

Debbie Tidwell is an Associate Professor in the Department of Curriculum and Instruction at the University of Northern Iowa. She is the Director of the UNI Reading Clinic, and teaches undergraduate and graduate courses in reading education, the language arts, and bilingual education. Her research interests are in the relationships between teachers' beliefs and teaching practices and between teaching practices and learning.

Rena Upitis (EdD Harvard) is Dean of Education at Queen's University, Kingston, Ontario. She teaches courses on music and mathematics curriculum methods, integrated arts and technology, and research methodologies. A musician and composer as well as a teacher, Rena has worked as a music teacher in inner-city schools in Canada and the United States and has been a studio teacher of piano and music theory for over 25 years. Her two books on music teaching explore possibilities for teaching music through children's improvisation and composition in regular classroom settings (*This Too is Music* (1990) and *Can I Play You My Song? The Compositions and Invented Notations of Children*, (1992), Heinemann). She is co-author of *Creative Mathematics: Exploring Children's Understanding* (1997, Routledge).

Susan Wilcox is adviser on teaching and learning in the Instructional Development Centre, and Assistant Professor of adult education in the Faculty of Education, at Queen's University in Ontario.

Glenda Wilkes is a member of the faculty in Educational Psychology at the University of Arizona. She teaches courses in human development to pre-service teachers and graduate students. Her research interests fall into the broad area of cognitive change with several loosely-related projects. Her passions are her family, the mountains, and her friends.

Index